MUSICAL BELIEFS

Psychoacoustic, Mythical, and Educational Perspectives

MUSICAL BELIEFS

Psychoacoustic, Mythical, and Educational Perspectives

ROBERT WALKER

Teachers College, Columbia University
New York and London

Published by Teachers College Press, 1234 Amsterdam Avenue
New York, NY 10027

Library of Congress Cataloging-in-Publication Data

Walker, Robert, 1936–
  Musical beliefs : psychoacoustic, mythical, and educational
perspectives / Robert Walker.
      p.   cm.
  Includes bibliographical references.
    ISBN 0-8077-3008-4 (alk. paper). — ISBN 0-8077-3007-6 (pbk. :
alk. paper)
    1. Music—Psychology.   2. Music and society.   3. Music—Philosophy
and aesthetics.   I. Title.
ML3838.W2   1990   89-20681
781'.11—dc20   CIP
                                                             MN

ISBN 0-8077-3008-4
ISBN 0-8077-3007-6 (pbk.)

Printed on acid-free paper

Manufactured in the United States of America

97 96 95 94 93 92 91 90   8 7 6 5 4 3 2 1

To my mother
and in memory of my father

Contents

Preface

Throughout the course of the Western rationalist quest to understand music, the assumption has been that there exist some fundamental laws to do with sound that affect all musical behavior. One has only to study the musical sound of one particular culture, Western for example, in order to find these laws. This is the generally accepted approach. Evidence is sought, therefore, in Western scales and musical harmony, and in Western musical theory, which, it is hoped, can provide clues to the nature of universals in musical behavior. Educational programs in music are based on the findings of this quest.

Such an assumption as that outlined above relies less on the role of culture and its possibly confounding effects, and more on a very ancient belief that music is out there waiting to be discovered. This is not at all surprising, except in the sense that it has survived from more primitive and superstitious times. All cultures, including the Western, have held the belief that music is, variously, the language of entities that lie above and beyond human existence, that it is the concretization of unknown forces that hold the cosmos in place, the repository of special powers of spirit beings or entities that can be tapped by humans through their musical practices, or that it is the means of communication with the supernatural world lying above the mundane existence of humans.

This much does appear to be universal: music is something to do with realms beyond the human. What is surprising is that this notion of music being out there in unknown realms is viewed less as a product of a possibly universal developmental trait in human behavior, akin to beliefs that gods lived on Mount Olympus, and more as a clue for modern science in its quest to understand musical sound and behavior. My view, and the one argued in this book, is that more attention should be paid to the varied effects of cultural beliefs about music in any quest to understand musical behavior. But before explaining this and introducing the content of the book, it is pertinent to raise some questions concerning the role of culture and to ask what its role might be in relation to the world out there! Does culture merely provide meaning to humanity's experiences, whatever they are, through defining or describing them, or does it have a more central role in the sense of actually providing the experience?

For example, if all persons experience the same thing, but culture provides varying means of describing and understanding this same thing, then the role of culture is relatively superficial in that it merely affects how we have perceived and understood. The same thing is out there, but each culture views it differently; culture does not extend to the actual thing causing the experience. But suppose culture has a more profound role, one that actually determines the object or event being experienced as well as the description or definition of it. In other words, suppose one culture can say that there is some entity out there that other cultures will not be able to perceive, that it will do this or that to you, and that this is how you will experience and perceive it. If such is the case, then culture becomes both the source of the thing being experienced and the definition of the experience it causes.

Historically, various cultures have invented descriptions of powers or forces that they believed could be brought to bear on their daily lives, influencing the outcomes of such states as illness or such activities as hunting. It was often believed that there was a power out there that could not be perceived by any of the human senses but could be summoned by music. Since one could not perceive this power, it is pertinent to ask how cultures knew it was there. If they did not invent it, how could it be related to some sensory input in humans? In other words, if someone who was ill suddenly got better, and a culture invented a healing power through some accidentally associated occurrence that it assumed was responsible for an improvement in health, what are we dealing with? Is it an invention, a pure fiction? Or is there really something out there that has been perceived and conceptualized culturally?

For example, if the illness was an intestinal blockage that somehow cleared itself through the natural motions of the intestines, yet at the same time someone was singing a song and the cultural wisdom assumed that the song had powers to heal this illness, would this culture have invented something that conformed to their cultural beliefs, or would it have witnessed something that was out there and that was somehow intrinsically connected with the song? In the latter case, but not in the former, there would be some point in examining the intrinsic properties of the song. Science tells us that songs cannot cure illness, yet science studies musical sound in attempts to discover intrinsic acoustic properties that might give clues to beliefs about musical meaning.

As another example, suppose that someone who was ill believed that music could effect a cure by means of a particular person's singing a specific song. Suppose the song was sung and the person was cured, as is often reported in ancient writings. What would have been responsible for the cure—the physical properties of the sounds of the song or the psychological effects of hearing the song, which was believed to be curative and which worked because of this belief? In the latter case, it could have been any song given such an assignment by the culture. We might well ask how this latter could happen, and empirical science might search for some cause-and-effect interactions. We do not, of course, entirely know how the brain functions. For someone holding a belief about the powers of a certain song, it is possible that hearing it will trigger some reaction in brain function that can have healing effects. The quest would be to find out whether there was something in the sounds of the particular song that interacted with brain function or whether the actual sounds of the song had little or nothing to do with the effect of the musical performance on the listener.

Extrapolating to more general musical behavior, should we, therefore, look to the intrinsic properties of sound for clues to understanding musical behavior, or should we look to the effects of belief per se on human behavior generally and beliefs about music specifically? This is an important question. It raises issues that lie at the very core of Western aesthetics. The search for universals leads many to investigate intrinsic properties of sound for such clues, and this has been the major thrust of inquiry in Western music. If the intrinsic properties of sound are of little consequence compared to the overarching role and function of invented belief systems, then much of the edifice of Western aesthetic inquiry into music has been an interesting but fruitless repetition of ancient Pythagoreanism through the ages.

There are three possible ways of explaining the significance for humans of the intrinsic properties of musical sound:

1. It is based on universal laws determined by the physiological and electrochemical makeup of the human auditory system.
2. It is the arbitrary product of the human imagination.
3. It is some mixture of the first two.

Throughout this book I argue that the third option is most tenable but that the second is of such importance that it can subsume the first. Certainly, the first possibility is inadequate to explain musical behavior in all its cultural variety.

Music can best be understood by knowing the universal laws applicable to the human auditory system, and acknowledging the role of the marvelously inventive human mind. Musical sound has fascinated humans to the point where elaborate systems surrounding sound and its relationship to unknown forces have been invented. These have become belief systems and have taken powerful hold over our lives.

Through a study of inventions in the form of beliefs, systems, behaviors, and structures, one may learn to understand music more profoundly than through the lens of investigative disciplines. But more than simply a study of the beliefs and systems, as well as their origins, is necessary to achieve such understanding. Through the music these things have produced, one can gain access to the profundity, and the essential humanity, of musical activity.

This book attempts to approach music in this manner. By tracing the origins, developments, and interpretations of beliefs and theories within music in Western culture, and by relating these to Western composers, it is possible to see the sheer inventiveness of humans in action. A great deal of space is spent on Western music simply because there is so much information available. However, by extrapolation to other cultures from the conclusions drawn from studies in Western musical beliefs, it is possible to draw comparisons and show distinctions. One non-Western culture is studied in some detail—the Pacific Northwest Indian—in order to show how this culture has selected musical materials to suit the needs of cultural beliefs and musical functions in daily life, much as Western musicians have done. The similarity ends there, however. Each musical culture produces its own special sounds, and this is an important focus in the book.

There are some physiological and environmental reasons for the distinctiveness of each culture's sounds in music. This is explained in some detail, and suggestions are put forward for identifying unknown scales based on a careful combination of knowledge about the acoustics of instruments, human perception of sound, and the human proclivity to place stimuli into categories rather than to treat them as discrete, isolated events. All things that happen to humans, it appears, need to be placed into some category in order that meaning can be assigned. The evidence, as far as music cognition is concerned, is presented as it relates to behavior in both Western and non-Western musical cultures.

In the explanations of musical perception the focus is centered on pitch. This is for a good reason. All cultures produce their own special sound, which is characterized by the particular spectral components of sounds. Since auditory perception is an activity whereby the ear performs a pattern analysis on wave forms, it follows that the most significant aspect of any sound is that concerning the complete wave form as far as human perception is concerned. It might even be claimed that, despite the rhythmic nature of some music, the most salient feature for our perceptual apparatus is the whole pattern of the wave form. Some evidence is presented to explain this, and examples from actual music that demonstrate the importance of pattern perception in musical cognition are provided.

Some basic issues in studies of music concern aesthetics. A frequent question centers on what music means. The answer suggested in this book is simply that humans invent their own meaning for their music and expect listeners to perceive that meaning. The invention of meaning is a major theme in the book. A good deal of space is allocated to explaining the epistemological origins of belief systems in music, which in turn provide us with musical meaning. It is suggested that without knowledge of these belief systems it is impossible to know the meaning of music.

Finally, the content referred to suggests a need for radical changes in some current music education practices. The last chapter makes some suggestions in this respect, providing some of the details thought necessary for actual classroom use in schools and postsecondary institutions. These activities are a direct consequence of the arguments presented in the first six chapters. If the arguments are not as explicit as they should be in the opinion of some, that would be my omission. At the expense of detail that might have turned out to be too cumbersome, too remote and labyrinthine, selective materials are presented and examined in a sequence that, it is hoped, makes the arguments sensible and logical. If this is not the case, then it is hoped that the intrinsic merit of the arguments may show sufficiently at least to arouse interest.

ACKNOWLEDGMENTS: I am grateful to Susan Liddicoat and Peter Sieger of Teachers College Press for their invaluable suggestions in the preparation of this text. I would also like to thank Professor Barry Truax of Simon Fraser University for his help in clarifying and simplifying the technical details, particularly in Chapter 2. Finally, I want to thank my wife, Pamela, for her continued encouragement and support. After such help, if any of the text is opaque, then the blame lies with me.

MUSICAL BELIEFS

Psychoacoustic, Mythical, and Educational Perspectives

CHAPTER 1

Musical Style
and Cultural Context

It is axiomatic that artists of all kinds reflect, at the very least, some aspects of their inherited culture, of their knowledge, experiences and interactions with their cultural surroundings. Musicians, common sense would dictate, are inevitably constrained by the available technology and performance techniques for musical creation, just as they are confronted by whatever social, political, and economic structures prevail in the setting within which their music is to be received. Again, common sense tells us that it is no more possible for a Beethoven, as we know him or as his contemporaries knew him, to have emerged from a seventeenth-century Italian court than it would be for a Picasso, as we know him, to have emerged in the sixteenth century to produce cubist symbols of Christ and the apostles for the ceiling of the Sistine Chapel. A great deal of cultural information derived from the beliefs and activities of both previous generations and contemporary society lies behind the artistic output and appreciation of a Beethoven or a Picasso.

These claims, of course, relate not so much to the unique or heroic qualities of either but more to the general role of cultural background and beliefs in motivating and guiding artistic activities. But this tells us little or nothing about why such artists utilized the materials they did in the manner they chose. Some would claim all this raises philosophical issues concerning rationalism and empiricism, or nominalism and Platonic realism. Why, for example, would common sense tell us that a Beethoven would not be likely to emerge from the seventeenth-century courts of Florence or Venice? One good and obvious reason is that Beethoven, like such poets of the day as Wordsworth, was strongly influenced by the ideals that fired revolutionary France; he supported the French Revolution and the notion of equal opportunity for all, irrespective of birthright. For sure, such views

1

would not have gone down well in seventeenth-century Italy. And from where would he have got such ideas, since they did not emerge in the literature until much later? But if he had held such views and kept them a secret, could we know about them from his music?

This last question raises a most important issue: Can we tell such things merely by listening to music or looking at musical notations? Empirically, we might claim that the early-nineteenth-century Beethoven of Vienna was known for such views. His music was received as indicating the *ethos* of the new age of freedom, and he wrote music that overtly represented the struggle for freedom: the incidental music to Goethe's drama *Egmont* and the opera *Fidelio*, for example, or the Ninth Symphony. Rationally, it might be argued that the musical structures and content he used had essentially no more to do with such social and political ideals than did those of Haydn, his teacher, or Mozart, whose music he knew and admired. It would certainly be very difficult to attribute such meanings to the music of Haydn, who employed very similar, and in some cases the same, musical elements. A nominalist might accept that the same or similar musical elements could be imbued with different associated cultural meanings, but a Platonic realist would have difficulty accepting such relativist notions.

For the latter, certain chords or melodies would contain particular essences of meaning or representational properties that would be unchangeable, a notion that has been at the core of Western aesthetic theory. Nowadays, particularly in view of both developments in 2,000 years of Western music and knowledge of different musical practices across the world's cultures, such a philosophical paradigm leads to nowhere artistically interesting to contemporary musicians—a point that will be explored in subsequent chapters. However, if philosophical labels have to be applied to discussions on music and meaning, then it is proposed to take more empiricist and nominalist starting points in order to examine the following propositions:

- There are no universals in music that can be defined in musical terms.
- We can, and do, imbue almost any sound with specific cultural significance for reasons other than the presence of universal semantic properties.
- The most important force in musical behavior and choice of sounds for music is culturally derived belief about their efficacy.
- The only universal affecting music across all cultures and epochs is that concerning the effects of the functioning of the

human auditory apparatus in perception and cognition, and the relationship of these human abilities to objective knowledge of the physics of sound.

A purpose of this book is to examine such issues.

THE IMPORTANCE OF EXPERIENCE IN COGNITION

There are implications for our understanding of musical cognition if such propositions are substantially supportable. Principally, it must be the case that the human organism, tuned as it were to certain beliefs about the cultural significance of certain sounds, will seek out the sounds to which it can ascribe meaning. The laws of the physics of sound are substantially the same all over the world. All humans are capable of perceiving the same range of sounds, and their auditory mechanisms respond according to the same principles. These principles are important to our understanding of the general phenomenon of music and, as will be demonstrated, have some bearing on the choices of musical sound made by specific cultures. This is not intended, however, as a key to knowledge about the cultural significance placed on some sounds but not others. This knowledge can only be acquired through experience and learning the musical codes invented by each culture.

Many cognitive scientists have pointed to the importance of individual interpretation of perceptual phenomena and of experience and learning in cognitive acts. Miller (1964), for example, states that:

> More and more psychologists . . . are beginning to ask . . . how can I discover the transformations that a perceiver can impose upon the information he takes in? And with each step forward in understanding the transformations, one gains increased respect for both the complexity and the beauty of our perceptual machinery. (p. 113)

Bruner (1973) quotes L. L. Thurstone in supporting the importance of individual experience: "In these days when we insist so frequently upon the interdependence of all aspects of personality, it would be difficult to maintain that any of these functions, such as perception, is isolated from the rest of the dynamical system that constitutes a person" (p. 44). Bryant (1974) puts it more forcibly: "Past experience is . . . crucially important . . . it must influence the way a person perceives" (p. 4). And Bruner (1973) explains that the perceiver "actively selects information, forms hypotheses, and, on occasion, distorts the input in the service of reducing surprise and of attaining valued objects'' (p. 3).

The musical corollary is that musical meaning must be a product of a learned belief system about musical sounds and their culturally imposed semantic properties, not simply a matter of perception of properties intrinsic to the particular musical sound. Therefore, understanding the forces that drive acts of musical cognition, as it were, is more a matter of understanding the musical belief system that imbues certain sounds with particular meaning than of investigating reactions to purely noncontextual sonic elements of music per se. A main purpose of this book is to expose the details of musical belief systems and to show how beliefs can attune us to acts of musical cognition in the manner suggested above.

THE SPECIAL NATURE OF MUSICAL SYMBOLISM

One basic difficulty in dealing with musical cognition is that the sounds of music are vague as symbols. One cannot really pin down a musical sound that can be said to have obviously heroic or cowardly properties or to signify such things in the way visual art or language can. Some aspects of contemporary culture that can be linked in some way with a composer's intentions can always be found; the problem arises in identifying the actual musical elements and showing that they do represent or reflect the influence of nonmusical objects. By way of illustration, we would not expect to find evidence of Marxist aesthetic theory in Palestrina's masses, nor any influence of the Counter-Reformation and the edicts of the Council of Trent in Cornelius Cardew's music. However, we might reasonably expect to find some evidence existing for the reverse associations: Palestrina was held up as the musical exemplar of the newly prescribed aesthetic of the Council of Trent, and Cardew has avowedly composed Marxist music.

But having suggested this, there remains the problem of identifying the evidence for such associated meanings. We cannot easily point to musical sounds that are clearly Marxist, any more than we can find readily distinguishable musical sounds that relate to Adam Smith's free-market theories. It is a curious but observable fact that a good deal of the music approved by post–World War II revolutionary Marxist regimes as being suitably collective in content and appeal is surprisingly dull, predictable, and most unrevolutionary in its musical content. Intentionally Marxist music written within capitalist regimes is usually, by contrast, extremely recondite, comparatively esoteric, and decidedly uncollective in its appeal and content. Even more curious, considering the ideological extremities and the notion that music reflects and symbolizes its era, are the noticeable similarities between music written for nineteenth-century capitalist, jingoistic regimes and that approved by some twentieth-century Marxist governments for state occasions. It would seem to follow, then, that musical symbolism is not a simple matter of matching each symbolized object with a different and appropriate sound so as to form a sort of universal lexicon of musical symbols.

It could be claimed, even, that music is such a highly abstract artform in Western traditions that it is comprised of sounds having no clear or fixed symbolic function or association at all, save that attributed by the composer. If this is the case, then music is a most idiosyncratic and esoteric form of communication. In contrast, shapes in visual art can readily resemble outlines of everyday objects familiar to the observer, and words in language have more or less fixed meanings, most of which can be translated into different languages. All cultures, for example, have words that are used as a label for sunrise and that are usually different from those used for sunset. However, it is quite possible in music to use the same sounds for either and not in any way compromise the intended meanings of the musical sounds, provided the composer states his or her intention. In fact, we cannot know purely from the musical sounds what they are intended to represent unless they clearly imitate some natural sound, such as a birdcall or a barking dog; but musical art, of course, operates on a different level from this kind of simple, literal reproduction.

It might be argued that language also comprises word sounds that are incomprehensible without their cultural reference. But with word sounds, each social group agrees on their fixed meanings, which can then be translated into other languages so that other social groups or cultures can understand their meaning. Thus in each language there is not only clear symbolic meaning for words but also grammatical and syntactical structure. This enables someone to make a statement that the sun has risen in one language and have it translated into another language so that it comes out with the same meaning in both. With music, Western music in particular, this is not the case. Composers can invent their own musical language and its symbolic reference that few but themselves might fully understand.

The history of modern Western music has many examples of such composers; one of the most recent of these is Olivier Messiaen (1944), who felt the need to write a book explaining his new musical language. There would be little point in inventing your own verbal language because there would be no one to communicate with except yourself. In any case, inventing an entirely unique and esoteric verbal language could only be an act of extreme mental isolation signifying a conscious desire to deny to language the very purpose of its existence: to facilitate communication between humans. With music this does not seem to apply, judging by recent developments in Western music. As later chapters will illustrate, there appears to be no convincing evidence, even within a specific musical culture, of the necessity for a common musical grammar whereby such elements as melody, harmony, and rhythm must conform to some basic structural principles, as is the case with the words and groups of words that make up language structure. This is particularly so across different musical cultures. In Western culture, in fact, it is more often than not considered to be a mark of musical greatness to establish new forms, structures, and sound patterns, rather than merely to show continuity and links with the past. Where composers considered great acknowledged the past they did so in music that was essentially new and different. Brahms, in his Fourth Symphony, for example, and some twentieth-century composers, such as Vaughan Williams and Bartók, forged links with the past by a deliberate use of archaic forms or musical idioms within new or modern structures.

Returning to the specific problem of musical symbolism and the difficulty of identifying relationships between musical sound and symbolized object, let us explore a little the contention that such relationships are perceivable more from the heuristics of musical style and the composer's intentions than the identification of literal or implied semantic analogies. We cannot derive information about the spiritual role for music in the liturgy assigned by the Council of Trent just by listening to a Palestrina motet; we need to engage in a detailed and serious study of Palestrina's style in order to contrast it to that of some of his contemporaries whose style was banned from liturgical use. The evidence in this case would relate to an absence in Palestrina's work of certain characteristics that the Council decided were unhelpful to proper spiritual contemplation. These characteristics had mainly to do with sounds that were thought to induce physical rather than spiritual responses; in particular, rhythms thought more suitable for dancing were banned. Today, four centuries later, many churches would be empty if dance rhythms inducing bodily reactions were suddenly banned from all music performed in them.

The Counter-Reformation was intended to rebut the criticisms of the Reformers that the Roman Church had become lax and dissolute.

By banning dancelike rhythms in liturgical music, it was hoped to keep some of the more doctrinaire and devout from leaving the Catholic Church. The hoped-for musical result of this was the imbuing of Palestrina's music with a greater spirituality than that of some of his contemporaries by virtue of the absence of certain rhythmic qualities. Thus both the composer's intent and the listener's belief about musical meaning were clearly prescribed for devout Catholics.

On the other hand, we can see a level of spiritual commitment no less devout actively expressed through the dancelike rhythms in the Gospel music of the American South; though not identical, these are the very *types* of rhythms banned by the Roman Church of the sixteenth century. The Gospel traditions emanate, of course, from African-American cultural sources, which are quite different from those of sixteenth-century Rome. To have two such distinctly opposed ways of expressing presumably the same spirituality in the service of the same God inevitably invokes issues of cultural relativism. We really cannot say that African-American bodily expressions in religious worship are any less devout or spiritual in intent and achievement than the intellectual effects of Palestrina's mystical polyphony. Neither is an absolute; both certainly rely on beliefs and intentions for their musical, spiritual, and semantic validity.

The same kind of semantic and aesthetic problem arises even within the boundaries of a single culture and epoch. More often than not this emanates from opposing semantic uses of the same musical elements. The famous self-borrowings of Handel illustrate the dilemma well. Many of the most devotional arias and choruses from his *Messiah* use music lifted straight from his own youthful settings of Italian erotic poems (Hanslick, 1854/1957). If there is absolute meaning in musical sound, or the type of meaning comparable to the information we perceive visually when we recognize the outlines of something we know from our everyday experience, how can identical musical elements have different—in fact, opposite—significance? Visually a shape cannot look like both a table and a cat without artistic distortion in the way musical elements can, chameleonlike, assume almost any meaning. How does one show that the famous Tristan chords actually symbolize romantic sexual longings, as Wagner intimates? Even within the technical context of nineteenth-century harmonic language, it would be misleading to assign such meaning exclusively and totally ignore other meanings that other composers have applied to the same or similar chords. Passages of similar richly chromatic harmony can be found in the music of many composers from Liszt, in his religiously inspired works, to Elgar, in *The Dream of*

Gerontius; clearly they are meant to symbolize entirely different moods and feelings.

In contrast, there can be no doubt about the subject matter of certain erotic paintings or drawings in Western or Oriental art. It is not possible as it is in music, for such artists to use the same shapes and forms to represent perceptually something entirely different—opposite, in fact. The artist uses our visual perceptual apparatus in various imaginative ways in order to make us think visually (Arnheim, 1969). This is possible because of the effects of visual images from our everyday experiences in fixing meaning to visual shapes with which the artist can tantalize our perceptions by presenting patterns and contrasts that challenge our assumptions. From Picasso's juxtapositions of machines and animals, depicting bull's horns as bicycle handlebars, for example, to Jackson Pollock's mobiles, we are confronted by an admixture of shapes that relate to our everyday visual knowledge of the world.

Historically, painters attempted to recreate the visual world around them by using figures and shapes that made up that world. But as artistic sensibility developed, it became possible to juxtapose fantasy with reality or merely to re-create real life through the eyes of the artist. Two-dimensional shapes displaying humans in erotic poses, for example, cannot, perceptually, provide different information than that relating to humans in erotic poses. There are certain ambiguous visual shapes, such as the two wine goblets in silhouette that can oscillate perceptually between the outlines of two human faces and the edges of goblets (see Gregory, 1966). But most visual art depicting the human form lies well beyond such perceptual thresholds, enabling us to recognize clearly the shape it depicts. Such clearly delineated perceptual categories cannot be found in musical representation: music is, representationally, not so much ambiguous as incorporeal and utterly abstract.

The assignment of symbolic reference to musical sounds is in one sense, then, quite arbitrary. The composer chooses a sound to be a symbol of something, and by musical convention that sound acquires particular evocation or representative powers within the context of a particular milieu. Successive composers may, or may not, imitate this symbolism, or they may invent entirely new ones. Listeners are obliged to discover and learn each new development in musical composition or remain rooted in outmoded or defunct musical referents, thus running the risk of misunderstanding the intentions of the composer. Moreover, the translation of specific musical imagery from one musical culture to another is impossible; each has to be accepted on its own merits, as the succeeding chapters will elucidate.

In the case of the tonal grammar that evolved in the eighteenth and nineteenth centuries in Western Europe, no equivalents can exist outside Western musical culture of that period for such things as a perfect cadence, tonal entries in a fugue, affective melody, or musical representations of rivers or mountains; all are culture- and composer-specific modes of musical behavior. The same can be said of certain aspects of Western musical culture from this century: no equivalents exist either in earlier Western culture or across other musical cultures for such things as moment form or integral serialism. The traditions of Balinese and Javanese gamelan music and the individually owned and mystically received spirit songs of the Pacific Northwest Indians of Washington State and British Columbia cannot be expressed in other musical cultures the way a Shakespeare play can be translated into other languages. They are all abstractions peculiar both to music and to a specific musical culture. They have no perceptual features that relate to everyday objects known to a culture in the way visual art does. Each musical culture is driven by self-contained musical beliefs and practices—self-contained in the sense that the sounds of each culture have no relevance or translatability outside their individual cultural milieu. They are abstractions in sound relating only to a specific culture, a notion that later chapters attempt to explain and elucidate.

The contention is, then, that the intended musical symbolization, or representation, can only be apprehended through appropriate cultural knowledge. Nonetheless, within each musical system there are clear and well-defined symbol systems in operation. The problem is that each system is, more often than not, confined to a single composer or, at most, group of composers. Composers can and do invent their own semantic systems. Despite this, their music attracts audiences who will listen and understand, indicating that the invention of a personal musical language is no barrier to communication in the way it would be in the case of verbal language, provided one both believes in the efficacy of the personal musical language and has access to its esoteric codes. Thus musical communication occurs despite the relatively abstract constructions in sound that make up musical events. Rather than engage in a possibly fruitless search for intra- or cross-cultural similarities or universals, it therefore seems of greater import to know how different musical cultures have used sound as a means of communication and why certain sounds and not others were chosen.

It is evident, then, that despite the absence of an acoustic equivalent in music to the identifiable visual forms and shapes in visual art that match everyday experience of objects, or to verbal semantic precision used in everyday discourse or literature, musical practices have arisen that rely on acceptance of acoustic forms of communication as reflective of some set of beliefs about the significance of such forms. Such beliefs about sounds are necessary for music to sustain meaning. The same would not be true so much of visual art, in the sense that belief here would relate to the object being visually represented rather than the actual visual shapes of the artwork. Since music cannot represent objects or feelings in the same fashion as visual art, the belief, in the case of music, must relate to the sounds of music.

For example, recognizing that a visual shape represents a cat, however stylistically modified it might be (as in cubist or expressionist paintings), does not require a set of beliefs. It looks either like a cat or like something else. Our perceptual senses and cognitive apparatus confirm the identity of a shape with a minimum amount of visual information; with far less than a full outline, we can say the shape is meant to be a cat. This is not the case with musical sounds, which cannot relate to everyday auditory objects. Therefore, more than with any other mode of communication, accepting beliefs about the intentions of those communicating—the musicians—is of paramount importance. There appears to be little else upon which to base our assignment of meaning to musical sounds.

MUSIC AS A CULTURAL SYSTEM IN ITSELF

Across different cultures there is a common thread concerning music's representational properties. Musical sound seems universally to be assigned some kind of affinity with the supernatural, either in the form of spirit beings or entities or in the way in which the actual elements of musical sound relate. In the latter case these elements are thought ideally to reflect the perfect harmony observable in the environment, particularly in the way planets appear to exist in perfect harmony. In the West we know this as Pythagoreanism, but this perspective had its origins in the civilizations of ancient Mesopotamia, Egypt, China, and India; from it there arose a notion that universal semantic properties are contained in musical sounds. In the West this was expounded by Plato and his successors as the theory of *ethos*. As modern Western music evolved in response to such theory, individual composers began to interpret the theory in increasingly esoteric fashion, as explained in later chapters. This is particularly so with more

modern Western musical practices, where the autonomy of composers has become such that they virtually create their own musical uni-
verses, complete with belief systems.

Such belief would presuppose a distinction between the esoteric,
the "in" group around the composer whose members know the
acoustic codes utilized, and the exoteric, the outsiders who have yet
to identify the codes and learn their surrounding beliefs and significance. Within Western culture examples of this are legion and cover a
wide range of compositional and performance practices: the musicians at St. Marks, Venice, in the sixteenth and seventeenth centuries,
which became a mecca for ambitious musicians from all over Europe
who were eager to learn the Venetian musical secrets; an orchestra
such as the Vienna Philharmonic, whose long-time members know
from each other (in an almost telepathic manner), and from such
apparently innocuous signals as an eye or shoulder movement by their
conductor, precisely what to do musically; an anciently established
choir such as King's College in Cambridge, where subtle and unobtru-
sive hand or finger signals indicate an extra beat here, a pause there; or
the improvisational music of Stockhausen, where those performers in
the know can readily construct a piece of music from a mysterious
and cryptic verbal score such as *From the Seven Days*. Examples of
the esoteric in Western musical practices extend as well into modern
popular forms—one need only think of the great traditions of jazz
improvisation.

Access to the "rituals" is only obtainable from within the group.
Two examples illustrate how this applies to performance practices as
well as composition: Haydn's symphonies presented some problems
to players of the Philharmonic Society Orchestra in London, and he
had to demonstrate personally during his visits to London how to play
some passages and make a viable performance of the whole symphony (Carse, 1948); Viennese orchestral players derided Schubert's
Great C Major Symphony as unplayable during the nineteenth century.

Numerous other examples can be cited of composers whose music
remained incomprehensible to many listeners for some time simply
because it contained recondite or unknown musical semantic codes,
which also had implications for performers. Often, as in the case of
Samuel Wesley's and Mendelssohn's reviving the music of J. S. Bach, it
took someone with extraordinary insight to unlock the secrets and
make the music intellectually accessible.

Such examples indicate that intraculturally there are some musical
practices that are not immediately accessible or acceptable to all members of the culture. These represent but one facet, of course: not all

Western music is remote from general public acceptance and understanding. Some has had immediate appeal and popular acclaim, even
to the point of gaining popularity through mass involvement in its
performance. The varying needs of Western society are reflected in
the multifarious social and political uses to which music has been put:
nineteenth-century social changes favored mass involvement in performing sacred choral works; the ubiquitous radio, phonograph, and
cinema of the 1940s and 1950s were responsible for promoting various popular musicians; the more recent rise of specialized music-
appreciation groups provided opportunities for musicians with more
aesthetically profound intentions to perform their music. Thus within
Western culture there is music intended for mass consumption as well
as music that is accessible to only a few who are "in the know."

Social and educational institutions in nineteenth-century Western
culture made clear distinctions, as educational provisions expanded to
all members of society, between the music thought suitable for the
working classes and that thought more suitable for the middle and
upper classes. The former comprised suitably moralistic songs, whereas the latter included contemporary art music serving a perceived
need for engendering intellectual development and the pursuit of leisure. The two had little in common in terms of curricular aims and
content (Rainbow, 1967; Walker, 1984).

The situation in other cultures is similar, but only in the sense that
there are different social functions for music. Although Western social
and economic structures are not reflected in terms of musical utility
and accessibility, a clear distinction is usually made between music
used in the public domain and that used more privately. The personal
songs owned by Pacific Northwest Indians are passed on from one
individual to another, and often no one else is allowed to sing them.
Only close family members would know such songs, but even they are
usually forbidden to sing them without the owner's permission. Australian aboriginal "dream songs," which relate to totemistic objects
over a particular territory, are "given" during initiation rites. Their
significance is generally unknown outside the group and territories
involved. Almost every culture has similar guardianship over certain
musical secrets, just as they have other music that is intended for mass
performance and assimilation. Within any culture there are, it seems,
certain musical behaviors that are esoteric compared to other, more
public and accessible, musical behaviors.

In a more general sense, the situation of the outsider trying to
understand unknown musical sounds and behavior is similar to that
experienced by anthropologists when they seek to investigate some

unknown culture. Music poses problems in this regard because its sonic structural and symbolic systems obey different laws from those of language, or those of visual art, making it a most difficult form of communication to understand from the outside, that is to say, outside the particular musical culture. Unlike the sounds of language or the shapes of visual art, the sounds of music relate only to music. The sounds of language contain certain universal sounds, such as sighs, cries, or laughter, as well as culturally fixed meanings that relate to observable everyday objects in ways musical sounds cannot. The shapes of visual art are those of our everyday visual experiences, even though they may be arranged to suit artistic spatial criteria. The sounds of music are not the sounds of everyday life.

The general problem in music thus hinges on the difficulties experienced by the outsider attempting to decode communications that are known by the insider—someone who has grown up with the musical code. More specifically, the problem in music concerns decoding and understanding the significance of the particular choices of sound made by each musical culture, which will tend to be very different from each other. As will be explicated throughout this book, it is in such choices that cultural belief systems are reflected. One understands the choices in terms of the belief system, not the other way round, and in such understanding lies the key to the musical and cultural significance of musical sound.

GAINING ACCESS TO MUSICAL CODES

Using Musical Metaphors

The choices of sound in Western musical practices are susceptible to identification and description, and the reasons for such choices are well documented through the ages. One object of this book is to expose as fully as possible both the choices and the reasons for making them. Since this subject is addressed in documents stretching back over 2,000 years, there is a great deal of information available and considerable space is herein devoted to it. Less information of a reliable nature is available from cultures that possess essentially no written record, even though they may have existed for many thousands of years. By explaining how profoundly a documented belief system has affected all aspects of musical practice, as in Western culture, it is possible to trace connections between belief, meaning, and choices of musical sound. In cultures that possess little such documentation, it might be possible to establish such links by extrapolation, assuming that at some fundamental level of operation all human cultures adhere to similar basic laws of function. Thus if one knows something of the belief system in a culture, such as that of the Pacific Northwest Indian, and knows something of the meanings intended for its music, then it might be possible to develop some sort of hypothesis about the culture's choices for sound, particularly in the case of melody, the control of which is peculiar to humans in an activity such as music-making.

Some anthropological theories hold that humans essentially invent their own culture in order to acquire some control and understanding of the forces that shape their environment. Similarly, composers invent their own musical language in order to express in musical sound the various effects of the environment on their sensibilities. Wagner (1981) explains that in order to get to know another culture we also have to invent it. Referring to the situation of the outsider trying to gain "inside" knowledge, he maintains that *culture* is a term used to describe esoteric ways of behaving that develop in a group of people. These behaviors derive from particular physical conditions, the effects of historical lifestyles and beliefs, and other social and economic factors. Wagner explains that someone from another culture has to learn to appreciate the full significance of the esoteric and translate from his or her own exoteric standpoint to the esoteric one. In order to do this, it is necessary to use metaphors or tropes, essentially, to "invent" the other culture in attempts to understand it. The invention arises from using terms from one culture to represent metaphorically what is observed of another; in essence, to use words that stand in place of the other culture as a means of objectifying it.

In this way it is possible to gain some access to the individual experiences that motivate perception and cognition. The effect of the specially "tuned" organism, to borrow a term from the psychologist's explanation of the crucial role of experience in interpreting sensory data, is akin to the effect of belief systems on our behavior. The use of behavioral choices to represent mental acts in experiments investigating mental operations is akin to Wagner's explanation of the use of metaphors in objectifying both cultural knowledge and the semantic properties of cultural behaviors or artifacts.

There are considerable heuristic advantages in investigating the secrets of a musical culture by using metaphors in this way. It encourages a greater sense of respect for the possible uniqueness of the unfamiliar. And through acknowledgment of the use of descriptors from one's own culture, there is a tacit acceptance of their probable inadequacy for fully representing another cultural mode of thinking and behaving. This point is worth illustrating further in a musical context.

During the late nineteenth century and the early years of this century, when non-European music was commonly referred to as folk music, a great deal of immensely valuable fieldwork, the collection of songs from many different parts of the world, was done. All the songs were meticulously recorded using Western music staff notations. Because of its rigidity and ethnocentric nature, this notational system was unable to account for the enormous diversity of melody, rhythm, and timbre found across different cultures. At its worst it made aboriginal music from Australia appear, on paper, to look little different from crude attempts at writing Schubert *Lieder*.

Many fieldworkers acknowledged this and attempted to reflect deviations from non-Western musical elements by means of ingenious modifications to staff notation. Basically, however, melody was represented on the staff using the Western diatonic system and rhythm by means of Western metric notation. Melodically, for example, it did look as though Australian aboriginals and Canadian Inuit both used diatonic intervals, such as minor thirds, in their melodies, despite the miraculous coincidence of this occurring in two such extremely distant and remote cultures. Ethnologically, it enabled the more extreme to cite folk music as containing evidence of Darwinian evolutionary progress toward the more ''perfect'' diatonic Western scale system, since incipient diatonic intervals could be ''observed'' in ''primitive'' music. Ethnomusicology today uses more sophisticated procedures that account for cultural differences more sympathetically, but discovery of a universal method of musical analysis across different cultures is still more impossible than merely elusive.

The difficulties inherent in metaphorically representing one musical culture in terms taken from another musical system is similar to those that exist within Western art music when the ideas of a composer confront those of listeners who are naive and unfamiliar with the composer's style and content. In the case of a composer who essentially invents his or her own musical language, inside knowledge concerns ways of organizing sound in order to express oneself or represent one's cultural ideals in sound. Since the outsiders, or listeners, unfamiliar with the invented musical language have only an exoteric access to such things, they are obliged to find metaphors for what is experienced from within their own experiences in order to facilitate understanding. If they know only tonal melody and metrical rhythm, they will employ these as metaphors in their descriptions and interpretations of the unknown music.

Problems arise from the inevitable loss between the exoteric and esoteric, between the knowing that occurs from within the musical system under scrutiny and that which occurs in the mind of the outsider. Or, put another way, between the knowing that occurs within the mind of the composer who invents the musical composition and that which occurs in the mind of the outsider—the listener who is trying to gain access to the musical codes that result from the composer's inventions. Of course, the listener has a right to interpret purely as a listener, with no obligation to observe the intentions of the composer.

Total ignorance of and indifference to the composer's intentions will, however, undoubtedly render musical art innocuous, just as they will, if applied to minority cultural needs in political and social matters, render the people of such cultures less than they are as humans.

The esoteric is manifest in various behaviors by members of a particular cultural group whose cultural beliefs determine the significance of such behaviors. The exoteric is manifest in attempts to bridge the gap between different beliefs, albeit using products of the beliefs of one as metaphors for understanding the other. In this sense, the term *belief* refers to more than simply what someone believes to be true. It refers to the knowledge system about the world, or, as in this case, about music, which arises from a set of principles believed to be true. Our knowledge system is comprehensively supportive of our actions and acquired behavioral patterns. This suggests that *belief* is a sort of umbrella term that subsumes all kinds of logical systems for explaining, predicting, and defining the environment. It includes, on the one hand, rational and empirical ways of knowing, and on the other, the more mystical or superstitious ways of explaining phenomena. Basically, the term *belief* can be said to apply to the set of guiding principles upon which a particular lifestyle of behavioral pattern is based; regarding music, it applies to the set of principles upon which the musician invents musical structures and behaviors.

In the case of music, the most obvious exoteric approach is through an acoustic or other objective explanation or representation of the sounds used, such as scientific symbols and formulae or musical notations and formal musical analysis. Esoteric musical knowledge, in contrast, springs from "inside" knowledge, or an examination of the belief systems that motivate musicians in their musical inventions, and it often involves information that cannot easily be expressed metaphorically. Chapters 3–6 examine the genesis and evolution of what are suggested to be esoteric beliefs that have motivated music-making throughout the development of Western and some other cultures. These chapters attempt to explain the esoteric in music from a standpoint within the milieu sustaining and motivating the musician. In effect, they attempt to expose and explain the esoteric through explication of the various theories supplied by actual composers, their teachers, or others intimately connected to their musical belief systems.

Prior to this undertaking, however, Chapter 2 explores a more obviously exoteric approach to understanding musical sound: that of defining its acoustic parameters. Other chapters will show, by contrast, the difference between this exoteric approach and the more obviously esoteric one and, it is hoped, highlight the importance of both to our quest for a deeper understanding of musical cognition.

Using Purely Objective Metaphors

Perhaps the most objective and extreme exoteric viewpoints from which to examine musical sound and behavior are those of acoustics and psychoacoustics. And although modern science has made great strides in understanding the workings of the human ear in its responses to sound, the search for scientific or objective explanations for the musical sounds chosen by musicians has very ancient origins. The ancient civilizations of China and the Middle and Near East included the study of musical sound as an important part of their scientific activities. They were certainly aware of the fact that vibrating objects caused some sort of disturbance in the air that affected the ear in some way, enabling us to hear and respond.

In order to match these effects with the behavior of vibrating objects, such as strings or columns of air in tubular lengths of metal, the ancient Greeks developed an elaborate system of mathematical proportions that were meant to be an analogue of melodic movement—a scientific metaphor for the magic of song that itself became part of the esoteric tradition. Elaborate theories carried the metaphor to such lengths as establishing relationships between certain special proportions, or ratios, and melodic movement that was considered to be especially beautiful or perfect. This desire to find a scientific metaphor for musical activity has continued throughout the development of Western culture, becoming today the highly sophisticated science of psychoacoustics—the matching of mental phenomena with acoustic objects.

It was not until modern times, however, that the true nature of the behavior of a vibrating object was known. The activities of a vibrating string are far more complicated than Pythagoras or his Babylonian and Chinese antecedents realized. During the late Renaissance, scientists became aware of something of the complexity of the disturbance in the air caused by a vibrating string or column of air; as a result, applications of ideal mathematical relationships between harmonic partials of a musical tone were included in the scientific metaphor of musical sound. Nevertheless, as we shall see in Chapters 3 and 4, this scientific advance did not destroy the validity of the more ancient metaphor—proportional lengths of a string.

Modern science tells us that musical sounds comprise what are termed "complex waveforms," that is, waveforms that contain a number of partials, each vibrating simultaneously in some mathematical relationship to the basic rate of vibration of the whole waveform. Simple waveforms, that is, those with no partials, do not exist in isolation in nature and were not found, as such, in musical practices until the present age of electronic generation and manipulation of sound. The ear seems to respond differentially to these different partials and, indeed, to different repetition rates of a vibrating pattern. Such observable phenomena have continued to inspire scientists to speculate on relationships among musical sounds, mathematical metaphors for sound, and physiological and mental effects in the listener.

If the ear responds differentially, it is argued, there must be some sounds that excite more pleasure, or sense of beauty, than others, and the auditory perceptual apparatus will respond appropriately to give us such sensations. Thus the notion of matching culturally accepted musical beauty or perfection with auditory perception and the workings of the ear using the metaphor of mathematics became a seductive objective. The intractable problem of establishing common standards of beauty with which to match objective criteria across different musical cultures still precludes the possibility of real advance. Yet, nevertheless, as science continues its quest to find objective metaphors for Western musical behavior, the metaphor has today been extended to include matching with neural firing rates and codes utilized along the auditory pathways in the brain (Patterson, 1986).

In any explanation of human behavior, the tendency to invent one's own culture presents enormous problems in the quest for rational scientific metaphors for such things as musical behavior. Yet in Western music, more than in any other musical tradition, there has persisted a tradition that links rational scientific thought to musical theory and practice. The main purpose of this book is to explore the invention of musical culture and describe the application of metaphors that purport to explain musical behavior. My contention is that the enormous edifice of Western musical theory and practice is just as much an artifact, a product of cultural beliefs, as is the music of the Pacific Northwest Indians or any other cultural group. No single musical culture can claim to owe its existence purely to objective, scientific laws any more than any other. The more interesting questions concern how and why musical systems emerged and developed as well as the nature of both the origins and the beliefs that motivated men and women to create and nurture such systems.

The range of musical beliefs and practices in the world is so diverse that the proclivity to invent a belief around some musical object and act in accordance with that belief seems a likely candidate for a universal that might explain, if not predict, musical behavior. After all, if it can be shown that the musical practices of Western culture are products of a belief system, and are the inexorable outcome of scientific laws only insofar as they apply to all human auditory perception of pressure waves from vibrating objects, then we surely cannot make different claims about music from other cultures.

CHAPTER 2

Musical Pitch
and Human Hearing

Traditionally, pitch is regarded as the most important aspect of Western musical sound. This is largely because of the central importance of pitch in Western musical theory and, as a consequence, the fascination it holds for scientific investigators. The purpose of this chapter is to explicate various theories of pitch perception and to expose the fallacy that Western musical pitch is more closely based on the natural workings of the human auditory mechanism than the pitched sounds of other musical cultures.

The range of Western musical pitch might be given as approximately C below the bass staff up to C above the treble staff, or four octaves, if relating to music written through the end of the eighteenth century. Thereafter, based on the piano and its popularity as well as the growth of the range of orchestral instruments, the range might be extended to seven octaves. These two ranges, translated into cycles per second, or Hertz (Hz), would be roughly 65 Hz to 1,050 Hz and 32 Hz to over 4,200 Hz, respectively. This does *not* mean that there is a different pitch for each different cycle per second. There are 48 or 84 musical pitches (four or seven octaves), respectively, within these two sets of frequencies. Considering the enormous variety of music in Western culture, this would seem, on the face of it, somewhat astonishing. How can just 48 different pitches be the source from which the music of Léonin, Machaut, Palestrina, Monteverdi, Buxtehude, and J. S. Bach sprang? Or how can just 84 different pitches provide the basic material for the variety of music produced by Wagner, Tchaikovsky, Debussy, Stravinsky, Stockhausen, Elvis Presley, Charlie Parker, John Cage, Prince, or Big Bill Broonzy?

Indeed, if the only information in music was that pertaining to the notes of musical scales we call pitch, it would be difficult to understand the wealth of musical invention that has been produced in any musical culture, not just that of the West. However, musical pitch, if defined as information relating only to the perceived position of a sound within a particular scale system, is only one part of the sound picture that makes up what we call music. Apart from rhythm, dynamics, and timbre, there are the complexities of musical language structure. Nevertheless, the development of the pitched scale system held a very important position in the development of Western music and may even have been the most crucial element. Without doubt, most of the scientific interest in Western music has been centered on pitch as the foundation of the entire edifice of Western musical theory.

To this extent it can be said that musical pitch is the most important element in Western musical history. And while perception of musical pitch might be described, in one sense, as a simple matter of identifying one or more of the small number of pitches found in Western music, it is certainly a far more complex matter to establish psychoacoustic correlations between the perception and the physical properties of the musical sound. A perceived musical pitch can be said to be simply the result of the mechanical and neural effects in the auditory apparatus of complex interactions caused by many or all of the physical aspects of the sound. But we would not normally describe all pitched sounds, in the musical sense, as having musical pitch qualities. Musical context is important, but so are the musical characteristics of sound in the sense that a single pitch would sound more musical sung by a trained singer than if sung by an untrained one. Musical pitch perception, therefore, suggests a more complex process than the purely mechanical business of pitch extraction. Researchers in psychoacoustics generally do not make a distinction between frequency discrimination and musical pitch perception where isolated sounds are concerned. I am suggesting that there are scientific as well as musical reasons why this distinction is important to our understanding of auditory perception in general and musical cognition in particular.

To a trained musical mind the sounds of a musical instrument playing middle C would constitute a musical pitch, as in the Bach C major Prelude and Fugue for organ. Few people, however, would automatically attribute the musical pitch of middle C to the sound of a truck horn they heard while driving down the freeway, even if it were at precisely 261.63 Hz (the concert pitch frequency of middle C); the context at least would be inappropriate. But more to the point, the character of the sound (by which I mean its amplitude, onset, and spectral characteristics, etc.) would not suggest a musical pitch, even

though the sound could be said, acoustically, to have pitch characteristics in that it has a regularly repeated wave form. An important part
of musical development in any culture is learning how to make and
recognize the special sounds that the particular culture regards as
musical. Common sense would suggest that there is a difference between musical sounds, which have musical pitch, and nonmusical
sounds—such as animal or machine sounds—that, acoustically, might
have the same repetition rate (frequency) but clearly are not part of
any particular musical traditions. But this does not mean that "nonmusical" sounds cannot under any circumstances be interpreted in
terms of musical scales: Anyone familiar with the behavior of music
students knows that they take great delight in identifying the note on
the treble or bass staff that is approximate to the "pitch" suggested by
animal or machine sounds. Although such sounds will not be considered musical simply by virtue of such identification, this does not
preclude their description in musical terms by someone musically
trained. In other words, there is more to the perceptual process of
attributing a musical pitch to a sound vibration than mere apprehension of the appropriate repetition rate.

There is a further complication in that we would readily attribute
the musical pitch of middle C to a violin string vibrating at 265 or 259
Hz (i.e., playing musically sharp or flat), yet not to a dog howling at
precisely 261.63 Hz. We would be influenced partly by the quality, or
timbre, of the sound—a dog howl is not one used in music, but a
violin is—and partly by our proclivity to accept approximately correct
frequencies as belonging to the pitch category intended and nearest to
them (Seashore, 1938). This latter tendency is called "categorical perception" (Siegel & Siegel, 1977a). On the other hand, let us imagine a
hypothetical human auditory receptor mechanism and perceptual system that does not know that 261.63 Hz signifies middle C. What
happens when, say, a violinist plays middle C accurately? The system
will not reject the information as outside its experience; it will respond in some way known to it simply because it is designed to. But it
will not attribute the musical pitch middle C to the sound in the
manner of suitably experienced listeners. These things suggest that
two essential and major factors, at least, are involved in the perception of a musical pitch: appropriate experience in the listener, and
appropriate information in the sound. They also indicate the importance to our perceptual processes of what Rousseau (1749/1966), in
his *Essay on the Origin of Languages*, termed the "moral" content of
a sound. By this he meant the special codes contained in the sound
that make it musical to a musician, or French to a Frenchman, or dog

language to a dog. I want to suggest that such "codes" are present as much in individual sounds as they are in the larger musical context of songs or instrumental pieces.

Until fairly modern times, humans did not know how they perceived sound because they did not know what sound actually was. The ancient Greeks and Chinese knew about vibrating strings, but they relied on their calculations of proportional lengths of strings to explain the phenomenon of different pitches. It was only during the last few hundred years that discoveries have been made about the true behavior of an object vibrating at sufficient speed to be heard as a sound. And it is only very recently that we have been able to generate sounds that lie outside the range of acoustic musical instruments. There are some interesting and pertinent issues raised by our knowledge of the higher frequencies to which the human ear responds.

The highest note on a piano—C four octaves above middle C—has a frequency of 4,186 Hz at concert pitch, and the lowest C three octaves below middle C—a frequency of 32.7 Hz. A large cathedral organ can produce a lower C, at 16.35 Hz, but its pitch at this level is hardly discernible without a C major chord played simultaneously at higher pitches. The limits of human functioning at the upper range of frequencies extend in most adults up to about 12,000 Hz, which is far in excess of the capabilities of acoustical musical instruments. Young children have a response range that extends even higher, reaching to about 20,000 Hz. From about the age of 20 years, the top frequencies begin to disappear from our hearing as a result of normal aging processes and our exposure to noise. Needless to say, there are no objects in a natural environment that are capable of producing periodic vibrations throughout this whole range, so we might reasonably ask why we need to hear such sounds at all. And here we are talking simply about hearing the fundamental rate of a vibration at, say, 12,000 Hz, not hearing the musical pitch associated with it. It seems obvious that no musical pitch could be associated with such a frequency, because no acoustic musical instruments can satisfactorily produce periodic vibrations much above the range of the piano; and, indeed, it has been verified experimentally that we cannot derive musical pitch from such extreme frequencies (Schouten, 1970).

There is a problem with such verification, however, because it does not take historical musical experience into account; it assumes that musical pitch perception is static across the millennia, and this assumption is, at the very least, open to question. For example, it is possible that the upper frequency limit for perception of musical pitch might have been only about 1,100 Hz in the year A.D. 1700 simply because of the limitations in the pitch range of existing musical instruments then. After all, it is difficult to see how pitch concepts can be developed for (musically) nonexistent sounds. Since the cochlea can respond to frequencies up to 12,000 Hz in adults, there seems to be no physical reason why humans cannot adjust to perceiving as musical much higher pitches than exist even in present-day musical practices. They apparently did it between the seventeenth century and the present!

Experimental evidence shows, however, that the higher frequencies, which lie within human hearing capabilities but do not appear to have a musical function, are important to pitch perception. The information contained in the higher frequencies of a complex sound is reflected in the musical ambiguity we feel when we hear our favorite tune played on a strange instrument instead of being sung by our favorite singer for that tune. We can still pick out the melody, but something is missing: the timbre or voice quality we are used to and value. Some acoustic correlates for this are contained in the frequency spectrum of the sound.

In fact, much of the complication associated with musical pitch perception arises out of the perceived relationship between the subjective pitch we hear and the various properties of the pressure wave to which we have responded. Some have argued that pitch is only obtained from the fundamental vibration rate (von Bekesy, 1960; Helmholtz, 1885/1954). Others refute this by demonstrating experimentally that we hear a pitch where no fundamental is present (Houtsma & Goldstein, 1972; Schouten, 1940). The former make it easy to equate acoustic pitch (i.e., a vibration rate) with a perceived musical pitch, since both are derived from the fundamental and suggest a more restricted view of musical art. The latter provide for the possibility of a more sensitive and responsive framework within which different musical cultures, as well as different musical fashions within a single culture, can be accounted for. They also enable us to accept and explain a perceptual distinction, which common sense tells us exists, to be drawn between purely acoustic and specifically musical phenomena given certain appropriate cultural contexts. Here one is drawing a distinction between the intentional perceptual act that applies musical meaning to a sound and that which does not. As we have seen above in the example of music students and machine noises, it is perfectly possible to apply some musical meaning to unmusical sounds, given certain basic properties in the sound, a humorous intent, and appropriate training in the perceiver. Acoustic definitions of sound can, however, help us identify which characteristics are essential for the sound to be acceptable as music, as well as which are necessary to provide the barest minimum for one to make a pseudomusical identification.

WESTERN MUSICAL SOUND AND ITS SPECTRAL CHARACTERISTICS

Modern acoustic theory tells us that any vibrating string or column of air produces a pattern of vibrations comprising a conglomeration of many simple vibrations superimposed and sounding simultaneously. In fact, any naturally occurring pitched sound can be broken down into its component parts if certain facts are known. The component parts are individual sinusoidal waves, so called because their waveform can be calculated using sine (or cosine) functions. Each component has its own amplitude and phase coefficients, which are called "Fourier coefficients." An ideal, or perfect, complex vibration is one in which each individual sine wave occurs theoretically at integral multiples of the overall rate of vibration. This means that such an ideal object vibrating at an overall rate of 200 times every second is also vibrating at 2 times, 3 times, 4 times, 5 times, 6 times, 7, 8, 9, 10 . . . n times the basic rate. These additional vibrations are called "harmonics." Numerically, this means that the vibration is a complex of patterns ranging from the overall, basic rate of 200 through 400, 600, 800, 1,000, 1,200 . . . $n \times 200$, all at the same time. Few objects can produce such ideal vibrations, however, and this fact is important to bear in mind when we consider the development of belief systems surrounding Western musical theory. This theory is based on Pythagorean beliefs about the metaphysical properties of proportional lengths of vibrating strings. Some Western musical instruments produce imperfect and inharmonic (i.e., nonintegral multiples of the basic repetition rate) vibrations in actual music-making. It follows that any musical system based on the notion of ideal or perfect physical relationships cannot be perfectly realized in practice, but, as will be seen in the case of Western music, belief in the ideal can drive the development of a musical tradition.

Vibration patterns can be seen visually on an oscilloscope or any microcomputer capable of dealing with auditory input by means of a digital-analog converter. Visually, a sine wave is represented as the projection of a point on a circle, but traveling through time. The top half of the circle is described in the normal fashion; but instead of going back underneath to complete the circle, the bottom half traveling through time is described in the adjacent space. This shape represents the simple harmonic motion of a vibrating body moving through time from a state of stasis to one extreme determined by the energy applied to it, back to the midpoint, the stasis point, but with momentum to carry it beyond to the "negative" side and back again to rest. It represents one single cycle of a vibration. In the natural world, however, such a pure vibration does not exist, although it can be approximated by a tuning fork. When such a vibration is modified by the addition of other single vibrations in the form of harmonics, whether perfect integral multiples of the basic rate or not, its shape becomes less circular as different rates of vibration are superimposed to form a very complex trace of movement.

In theory, every complex vibration that is periodic (cyclic) can be broken down mathematically into its constituent parts. The French mathematician J. B. Fourier (1768–1830) developed a theorem for expressing a periodic function (i.e., a regularly vibrating object) as the sum of a series of sine or cosine terms. This is known as "Fourier analysis." Its opposite is Fourier synthesis, wherein the series is added together to compose a regularly vibrating pattern, as is the practice in electronic music synthesis. For a typical violin string these harmonic rates of vibration could go as high as about 6,000 Hz, or the 30th harmonic, for a basic or fundamental rate of 200 Hz, though at this high rate of vibration there would be far less energy and little that the ear could pick up. This brings us to the important point that the energy level is not uniform for each of the harmonics due to factors such as the nature of the vibration source, shape and consistency of the materials making up the instrument, and manner of playing. In fact, energy normally decreases with higher and higher harmonics.

From this brief and sketchy explanation of the harmonic content of a complex periodic sound, the sort that we hear in Western music, it can be deduced that there is much more to musical sound than merely the number of pitches contained in a musical scale. The harmonic content of a musical sound contains special codes for our ears to learn to respond to. These are similar to the codes that we all learn to assimilate as infants when we hear speech sounds. They enable infants to recognize their mother's voice as a sound distinct from another woman's voice. The different energy levels of different harmonics forming peaks and valleys (i.e., the spectral envelope) in a complex periodic sound provide a wealth of information, all of which is crucially important in our perceptions of both speech and music. There are other important aspects of such a sound, particularly those having to do with the amplitude envelope: such characteristics as onset and release time, for example. But in the musical traditions of the West, the steady state of a signal from a musical instrument assumes more importance for musical theory than its onset characteristics, which merely help to distinguish, say, the sound of a trumpet from that of a violin. Acoustically speaking, it is from the steady state of a musical sound that the frequency ratios, so crucial to Western musical theory, are calculated, whether they are made by a violin, a trumpet, or a human voice, each of which have vastly different onset and release characteristics.

To define the characteristics of the steady state of a musical sound in more detail, let us consider the human voice. At the vocal folds the sound produced as the column of air passes up from the lungs contains all the harmonics, from the fundamental and beyond, but at decreasing energy levels. This can be described as a linear relationship between frequency and amplitude, where energy diminishes between each harmonic to the point where the higher harmonics are nearly at rest (see Figure 2.1). This complex vibration reaches the vocal tract, which is the area from the vocal folds to the mouth. The unmanipulated vocal tract is about 17 cm long and has a cross-sectional area of about 5 square cm, with a diameter of 2.5 cm in male adults (Fry, 1979). In children it may be as short as only 7 or 10 cm (Sundberg, 1987), with correspondingly smaller cross-sectional areas. The tract has a bend in it where our mouth joins our throat. The sides of the tract are flexible; we can move our tongue and muscles in our mouth and throat at will, thus changing the shape of the tract. In fact, we do this automatically as we say words. We make a different shape for the vowel *e* than for the vowel *a*, and so on. These changes in the shape of

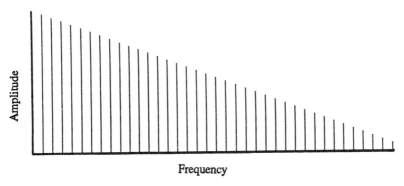

FIGURE 2.1 Idealized harmonic spectrum of pressure waves from the vocal folds

the vocal tract act upon the energy wave coming from the vocal folds in such a way as to alter the energy distribution from a linear one, wherein the lowest component has the highest level, to a curvilinear function, wherein different harmonics have different energy levels. This phenomenon is called "resonance."

Adult males can vary the cross-sectional area of the tract from as large as about 12 square cm to as small as 1 square cm at certain points (Sundberg, 1987). Our vocal tract, in fact, performs like a natural synthesizer as it filters and modulates the pressure wave emanating from our vocal folds, in much the same way that we can by setting various electronic controls to filter and modulate the waveform generated from a voltage or digitally controlled oscillator in an electronic synthesizer.

What happens is that the peaks of energy move from the fundamental rate of vibration (e.g., 200 Hz) at the vocal folds, up to various levels that conform to the natural resonance characteristics of an unmanipulated tube 17 cm in length. These resonance peaks occur naturally at around 500 Hz, 1,500 Hz, and 2,500 Hz as the wave is filtered by the vocal tract. But this is assuming a perfectly shaped tube. The precise location of these peaks depends upon the shape of the mouth and lips, the position of the tongue, and other conditions within our vocal tract that result from our shaping of consonants and vowels; they are more often than not centered at other points in the harmonic spectrum. Such peaks include several individual harmonics gathered together to form large peaks followed by troughs. These peaks, called "formants," are responsible for the special qualities of a vowel sound as well as the special qualities of a person's voice. It is the steady state of these spectral characteristics that we perceive as musical pitches or as vowel sounds in speech.

The first formant (500 Hz) can be raised or lowered from between 250 Hz and 1,000 Hz by increasing or decreasing the size of the jaw opening, respectively. The second formant (1,500 Hz) can be varied between 600 Hz and 2,500 Hz by the tongue position. The third formant can be raised to about 3,500 Hz or lowered to about 1,700 Hz by increasing or decreasing the size of the cavity behind the incisors, which is determined in part by the position of the tip of the tongue (Sundberg, 1987). Just as our fingerprints comprise very individual conglomerations of lines embedded on the skin of our fingers, so we have special and individual arrangements of formant peaks in the harmonic spectrum of the sounds our vocal tract produces. Each person has a special tone quality, just as each instrument in music does, and this special and unique quality is reflected in the formant peaks.

The differences between human-voiced sounds and those of musical instruments have to do with the nature of sound production employed. A column of air set into vibration by a pair of lips blowing into a mouthpiece and on into the tube of the instrument will produce different formant peaks than those set in motion by the vibrations of a reed and then traveling into the tube of the instrument (Benade, 1976; Roederer, 1979). Various other factors come into play, however, including the length, shape, and consistency of the tube and the addition of a bell-shaped end, as well as the nature of the waveform initiated from the mouthpiece. All these factors affect the harmonic nature of the waveform as well as its amplitude envelope characteristics. All combine to provide the necessary and sufficient information for our perceptual apparatus to process and recognize them as music in the Western traditions. Sounds not containing these necessary and sufficient characteristics are not, therefore, acceptable in this way. But such decisions are not made at the peripheral level of ear function. They are made by the higher-processing levels of the brain. For the moment, though, let us concentrate on identifying acoustic characteristics of musical sound.

Vibrations caused by a string set into motion and amplified in the body of a violin will have different amplitude characteristics, such as onset time and spectral envelope characteristics, than those induced by a vibrating column of air. Yet we still recognize them as musical sounds because they contain certain other characteristics essential to musical sounds in Western culture. The nature of these vibrations will be affected by such factors as pressure of bow on string, or lip position and air pressure emanating from the lips, as well as resonating characteristics of the body of the string instrument and the transmission of the vibrations from string to body through the bridge, or from mouthpiece to metal tube. All these elements can be manufactured to fit shapes as variable as those of the vocal tract if necessary, but such variability, of course, exists between instruments, not within a single one. Those from nonmusical sources, such as car horns, howling dogs, and so forth, contain other characteristics that lie outside those acceptable as musical sound. Even though the repetition rates of such sounds may approximate those of music, the spectral contents may not. Nonperiodic sounds will lack both periodicity (that is, any sense of pitch) and appropriate spectral characteristics. Such latter characteristics include lack of sufficient energy in several adjacent lower harmonics, which reinforce the sense of musical pitch (see below for an explanation of experimental evidence), or lack of a sufficient number of integrally related harmonics, which also can reinforce the sense of pitch.

PERCEPTION OF MUSICAL SOUNDS

Our ears have developed in such a way as to be able to analyze the pattern formed by the harmonic content of sounds in all its amazing intricacy. And this ability is not unique to humans. All animals have a capacity to recognize the special harmonic or spectral characteristics of the natural sounds of their environment. It enables animals to recognize their own kind and their enemies and provides other information they need for survival. A most interesting facet of this concerns how humans use spectral content not only to tell the difference between musical instruments or different people's voices but also as a source for deriving pitch from any complex periodic sounds.

Empirical studies have shown that humans and animals (Chung & Colavita, 1976; Cynx & Shapiro, 1986; Javel, 1980) in general can recognize the acoustic pitch (which we might for the present define as the fundamental rate of vibration that we equate with pitch) of a complex periodic sound from a group of adjacent harmonics, whether or not the fundamental rate of vibration (i.e., the lowest) is present. In terms of sharp G below middle C (i.e., 200 Hz), this means that if two or more adjacent harmonics only are sounded (e.g., 600 and 800 Hz), our ears will respond as though a vibration of 200 Hz were present (Houtsma & Goldstein, 1972). The more harmonics that are sounded (e.g., 400 and 1,000 Hz), the more the 200 Hz vibration will come into auditory focus. By analogy, a few visual cues, giving us only parts of a visual shape, can nonetheless enable us to fill in the missing parts; as more and more visual cues are added, the identity of the shape is confirmed. There is some evidence (Javel, 1980) that neurons in the auditory nerve respond to waveform envelopes in a highly sophisticated manner, such that different neurons respond to different subjective pitch characteristics.

We are used to incomplete sounds (i.e., sounds without energy at the fundamental repetition rate) in our everyday life. In normal speech, and often in singing, most human voices contain little energy at the fundamental repetition rate. Telephone speakers and small transistor radio speakers both produce sounds with missing fundamentals, containing only harmonics. A brief examination of the technical specifications of such speakers will show that they are unable to respond to vibrations below about 250–300 Hz, or even higher in some cases, and those responses at that low end are of such a low energy level that we can hardly hear them. This means that melodies with notes lying below about D or E at the bottom of the treble staff are not represented except by their harmonics, yet we still hear them and recognize them.

(Of course, the manufacturers of telephones and radios knew the workings of the ear before they marketed their products.) Contemporary evidence would suggest that the ear has evolved to recognize human speech and music through the patterns formed by spectral contents, rather than simply from fundamental vibration rates (de Boer, 1976). Although certain aspects of these spectral patterns and the fundamental repetition rates do correspond, as explained below, there is significant perceptual information in the spectral content of sound, such that the presence of high energy levels at the fundamental rate is not essential to pitch perception.

In Western music, concert and opera singers are specially trained to add the spectral energy to their singing voice in what is known as the "singer's formant," in the region of 2,500–3,000 Hz. This gives their voices the characteristic "ringing" sound associated with Western trained singers. The sound of a well-trained singer accompanied by equally well-trained instrumentalists gives the musical listener a clearly defined sense of Western musical pitch. This is because of high energy levels in many adjacent harmonics. If individuals experienced only in Western classical music were to hear an untrained singer who was unable to produce much spectral energy beyond, say, the first natural formant (i.e., around 500 Hz) of the human vocal tract, they would almost certainly say the sound is "unmusical," particularly if the context led them to expect a trained singer. And this would be the case despite high accuracy of tuning. The reason for this is that important information concerning musical pitch in the Western traditions is contained in the spectral content of periodic sounds intended as music. This information is derived from high energy levels in a number of adjacent harmonics from the 3rd upwards (Houtsma, 1971), as well as from the unique, specially induced formants that lie above the second natural formant (Sundberg, 1987). These enhance the sense of musical pitch associated with musical intervals based on Pythagorean proportional theory and their modern applications to melody and harmony in recent Western traditions.

Figure 2.2 shows comparisons of concentrations of spectral energy between untrained and trained singers in analyses of their respective spectral envelopes. It illustrates that little spectral energy is observed in the untrained child's voice above the first natural formant as compared with the trained child and the trained adult. Children's average formant frequencies generally lie about 32–38 percent above those of adult males (Sundberg, 1987). This would suggest that the child's first natural formant should lie at around 650–700 Hz because of their shorter and narrower vocal tract. Singers and singing teachers

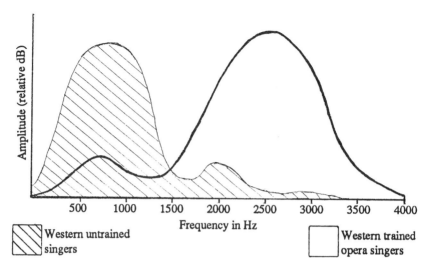

FIGURE 2.2 Relative distribution of spectral energy in sounds produced by Western trained and untrained singers

are, of course, fully aware of the need for vocal resonance, and they have long utilized many somewhat fanciful metaphors for the acoustic description of inducing unique formant peaks so as to give the voice a special ringing sound associated with Western trained singers. To this extent the development of Western musical practices has resulted in the exploitation of our cognitive capacity to respond to these aspects of the spectral content of sound. The fact that musical sounds in many other cultures, as well as in the ubiquitous popular-music culture of the West, use different distributions of spectral energy is particularly important to our understanding of the influence of culture on our perception of musical sound. It is important, to our understanding of cultural context, to the relationships between this context, the musical sound, and its acoustic properties, and to the development from birth of our cognitive abilities in music. Different musical practices employ different spectral and amplitude characteristics in their musical sounds, and these characteristics relate to the different belief systems underpinning such practices.

For example, the chanting of certain Tibetan lamas gives the impression of one man singing a chord (Smith, Stevens, & Tomlinson, 1967). By means of certain manipulations of the vocal folds and tract, certain harmonics, usually the 10th, can be emphasized and made individually audible. The importance of the fundamental frequency in Western music is a reflection of the importance of integer ratios between such frequencies in the definition of musical intervals in melody and harmony used in music theory. This is the case despite the ability of our perceptual apparatus to hear a pitch when no fundamental is present. The implication is clear: the theoretical basis for Western musical melody and harmony cannot be satisfactorily explained purely in terms of acoustic laws, whereby the latter illuminate and show correspondences with the tenets of the former. Before examining this proposition in more detail, it is interesting to consider the intuition of a composer, Arnold Schoenberg, concerning the importance of the spectral characteristics of sound in pitch perception and musical melody and harmony.

One of the most important insights displayed by Schoenberg was articulated in the final section of *Harmonielehre* (1911), where he postulated the idea of melody arising from tone color—*Klangfarbenmelodie*. Intuitively Schoenberg reached the conclusion that melody was a product of tone color: ''I cannot unreservedly agree with the distinction between color and pitch. I find that a note is perceived by its color, one of whose dimensions is pitch. Color, then is the great realm, pitch one of its provinces'' (p. 471).

He elevated color above melody in a number of his works during the period before the First World War, particularly in the third movement of Variations for Orchestra, opus 16 (1909), in which different instrumental timbres, or colors, provide the main focus rather than thematic material, which would traditionally have been the case. In this piece Schoenberg requires single chords to be played continuously by successive groups of instruments, thus giving the listener a continuously changing tone color.

There are, however, important musical and perceptual issues involved in Schoenberg's notion of *Klangfarbenmelodie*. Being a province of color, the musical implications of pitch, and therefore melody, are considerable. A melody becomes distinctive, musically, not so much by the vertical contours of melodic movement as by the tone color of the voice or instrument performing, that is, not so much by the movements of fundamental repetition rates of the musical pressure waves as by their spectral patterns. In practice, this means that for some there can be only Luciano Pavarotti to sing Italian opera, or for others only Placido Domingo, or other favorite singers. The tone qualities of the voice become so inextricably bound up with the melodic contours of operatic arias that they are regarded as inseparable.

The same phenomenon can be observed today in the pop/rock scene, where only a performance by the favored group is acceptable to fans for their favorite piece of music. It does not sound the same with anyone else performing, even though they may be playing the same notes. The associations between what might be called quality of sound and melodic perception are, therefore, crucial in the context of Schoenberg's artistic intuitions. I am aware of no evidence showing that Schoenberg was familiar with the nineteenth-century debate concerning auditory perception of pitch. Nevertheless, as will be explicated below, the possibility of a connection between spectral content and pitch perception had already been suggested by scientists around 1840, and, more important, research in the last few decades has tended to affirm that Schoenberg was indeed correct in that pitch perception is intimately bound up with perception of the patterns formed by the spectral contents of sounds—their timbre or color.

The connection between the timbre of a musical sound and its harmonic content was known about and used in the seventeenth and early eighteenth centuries, when violinists such as Tartini (1754) demonstrated the presence of such harmonic effects as difference and combination tones, though their possible connection to pitch perception was not suspected then. But the idea that the pitch of a complex periodic sound arises from the tone color of a sound—that is, from its harmonic content rather than simply from its fundamental vibration rate—was not entirely new to the twentieth century. Scientists were arguing about this possibility as early as the 1840s, even though some dismissed it out of hand. It was not until a century later, that the Dutch scientist J. F. Schouten (1940) demonstrated the so-called "residue" phenomenon and put forward an alternative theory of pitch perception (as will be explained in more detail later in the chapter).

Similarly, although the presence of harmonics in musical sounds had been known about since the seventeenth century at least, it was not generally thought that harmonics could have such an integral and crucial role in pitch perception until Schouten's "residue" theory appeared. Instead, scientists and musicians tended to use this knowledge of harmonic content to explain the developing theory of musical consonance and harmony. And this supposed scientific basis for Western tonal harmony was thought to be the reason that listeners found such sounds beautiful and pleasing. In the middle of the eighteenth century, Rameau (see Chapter 3) defended his theory of functional harmony by citing contemporary scientific knowledge of harmonic content in complex sounds and its connection with ancient Pythagorean proportionism.

MUSICAL PERCEPTION AND AUDITORY MECHANISMS

Until the "residue" theory appeared, pitch was thought to emanate entirely from perception of the fundamental vibration rate of a vibrating string or column of air. It was considered to be something of a mechanical process that left the perceiver with little or no input from learned experiences, that is, from the higher cognitive processes of the brain that interpret in accordance with experience, belief, preference, and the developed individuality of the species or organism. In this way Western musical pitch came to be regarded as the natural interpretation for a human on hearing a complex periodic sound, being rooted as it was in the Darwinian-based notion that the evolved mechanics of ear function are linked with the highest evolutionary level of musical practice and perception. The notion of the perfectness of the ideal harmonic series gave rise to the notion of the perfectness of Western tonal music, its melody and harmony. Further, musical dissonance and consonance, the very bedrock of Western melodic and harmonic expression, were thought to derive from acoustical dissonance and consonance and to be capable of mathematical description.

The actual process of pitch perception was thought to rely entirely on the response of the inner ear, the workings of the cochlea responding to the basic rate of vibration, or the fundamental period of the waveform, purely in terms of this rate's stimulating the appropriate part of the basilar membrane. Helmholtz (1885/1954) put forward a theory of frequency detection that incorporated Ohm's acoustic law (posited in 1843). Ohm suggested that the ear analyzes any composite mass of tone into its simpler components (Davies, 1978), that is, into sine wave components calculated according to Fourier's theorem. Helmholtz's theory of hearing took this as a basis and suggested:

1. The ear performs a frequency analysis of the waveform and is able to separate the harmonics in a limited way. This has importance, it was argued, for both pitch perception, timbre perception, and musical dissonance and consonance.
2. Each harmonic causes a particular resonator to react on the basilar membrane, which in turn excites a corresponding nerve fiber, resulting in a related pitch sensation. This is the main cause of our sense of pitch, it was argued, and is the origin of the place theory of pitch perception (de Boer, 1976).
3. Any acoustic dissonance, such as inharmonic partials, causes a disturbance to this process and results in musical dissonance.

The idea was that the vibrations of a musical sound would reach the oval window, the entrance to the cochlea, and set up a motion within the cochlea fluid. As the ear resolves, or separates, the harmonics, each would in turn stimulate a certain place on the basilar membrane, one of the two membranes that divide the cochlea. On this membrane is the organ of Corti, which contains rows of hair cells that act as triggers of neural activity, transmitting information to the brain. Helmholtz postulated that as the particular place on the organ of Corti was stimulated by the appropriate vibration rate, the particular individual hair would be activated and the message concerning the "pitch" of the vibration, as determined by the hair in a particular place on the organ of Corti, would go to the brain (de Boer, 1976).

It was thought that the basilar membrane was constructed such that harmonically related, or consonant, sounds were better received by it than were dissonant ones. In this way a particular harmonic vibration corresponded to a particular pitch in music in a fairly mechanistic fashion. A melody would thus be found by a process of tracking the energy outputs of the lowest frequency, the fundamental, irrespective of the type of overtone structure. In other words, the different overtone structures of different instruments or voices would not affect this process, a view opposite to that of Schoenberg. In a sense they are both correct. As we shall see, different waveforms, given a common musical pitch, do provide different pitch sensations, but they can also denote a common musical pitch if the musical context requires it, given our propensity for categorical perception. Helmholtz postulated that the higher tones would receive sympathetic responses in the hairs at the round window end of the cochlea and deeper tones at the apex end. In fact, later research has shown the opposite to be true (von Bekesy, 1960). Moreover, Helmholtz also suggested that the ability of the ear to perform a frequency analysis on complex waves explains the problem of timbre perception. This has been refuted by many researchers (Davies, 1978). But there are more serious problems with this theory when musical sounds having no energy at the fundamental, such as those made by the French horn or some singers, are considered. Also, our frequency sensitivity (jnd) is not consistent with the place theory.

Thus by the end of the nineteenth century theories of music perception comprised a mixture of mechanics of ear function, belief about the objective physical basis for consonance and dissonance in music, and the relationships between these and the musical value systems of Western culture: the perfect physical object induced perfect mechanical reactions in the ear, which in turn yielded an inner sense of perfection and aesthetic pleasure. This Platonic causal chain characterizes the so-called "place" theory, which holds that pitch resolution of complex periodic sound occurs mainly at the level of the inner ear and relies on tracking the fundamental vibration rate. The notion that the higher levels of brain function could intervene in the process was precluded on functional grounds. How could these higher levels intervene, it was argued, if pitch perception was such a relatively simple and mechanical affair occurring at this peripheral level of perception? Experiments investigating this phenomenon were carried out using pure tones to ensure adequate experimental controls, despite the fact that Western music uses only complex tones. However, it was not until fairly recently that convincing theories, discussed in fuller detail below, were developed concerning differences in the way the cochlea responds to pure and complex tones (Terhardt, 1970; von Walliser, 1969). These theories appear to indicate some differences between a musical perception involving complex tones and an experimentally derived one using pure tones. With complex tones, musical context would be an important factor, one totally lacking in the experimental context; thus no one-to-one relationships can be demonstrated between stimuli and responses in experimental conditions and musical contexts.

At this point one can contrast the applications to musical art of findings from the objective world of science with the intuitively insightful world of the musician. Helmholtz (1885/1954) had produced an acoustical correlate for musical dissonance and consonance by the mid-nineteenth century. During the next hundred years or so, musicians developed their musical uses of consonance and dissonance to the point where Helmholtz's theory seemed irrelevant. Moreover, the notion of functional harmony, formulated by Rameau and assimilated by Helmholtz into a psychoacoustic theory of music, was deliberately broken down. Wagner, Mahler, Debussy, Scriabin, Schoenberg, Webern, Stravinsky, and many others were using chords, including additional musically "dissonant" notes, merely as entities in themselves rather than as part of some logical and functional harmonic progression. These composers often required acoustic dissonance, or beats, in their musical sounds. Since Helmholtz, dissonance has been associated with beats. It is well known that a group of stringed instruments with slight mistunings create acoustic beats in their normal playing (Benade, 1976). Beats are extra sinusoidal waveforms created for each single vibration when two such vibrations lie only a few cycles apart. Usually stringed instruments create only three or four beats per second when playing in tune. Badly out-of-tune piano strings, where there are two or more strings to a single pitch, can create many more vibrations per second, up to the actual vibration rate of one of the strings. Many combinations of musical sounds produce beats in actual performance, but the musical context has such an effect on our perceptions that we take them as part of the musical sound.

Such musical practices tended to ignore views expressed in acoustic science that, to many people, suggested clear relationships between musical consonance and dissonance and the natural workings of the ear. Many of the critics of composers who used musical dissonance cited scientific knowledge of human auditory functioning as reasons for dismissing their music as an aberration. In particular, Helmholtz's argument that there was a clear relationship between consonance and dissonance in both musical harmony and acoustic theory, as demonstrated in acoustical science by means of identifying beats, was regarded as powerful. Additionally, some music was described as unmelodic because some "dissonant" combinations of notes in harmony were thought to destroy the natural sense of pitch obtainable from "purer" sounds. The dissonances found in the music of Liszt and Wagner, and then of Mahler, Debussy, Ravel, and Schoenberg, were all regarded by some as outside the realm of acceptable musical sound largely because they were thought to violate acoustical laws. Today we can see how false this notion is. With hindsight, we can now see that the science of Debussy's, Schoenberg's, and Stravinsky's time provided only a part of the explanation of the workings of the ear, and that what we now know puts things into different perspective, particularly concerning those arguments that seek to justify particular musical practices in preference to others by citing mechanical workings of the ear.

Some modern acoustic theories hold that there is no fixed and immutable connection between musical dissonance, acoustical dissonance, and the workings of the ear (Houtsma, 1971). However, it should be mentioned that Plomp and Level (1965) show that consonance can be described as occurring when the frequency difference of two tones reaches the critical bandwidth in their action on the basilar membrane (see Truax, 1978). But apart from this scientific controversy, musical practices over the last century have shown that both acoustical and musical dissonance can provide a pleasing aesthetic experience, if given the appropriate artistic context. Moreover, the ear does not act in a purely mechanical way by attributing the pitch of a sound simply from the place of stimulation on the basilar membrane (de Boer, 1976). Hence the notion is false that Western musical harmony, rooted in the ideal Pythagorean harmonic ratios formed by the harmonic partials of an ideal complex periodic pressure wave, represents something like the highest level of artistic attainment possible, primarily because of its scientific and mathematical bases. Western tonal harmony may well be one of the most impressive examples of human artistry, but not for these reasons. The intuition of some musicians that Helmholtz was incorrect turned out to be justified. Schouten's "residue" theory, and the many experiments that have been carried out since the 1940s, have all shown that the most important influence on pitch perception is not that of the peripheral mechanisms of the ear but the processes of higher cognitive functioning at the central levels of the brain and its role in interpreting the messages resulting from the stimulation of the cochlea. That being the case, the role of learning and of the experience of the individual within a particular cultural context assumes some importance, as will be argued below.

THE PROBLEM OF THE MISSING FUNDAMENTAL

In one of Schouten's original papers (1940), he explains how he deduced that the "place" theory was inadequate to explain pitch perception. He showed experimentally that individuals attributed pitch to sounds in conditions in which the theory could not apply because the appropriate place on the basilar membrane could not have been stimulated to give the sense of pitch they obviously felt: there was little or no energy at the fundamental repetition rate. At this point, it is interesting and helpful to examine briefly the arguments that took place between some nineteenth-century scientists who were instrumental in developing theories of pitch perception. It was from these arguments that Schouten developed his "residue" theory.

In 1841, Seebeck put forward a theory of auditory perception which suggested that the pitch of a musical sound is determined not by the frequency of the lowest Fourier component but by the period of the signal's waveform. Although this amounted to the same thing, in that the period equals the rate of vibration of the lowest component, it suggests a crucial difference for the process of pitch perception from that implied later by Helmholtz. Ohm, as we have already seen, suggested that the frequency of the lowest component, the fundamental, determines the pitch of a musical sound. But as Seebeck realized, this does not account for musical sounds where there is little or no energy at the fundamental. He therefore postulated that the ear itself can add energy at the fundamental through quadratic distortion, producing a difference tone that corresponds to the fundamental.

The two argued over this, and Ohm produced the well-known version of his acoustical law in 1843 in response to Seebeck's position. In the same year Seebeck stated his criticism a second time. He argued that the higher harmonics might collaborate to enhance the strength of the first, and that these higher harmonics might interact in some way so as to produce a tone that has the pitch of the fundamental without the actual presence of the fundamental—the notion of the missing fundamental. In 1844 Ohm replied in an unscientific tone, rebutting Seebeck a second time while admitting that he did not use his ears in his experiments because "nature had completely denied him a musical ear" (quoted in de Boer, 1976, p. 495). This is illuminating in that it betrays a belief in connections between possessing an innate "musical ear" and ability to derive pitch from sounds. In 1863 Helmholtz entered the debate, coming down on the side of Ohm. He essentially ignored Seebeck's theory and was largely responsible for establishing the preeminence of the "place" theory and the role of the fundamental rate of vibration in theories of pitch perception until the 1940s. In its purest form the theory assumes perfect isolation of all Fourier components in the cochlea, such that this part of the ear becomes a kind of frequency analyzer. Since the fundamental frequency, the lowest component, will always be the strongest, it was argued, it follows that the sensation of pitch arises from this strongest part of the excitation.

The "place" theory suggested, then, that pitch sensations are due to the place stimulated in the cochlea corresponding to the maximum stimulation that the fundamental would inevitably cause, assuming most energy in the waveform occurred at the fundamental repetition rate. The advent of the telephone provided further information, however, that caused some scientists to cast doubts on the theory as far as the role of the fundamental was concerned. For example, in 1929 Fletcher wrote his first book, *Speech and Hearing*, in which he referred to the "case of the missing fundamental" (quoted in de Boer, 1976, p. 497). This concerns the fact that although telephone exchange circuits carry signals in which the fundamental frequency of the human voice cannot be present, people nonetheless hear the voice at the pitch of the fundamental. It was explained away, according to Helmholtz's theory, as the product of aural distortion. Later, von Bekesy (1960) carried out experiments with pure tones (i.e., sinusoidal tones) demonstrating that spatial analysis of sound does occur in the cochlea, thereby giving further support to the "place" theory of pitch perception.

There were two principles in the theory by the mid-twentieth century:

1. A particular frequency will be directed in the cochlea to a specific location where it will induce the maximum vibration.
2. Stimulation of the nerve fibers at any particular location and the consequent neural message to the brain will give rise to a sensation of pitch that is associated with that particular place in the cochlea.

The first principle is known to be true. The basilar membrane is stimulated in places according to the frequency of the stimulus. Higher frequencies are quickly damped in the cochlea and thus stimulate the end nearest to the oval window, the beginning of the cochlear tube (von Bekesy, 1960). Lower frequencies retain their energy more effectively and therefore travel farther toward the apex. Thus it can be shown that each frequency will stimulate a certain place in the cochlea. In the late 1930s, however, Schouten had demonstrated that the "place" theory could not completely explain perception of complex tones. By experimentally manipulating the harmonic content of a complex periodic wave, including removing various harmonics so that only a few adjacent harmonics were present (the 4th, 5th, and 6th, for example), he found that the fundamental pitch could still be heard.

THE PERCEPTUAL IMPORTANCE OF
SPECTRAL COMPONENTS

As a result Schouten extended Ohm's law to state that although the ear analyzes a complex sound into its components (i.e., its harmonic, or Fourier, components, many of which can be heard individually in certain circumstances), there is another component present that corresponds not to any individual harmonic but to the collective effect of several harmonics. He called this a "residue," which, he claimed, gives the sensation of pitch. He explained this phenomenon further by showing how the ear can resolve lower harmonics individually up to about the 7th or 8th harmonic, beyond which they tend to fuse together to form an overall pattern common to all of them. This pattern repeats itself the same number of times as the fundamental repetition rate, so that this fusion, in fact, gives the impression of the fundamental pitch of the whole waveform. This fusion can be seen quite clearly in Figure 2.3, where, by the 8th harmonic, the individual Fourier

FIGURE 2.3 Idealized representation of fusion of harmonic components into a pattern repeated at the same rate as the fundamental period of the waveform

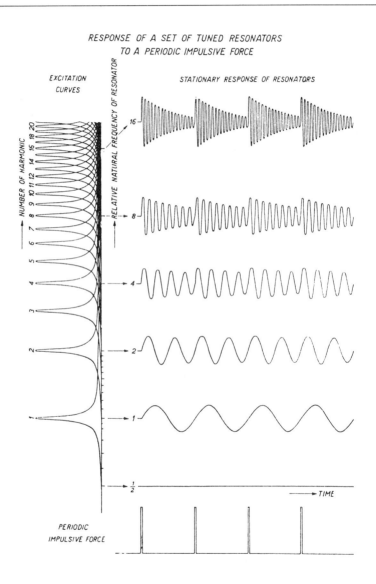

After Schouten (1940)

components appear to have merged to form a pattern that is repeated at the fundamental rate of repetition.

Helmholtz claimed to have heard up to the 16th harmonic, but he did so with the aid of resonators in the form of hollow spheres, the so-called Helmholtz resonators. Helmholtz's feat did not invalidate the position of later acoustic researchers, since it was not accomplished with the unaided ear. At the time, however, it did enhance his position concerning the importance of the ability of the ear to resolve individual harmonics, thereby giving more credence to the importance of place of stimulation on the basilar membrane in pitch perception.

The notion of a residue to explain pitch perception of complex tones, such as occur in musical sounds, has been developed extensively over the last few decades by many researchers. Ritsma (1962), for example, suggested a harmonic region where it might exist to best advantage—several adjacent lower harmonics. Using just three neighboring harmonics, he showed that as the strength of individual harmonics deteriorates, so does the sense of pitch. This indicates that there are probably optimum levels for the components of a complex periodic wave for musical pitch sensations of sufficient strength to be induced. While acoustically it can be said that any periodic sound has acoustic pitch, it is obvious to a musically trained ear that some sounds have qualities that appear more appropriate than others in terms of defining musical pitch, and these qualities are largely determined by the spectral components if we are dealing with a steady state of sound.

Perception of Pure Tones

For example, the sounds of the clarinet and flute in certain circumstances at certain pitch levels are almost pure, sinusoidal waveforms. Experimental evidence suggests that there is some difference between pitch perceptions of pure, or sinusoidal, tones and complex tones, even when both have the same fundamental rate of repetition. Von Walliser (1969) demonstrated that complex tones are perceived as having slightly lower pitches than pure tones with the same fundamental repetition rate at certain frequencies. Since there is no spectral information present in pure tones, although there is some evidence that the ear may well supply some through nonlinear distortion proclivities of the inner ear function, the cochlea obviously responds more to the place stimulated than to a pattern normally associated with a complex sound. Consequently, the central processing mechanism also appears to respond somewhat differentially in this regard in that purer tones (i.e., ones that are sinusoidal) will tend to sound musically sharp in direct comparison with complex tones of the same repetition rate. Terhardt (1970, 1979) put forward a convincing theory that the pitches of pure and complex tones are basically different perceptual entities. Meyer (1978) demonstrated that spectral components influence pitch perception in that different spectral contents induce different pitch sensations, even though the fundamental repetition rate is the same throughout.

A number of other researchers have confirmed such differences experimentally (e.g., Ohgushi, 1978), and musically there are parallels. It is not unknown for those instruments capable of producing nearly pure tones to sound out of tune in some orchestral passages. The third movement of Scriabin's First Symphony, for example, requires the clarinet to play solo passages much higher in pitch than the accompanying harmonies. Without some compensating adjustments by the wind player, this can easily sound out of tune. There are many such instances in the orchestral repertoire, and musicians have known about them and how to deal with them since long before experimental science supplied some proof that, given the same repetition rate, pure tones appear to have different pitches from those of complex tones in certain circumstances. This would cast serious doubts on any theory that based pitch perception exclusively on fundamental repetition rates.

Perception of Complex Tones

A significant line of research is that by Houtsma and Goldstein (1972) in which they showed that any two adjacent harmonics below the 10th could induce a sense of pitch. They reported that in their experiments a number of trained musicians could identify the fundamental of two-harmonic waveforms at far better than chance levels, in some circumstance achieving nearly total accuracy. They showed that neither fundamental periods nor energy are necessary conditions for fundamental tracking to occur. Further experiments using dichotic techniques, whereby each ear is fed a different harmonic, demonstrated that some centrally located mechanism lying beyond the cochlea operates on signals derived from separate partials to yield a sense of pitch. These experiments show conclusively that Helmholtz's theory that the fundamental frequency is the only conveyer of musical pitch is incorrect. They further show that the sense of musical pitch is enhanced as more harmonics are added. Two harmonics can provide a sense of pitch, but four or even six will enhance this sense considerably. They also found that all harmonics, even the higher ones, contribute to a sense of pitch, but lower harmonics contribute most powerfully. For example, ambiguity of pitch sense occurs for Western listeners (Houtsma, 1971) when lower partials diverge from harmonicity (i.e., integrally related harmonics), as in bells or xylophones, but not in the case of the piano, where inharmonicity is found only in higher partials. This would indicate an important role in Western pitch perception for the lower harmonics below about the 10th.

HIGHER COGNITIVE PROCESSING AND MUSICAL PITCH IN DIFFERENT CULTURES

In contrasting the typical musical sounds of Western music with those of other cultures in the light of more recent theories of pitch perception, some distinct cultural differences can be accounted for. The sung sounds of aboriginal musicians, such as Native Americans or Australian aboriginals, clearly have pitch, but they do not *sound* like the pitches associated with Western music. Acoustically they are different objects: the spectral contents of Western and aboriginal sung sounds are quite different from each other. The Western singer is trained to produce high levels of spectral energy above the second natural formant (1,500 Hz) that show unique formant peaks, often reaching the level of the so-called singer's formant (usually associated with approximately 2,800 Hz). Such training enables the singer to widen the pharynx opening to about 6 or 7 times the size of the surrounding part of the vocal tract. This produces an acoustic mismatch, which, in turn, gives the voice the special ringing sound associated with the singer's formant (Sundberg, 1987). In contrast, the Indian singer of the Pacific Northwest produces virtually no energy above the second or third harmonic (see Figure 2.4) and very little energy above 1,000 Hz, preferring to concentrate most energy around the first natural formant of the vocal tract (Walker, 1986).

Pitch sensations for the Indian singer arise almost entirely from only two or three of the lowest harmonics, not from the "residue" in most cases. In contrast, the Western singer seeks to induce energy higher up the spectrum and across several harmonics, giving a sensation of pitch associated with the harmonic pattern analysis the ear carries out at the cochlea on such complex sounds. Subjectively, according to Terhardt (1972), the brain differentiates between the two types of vocal pitch. On a metaphysical level, one will match the rich pallet of harmonics associated with Western musical pitch and with Western aesthetic notions of beauty of sound; the other will be entire-

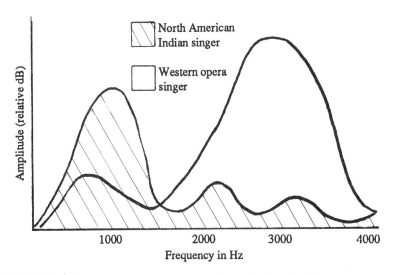

FIGURE 2.4 Spectral envelopes showing relative distribution of spectral energy in sounds produced by a Pacific Northwest Indian singer and a singer trained in Western opera techniques

ly appropriate for the intimate, personal, and intensely spiritual music that has been developed in the Kwakiutl Indian culture, in which music serves personal totemistic needs rather than public performance functions. The former has developed in cathedrals and concert halls whose acoustic properties tend to enhance the higher harmonics, which enables singers to be heard above the accompanying instruments (Benade, 1976). The latter tradition uses the open air in the Pacific Northwest rainforests, where higher frequencies disappear more rapidly than in confined areas where sound can be reflected off walls, ceiling, and floors. For the Kwakiutl Indian, singing forms an important part of a lifestyle intended to be at one with nature; the use of the first natural formant of the vocal tract for concentrating resonance explains, scientifically, how such singing practices form a musical corollary to the natural lifestyle. By contrast, unique formants to enhance higher harmonics developed in Western vocal practices, which are carried on in humanmade, artificial surroundings.

Thus there are not only acoustically definable differences between the sounds of different musical cultures; the effects of learning and assimilating cultural belief systems imbue these different acoustical objects with a sense of culturally discrete pitch and melodic systems. We can talk, therefore, of the pitch of Western music being derived from the unique formants and spectral envelope of periodic sounds produced by the Western trained singer's vocal tract, and of an entirely different sense of pitch being derived from the more natural, untrained (in the Western sense) spectral envelope displayed by the Indian singer of the Pacific Northwest.

During the last two decades or so, a number of scientists have put forward theories of perception suggesting various kinds of processing at the central level that rely upon the experience of the perceiver for pitch perception to occur, even for perception of pure or sinusoidal tones. All of this would indicate the crucial importance of experience and learning in apprehending pitch from any kind of periodic waveform. Acoustically we may talk of the pitch of any periodic sound as though it were in a single category of phenomena we know collectively as pitch. Yet it seems clear that this does not reflect how our perceptual system operates. The sound of an automobile braking may become periodic and may, therefore, have pitch purely acoustically, as would a wolf howl or a dog bark. However, our learning and experience operate on the information from the auditory perceptual mechanism in such a way as to enable us to distinguish clearly between those categories of periodic sounds that we know as being musical, according to our own particular culture, and those that acoustically have a similar periodic function but do not belong to the sound world we call "music." To this extent one may say that just as acoustical dissonance is not the same as musical dissonance, so acoustical pitch is, de facto, not necessarily the same as musical pitch.

Goldstein (1973), Terhardt (1974), Wightman (1973), and others all propose a multistage pitch-processing model, whereby incoming stimuli are subjected to initial peripheral analysis that yields information about the pattern of the stimulus. This information is then transmitted to the central processor for identification of the single "best-fitting" pitch. Some fairly convincing experimental evidence supporting the notion of a central processor is supplied by a number of researchers (e.g., Houtsma & Goldstein, 1972) using dichotic listening techniques, whereby different components of a complex waveform are fed into each ear, thus making it impossible for pitch resolution to occur at the peripheral auditory level. The consequent perceptions of pitch in such circumstances can only be a result of central processing, since inputs from both ears interact at this central level to form the pitch perception.

Such perceptions will involve not only the periodicity and timing of pulses of the waveform but also an entire complex of information, including its spectral distribution of energy and harmonic content, phase relationships, and amplitude contours (including attack and decay characteristics as well as duration). All of these interact to form a gestalt within the temporal and acoustical context in which the individual sound is situated. It is from the brain's interpretation of this complex information that we assign a particular category of pitch, be it musical, from whatever culture, spoken, machine-produced, or animal-produced. We learn to make such distinctions gradually from birth, as our auditory apparatus develops in response to the sounds of the environment and as we learn the values placed on these sounds by our culture.

THE ACQUISITION OF PITCH CONCEPTS

Of particular interest at this point in the discussion is the role of learning in the processes of attributing pitch to sounds. Equally interesting and relevant are the nature and functional abilities of the auditory apparatus of newborn infants. Rather than the ear and its receptor and interpretational mechanisms being the slave of the mechanical functioning of the cochlea, it seems certain that the reverse is true (de Boer, 1976; Goldstein, 1978; Terhardt, 1974, 1979). The cochlea is subject to the overarching control of the central processing mechanism in that whatever information is fed from the peripheral system to the central processing mechanism will be interpreted according to the latter's learned strategies and stored information for matching. Or, put another way, the experience of the perceiving organism will shape the auditory perceptual strategies that develop; as a consequence, these strategies will "tune" the peripheral mechanisms to recognize those culturally familiar inputs that are a product of conditioning by the surrounding auditory environment.

Terhardt's (1974) theory explicitly suggests this in a model of pitch acquisition that includes a learning paradigm. Divenyi (1979) provides some empirical support for the theory by citing two examples. Those who suffer congenital hearing loss, who have been unable to form the sound gestalts necessary to learning pitch concepts, are observed to perform far less effectively in frequency discrimination tasks than those with later, acquired hearing loss. For those whose hearing loss occurred after the age when auditory gestalts are formed, signals can retain some of their gestalt significance. For those whose loss occurred before the formation of auditory gestalts, inadequate controls over vocal pitch and poor pitch perception result. The second example pertains to musical culture. Terhardt's theory predicts that the frequency ratios that constitute musical scales proper to a given culture will reflect the pattern of harmonic (or inharmonic) partials present in the spectra of musical instruments. This is precisely the historical claim of Western musical theory (see succeeding chapters) in its explication of Pythagorean proportionism. As Divenyi points out, the inharmonic partials found in Javanese and Balinese gamelan sounds provide the basis for their scales and melodies. Each utilizes inharmonic ratios. Children assimilate such gestalts at an early age and accept them as musically appropriate, just as children in Western culture assimilate the use of harmonic ratios in the sounds of Western music.

Development of Hearing in Infancy

The experimental evidence concerning the development of hearing from infancy indicates how important the role of the central processing system is in our perceptions of pitch and how significant the role of learning becomes as the infant matures. It is clear from a number of researchers that the infant is born with an immature auditory perceptual apparatus. Infants from birth will respond to sound, but initially it is more of a defensive or curious type of behavior than one of responding with understanding. There appears to be an initially reflexive type of response that soon becomes an investigative one (Kearsley, 1973; Muir & Field, 1979). Very early, the infant begins to respond to sound within some kind of environmental context, not merely as an isolated phenomenon to be investigated or startled by. At the age of 1 month, infants are able to discriminate between different pure tone frequencies (Wormith, Pankerst, & Moffitt, 1975), and by 7 months they display clear evidence of being able to respond to different pitch categories in complex tones that lack a fundamental (Clarkson & Clifton, 1985); in other words, they are perceiving the residue of a complex tone from its higher harmonics, are able to categorize, and appear to be able to recognize the pitches associated with various residue effects. Such abilities must involve central processing.

However, it is not clear at what stage this ability to differentiate between different types of stimuli becomes something more psychologically sophisticated. Many researchers conclude that infants less than 7 or 8 months old are unable to extract pitch from complex tones in the way an adult does (Bundy, Columbo, & Singer, 1982), despite the evidence that 3-month-old infants possess a rudimentary ability to imitate pitches sung or played to them. In other words, the infant may be able to recognize that something is different in one stimulus as compared with another. This is not, however, the same as being able to recognize melody and musical pitch as distinct from acoustical pitch induced, for example, by animals or machines; such ability can be nurtured only by experience. Bundy and colleagues (1982) conclude that the mature forms of pitch perception we associate with adults are not present in infants; they develop with experience.

In an analysis of brainstem responses in infants aged 4 weeks and up (Teas, Klein, & Kramer, 1982), it was observed that low-frequency stimuli were received by the 4-week-old auditory system but that increasing age was a mediating factor with responses to higher-frequency stimuli. Another experimental study of auditory responses in infants aged 4 weeks and up (Trehub & Rabinovitch, 1972) demonstrated, through observations of nonnutritive sucking, that infants were able to detect the differences between synthetic and natural speech versions of the consonants *b*, *p*, *d*, and *t*. Clifton, Morrongiello, Kulig, and Dowd (1981) demonstrated that although newborn infants will orient to sound, their actions are related to maturation of the auditory cortex.

Differences Between Infant and Adult Perception

The assumption that infants and adults perceive pitch in the same way is challenged by a number of researchers in these and other reports over the last few years. The importance of pattern recognition in current theories of pitch perception associated with complex tones has led to many demonstrations that infants are unable to perform adult-type recognition tasks (Bundy et al., 1982). Cited in the arguments are the ability of adults and the inability of infants to recognize speech sounds when some information from the formant structure of the spectrum is removed, leaving just enough information for them to fill in the missing bits, just as an adult can do with incomplete written words. This points to the crucial role of experience and learning in such perceptions. Experience with naturally occurring sounds in a cultural environment is generally regarded as the most significant element in the development of auditory perceptual strategies. Bundy and colleagues showed that 4-month-old infants were unable, experimentally, to extract pitch contours from acoustic complexes that strongly suggest pitch to adults.

In tests of the ability of infants to discriminate between different pure tones, 4-month-old infants showed discrimination abilities almost as good as those of adults (Olsho, Schorn, Sakai, Turpin, &

Speduto, 1982). However, another research report (Trehub, Bull, & Thorp, 1984), also using pure tones, showed that 8- to 11-month-old infants were unable to discriminate differences between six-tone sequences when various transformations occurred, such as octave transpositions or other modifications that preserved the overall contour of the sequence. The researchers did confirm that with certain simpler tasks involving pure tones, the infants displayed abilities similar to those of adults. This would indicate that infants clearly possess a capability to discriminate both pure and complex tones but lack the experience to deal with the more complex configurations of either that result from semantic interactions. However, these abilities soon emerge, and by the age of 2 or 3 years they seem well developed.

THE ROLE OF EXPERIENCE IN PERCEPTION OF MUSICAL PITCH

In the work with infants mentioned immediately above, pitch perception is demonstrated by some action on the part of the infant subjects—usually head movements or changes in sucking rates—that indicates they have heard a change in the stimulus. By various sophisticated ways of manipulating stimulus variables, evidence can be obtained to determine which change in the stimulus elicits a response. However, the response is only an indication of a recognition of change; it tells us little about the cognitive processing that occurs at more central levels. Speculation by researchers has produced a number of theories that posit central processing as essential to acts of pitch perception (Goldstein, 1978; Terhardt, 1970, 1972, 1974; Wightman, 1973).

The psychoacoustic research into pitch perception is predominantly concerned with discovering properties of sound, activities in the ear mechanism, and correspondences between the two. It is important to know, however, why some subjects (usually trained musicians) will attribute pitch to certain auditory stimuli but others will not. What is noticeable in this respect is the proclivity among researchers to use musically experienced subjects, or ones with experience in psychophysical research. Houtsma and Goldstein (1972) and Ritsma (1962) all describe their subjects as experienced in one or both of these ways. This seems to indicate a tacit acceptance of the role of experience and training in perceptual activity relating to musical pitch. It also indicates acceptance of the American Standard Acoustical Terminology definition of pitch (quoted in Ward, 1954) as "that attribute of auditory sensation in terms of which sounds may be ordered on a scale extending from low to high, such as a musical scale." This leaves some doubt about pitch perception that is not obviously attributable to the location of sounds on a high-low continuum. Ward (1954) suggests that pitch perception implies that individuals possess internal, "subjective" scales of musical pitch that correspond in a one-to-one manner with some physically defined musical scale. It is certain that successfully trained musicians possess this, since it is the object of their training. What is unknown is the nature of the internal, "subjective" information about pitch existing in untrained minds.

Some evidence in the form of visual representations of pitch movement was obtained in a series of experiments requiring subjects to match auditory stimuli with visual responses (Walker, 1978, 1985, 1987a, 1987b). Four types of pitch movement using pure, or sinusoidal, tones provided the stimuli: two types of discrete pitch changes (upward and downward) and two types of glissandi, or pitch sliding (upward and downward). In all the tests there were clear, statistically significant differences between the responses of musically trained and untrained subjects. Musically trained subjects matched pitch movement with vertically placed visual metaphors, as in staff notation, whereas untrained subjects favored no particular visual metaphor over another. The visual metaphors ranged over many possible ways of arranging visual shapes in 2-dimensional space: vertical position, horizontal position, combination of these two, size, shape, shapes filled in with various patterns, outline shapes with no patterns, and so on. Some tests asked subjects to supply their own visual metaphors, while others provided subjects with a predetermined set of visual shapes from which to choose their favored metaphor for the particular sound stimulus. These findings also extended to the congenitally blind using tactile metaphors for sound (Walker, 1985). The trained musicians, whatever their age, always performed better than the untrained subjects in matching pitch movement with vertically placed visual metaphors for sound. The former had high scores, often in the range of 90 to 100 percent correct, while the latter appeared to produced no systematic choice of visual metaphors for pitched sounds. In two experiments (Walker, 1987a, 1987b) it was found that age and cultural background played some role in mediating responses, but not nearly as predominant a role as musical training. Other research (Fiske, 1989), using the same test battery and an additional one especially developed to include musical melody, showed essentially the same effect of musical training. This would seem to indicate that those without musical training do have difficulty relating pitch movement to a vertical continuum on which higher frequencies are matched with visual symbols placed higher than those matched with lower frequencies. It also seems to indicate that whatever internal representation exists, it is not one that naturally perceives movements in pitch as being on a vertical, high-low continuum unless the subject is specially trained to do so.

Musical pitch can therefore be said to refer to a specially trained response. And this is not confined to the complex tones in which musicians are trained; it also applies to pure tones, as demonstrated in the experimental evidence cited above. Terhardt, Gerhard, and Seewann (1982) refer to a dualism of pitch, one derived from pure tones and the other from complex tones. They mention the growing empirical evidence that the pitches of these two types of tones are basically different perceptual entities, involving different ways of stimulating the auditory mechanisms involved. Though Terhardt et al. may be correct with respect to the physics of hearing, they do not appear to be correct when the higher cognitive processes are involved, such as is the case with highly trained musicians. When asked to select visual metaphors for sounds, musically trained subjects tend to use musically related visual metaphors for both pure and complex tones, without distinction, in the experiments cited above (i.e., Walker, 1987a, 1987b). But we might expect this in view of the ability, mentioned earlier, such subjects have to identify periodic animal or machine sounds, for fun, in terms of musical scales.

The implication is that untrained subjects, although they might hear such stimulus differences as different fundamental frequencies, will not conceptualize them as being related on a high-low continuum. The question remains as to what, precisely, pitch means to untrained subjects. Clearly it cannot mean musical pitch, and since acoustical pitch is identical by definition with musical pitch, it seems to follow that only those who are musically trained can actually perceive pitch. Those without such training will respond to an auditory stimulus change that denotes pitch change, whether from the fundamental frequency or spectral components; but in view of the arguments above, their responses cannot be said to denote perceptions of pitch change, but merely perceptions of stimulus change. In the experiments dealing with pitch perception cited above (Walker, 1987a, 1987b), the responses from the untrained indicated no clear preference of visual metaphor—size difference, shape difference, and visual pattern difference were all preferred equally with vertically placed metaphors.

This would appear to have implications for the relationship between the higher cognitive processes and the peripheral perceptual auditory mechanism: it seems that only the learning and encoding of appropriate information at a higher level can ensure that appropriate stimulus change from whatever type of waveform can be interpreted as pitch change. Since many have postulated theories of pitch perception that include assimilation into the appropriate culture (e.g., Goldstein, 1973; Terhardt, 1974; Wightman, 1973), it would seem to follow that cultural definitions of pitch, rather than simply acoustic cues, are the determinants of pitch perception. The researchers described above who established the importance of the harmonic content of sound in pitch perception all used subjects trained in Western musical traditions. The use of subjects trained in other traditions, such as those of Bali or Java, might well yield different results with the same stimuli. These stimuli comprised integrally related harmonics, while the spectra of musical sounds in Bali and Java are not integrally related. Pitch perception would appear, therefore, to be more culturally induced than acoustically derived. All this might, in fact, refer to the special codes in sound alluded to by Rousseau (1749/1966) and mentioned earlier in this chapter.

CULTURALLY INFLUENCED CATEGORICAL PERCEPTION

An important perceptual proclivity displayed by adults, one that relies more obviously on experience, is categorical perception. There is also evidence that its incipient stages are present in infants. *Categorical perception* is a term referring to the tendency to group together a number of discrete sounds and categorize them as being all in one category rather than as a series of discrete events. The archetype for categorical perception was first described in a study by Liberman, Harris, Hoffman, and Griffith (1957), who noticed that subjects would almost always label randomly presented stimuli, such as /ba/, /da/, and /ga/, as one category or another (i.e., /ba/, /da/, etc.), even though the stimulus properties might deviate from either. Many further studies have shown that this proclivity is not confined to linguistic categories. Locke and Kellar (1973) and Siegel and Siegel (1977a) showed that musicians displayed categorical tendencies in their perceptions of musical stimuli.

Locke and Kellar (1973) asked musicians and nonmusicians to judge whether a series of pure tones in a low frequency range were the same or different. In each test three simultaneously presented sine tones were played: the first test varied the middle tone by 4 Hz, and the second test by intervals of 2 Hz, effectively spanning the interval from a major to a minor triad. Nonmusicians showed less sharp category boundaries than musicians, and the experimenters concluded that categorization into two categories, major and minor triads, was considerably more prominent among musicians than nonmusicians. This can only be attributed to the training the musicians received and thus suggests some importance for the role of the experience of the central mechanism in decoding this kind of information.

The experiment conducted by Siegel and Siegel (1977a) was more comprehensive in that a wider range of intervals was employed (unison up to a major third), and musicians with absolute pitch were asked to judge various single tones in relation to known standards. Again, sine tones were used as stimuli. They found that among nonmusicians the ability to categorize was severely limited. They attributed this to a lack of musical training, resulting in the subjects' greater reliance on stimulus context than musical knowledge. In contrast, musicians displayed clear categorical perceptions in all tests, despite the fact that most of the stimuli were out of tune. Basically, what was demonstrated was an innate proclivity to place stimuli in some known category regardless of any objective features that might preclude such placement—in this case, objective criteria of frequency difference. Subjects who did not know the categories placed stimuli randomly or in accordance with the experimental context. A further study by Siegel and Siegel (1977b) demonstrated that musicians are unable to tell sharp tones from flat ones when they are described as being within a specific category of pitch interval. In this experiment musicians were asked to place a series of tones supposedly relating to the intervals of a perfect fourth, an augmented fourth, and a perfect fifth. Each stimulus was varied in cents (see Chapter 3 for a fuller explanation of cents values) from the standard, and musicians were asked to make judgments. The results showed that musicians were unable to distinguish between sharp and flat tones within a category, a fact indicating that categorical perception took precedence over such fine discriminations.

A number of investigations into musical performance show that both vocalists and instrumentalists will produce considerable variations in pitch within the categories of musical intervals they intend to play. In fact, it appears that in both performance and perception musicians will employ categorical strategies. Seashore (1938) reports that singers and instrumentalists will vary the pitch of their vocalizations considerably during performance, often straying above and below the intended frequency—by nearly a semitone in some cases. Radocy and Boyle (1979) cite a number of later researchers who report the same phenomenon—string players, for example, who move between just, mean, and Pythagorean intonation within a single musical passage.

It is now well established that categorical perception is prevalent in perceptual activities other than linguistic ones, even that categorical perception may well be endemic to all perceptual activity (Beckman, 1988; Locke & Kellar, 1973). Most important, there is experimental evidence that it occurs in infants' perceptions. Eimas, Siqueland, Jusczyk, and Vigorito (1971) demonstrated experimentally that in discrimination of synthetic speech sounds, infants aged 1 to 4 months displayed discontinuity in discriminations that more or less coincided with the adult phonemic boundaries. Another experiment (Jusczyk, Rosner, Cutting, Foard, & Smith, 1977) also showed that 2-month-old infants perceive nonspeech sounds in a categorical manner. This would tend to support the position that the proclivity to categorize is innate, develops early, and is susceptible to training and other experiences.

Gestalt

Any particular culture, as represented in both speech and music, will supply the categories within which to place auditory stimuli. In the absence of a cultural influence enabling us to categorize sounds, we are either more reliant on the stimulus context than on its relevance to our acquired knowledge or we tend to impose pseudocategories on the stimulus. The role of culture and its belief systems in supplying us with categories for our perceptual apparatus to utilize would seem, therefore, to be of paramount importance in our auditory perceptual activity. It would seem that clear links are likely to exist between a culture, its developed belief systems, our innate perceptual proclivities, and our development of these proclivities.

These suggested links ought to work in a manner something like the following. The initial sound sources for both speech and music can be immensely variable in terms of both materials and how such materials are manipulated. The vocal folds, for example, can assume a great variety of shapes—some at will, some innately inherited. Similarly, our abilities to shape materials such as wood, metal, and plastic enable us to produce a great variety of shapes for mouthpieces or reeds, which provide the basic sound source for musical instruments to employ. From these initial sound sources vibrations pass into either the vocal tract or the main body of the musical instrument, where they are subject to another immensely variable set of possibilities. The shape of the vocal tract can be varied enormously at will or through special training techniques; innate factors are involved here as well, in that some vocal tracts are intrinsically wider or narrower in places than others. Similarly with musical instruments—we can shape the tubes of wood or metal, into which the vibrations from the basic sound sources pass, to suit our needs. Thus the pressure waves emanating from the basic sound sources can be modulated and filtered to produce a great variety of resonance characteristics, which we can recognize in the spectral envelopes of sounds. Yet despite this potential variety, the sounds of each culture are limited and confined to a culturally determined set of possibilities.

We will tend to shape the materials for producing sound to suit the needs of our particular culture. If we want to be understood in speech among others of our culture, we quickly learn to shape our vocal tract in such a manner as to make the correct speech sounds. Similarly, in music we will learn both to make instruments that produce appropriate sounds for our culture and to play them by making suitable physical movements to set them into vibration. Our perceptual mechanisms will learn to recognize appropriate cultural categories of speech and music sounds, whether phonemes or notes of a musical scale, and will tend to categorize both types of sound according to our perceptions of which category they best fit.

Thus there is a causal chain involving actions needed to make musical and spoken sounds, perceptions of such sounds, and the categories needed to guide our actions in making the sounds in the first place. A missing component in such a chain is the motivation for accepting one set of cultural sounds as opposed to another. This motivation must come, I suggest, from our beliefs in the efficacy of a particular culture. The role of belief systems in motivating a culture to use various categories of sound for both speech and music must play a major part in this causal chain. If it is believed, for whatever reason, that musical harmonic spectra and intervals whose frequency ratios do not exceed relationships between the numbers 1, 2, 3, and 4 form the best melodic sounds, as has been the case in Western culture, then that particular culture will tend to use only those sounds. Social pressures will ensure that such beliefs are adhered to and resultant practices followed. Another culture may believe that different harmonic contents of sounds and different spectral envelopes form the basic categories of musical sounds, as in the case of Balinese and Javanese culture; and yet another may believe that music and speech are virtually synonymous, as in the case of some aboriginal cultures. In this way appropriate perceptual categories will be formed to suit these particular beliefs about musical culture and its role in the general culture.

The apparently innate perceptual abilities of humans to respond to various aspects of sound in categorical fashion is not an indication that any particular category is also innate. Infants, with their innate abilities for pitch extraction and categorical perception, await acculturation; they will learn to respond to the categories favored by their cultures. Underpinning the formation of these categories are the belief systems that supply the basic reasons for using particular categories. I suggest, therefore, that the belief systems are a source of information about the music of a particular culture and are, therefore, of immense importance to our understanding not only of any culture but also of the processes of music perception.

We not only tune our organism to orientate and respond to particular sounds; we supply, through the process of acculturation, the perceptual categories our auditory apparatus adapts to. We invent both the category and the meaning it holds for us. And, to return to the notion expounded in the first chapter concerning the invention of culture, I suggest that as the infant learns a culture, the process described as inventing the culture must occur, just as it must for the outsider attempting to gain access to the culture. For the outsider learning the culture for the first time, it is through such invention that it may be possible to gain access to the kind of meaning and experiences known by those who form an intrinsic part of the culture. Adults teach infants by essentially inventing their own culture through various symbols so that the child can assimilate it. To gain understanding of belief systems that motivate cultural behavior, it is necessary to invent, or reinvent, the cultural beliefs by revisiting the events and important people who have contributed to the culture's formation.

In the case of music, there is clear evidence in many cultures of belief systems and how they operate on our perceptual acts, enabling us to extract the appropriate cultural information from auditory stimuli. The evidence and arguments presented above, while not definitive or even conclusive, strongly suggest that our perceptions are mediated in powerful fashion by our acquired beliefs and cultural knowledge, which supply the requirements our perceptual apparatus seems innately designed for. Subsequent chapters, therefore, will go through a process of reinventing musical culture by explicating the nature and development of different musical belief systems, beginning with that of Western culture. This musical culture, more than any other, holds the belief that its sounds are rooted in objective science and mathematics.

CHAPTER 3

The Belief System Surrounding Pythagoras' Music of the Spheres

There is evidence in many cultures of a belief in the existence of music in some spiritual dimension, some perfect state accessible only to certain groups or individuals who are able to induce appropriate states of mind. The desire to contact the spiritual world—or the infinite, or the supreme intelligence behind all life—is a most important force in the spiritual side of human existence. This spiritual side seeks access to the music of the perfect state of existence, music being regarded as the language of perfection and the means of communication between the imperfection of existence and the perfect state. The rational side of humans demands an explanation of the nature of perfection and the resultant music. Since we are limited in our music-making by our imperfections—by the limitations of the materials available for our music-making, for example—it was reasoned that there must be an ideal to aim for. This ideal was probably contained in the mysterious harmony that binds all physical things together, it was argued. Just as there are some musical sounds that are pleasant and sound well together, so must there be natural physical forces that work well or badly. Thus began the empirical uses of music as a means to understanding the workings of the universe, of nature, of humankind. People began to experiment, to speculate, to theorize about the concept of "harmony," using musical sound as an empirical tool. Where they could not make the actual sound, they postulated a perfect music, the music of the spheres, which was outside the sensory realm of humans.

In turn this led to the notion that some sounds were more "perfect" than others, were nearer to the mysterious universal force than others, and whose use, therefore, was quite potent in effect. It was argued that, ideally, music should be limited to certain sounds, in which case the use of music could be controlled and its powers utilized more effectively and efficiently. In all cultures there is evidence of qualitative distinctions between different musical sounds. Few cultures have simply used any sound that they could make as music; virtually all have imposed some kind of selection and classification on sounds.

The 84 frequencies (i.e., seven octaves), or repetition rates of waveforms, that more or less make up the pitches of post–eighteenth century Western music, are a product of certain specific mathematical ratios between any two such frequencies. All modern musicians are familiar with the ratios of two notes an octave apart (2 : 1), a fifth apart (3 : 2), or a fourth apart (4 : 3). One string or column of air, or any vibrating material that produces a sufficiently regular repetition rate, vibrating twice as fast, one and one-half times, or one and one-third times as fast as another will produce the musical intervals we in the West have come to recognize as the octave, fifth, and fourth, respectively. All other intervals in Western music can be similarly explained by means of proportions. Furthermore, modern science, particularly through the work of Fourier and others, has enabled us to break down the components of a complex waveform into its constituent sine wave parts, which are all related to the fundamental repetition rate, as discussed in Chapter 2. Ideally, this relationship is one of simple integer multiples of the fundamental repetition rate, but few, if any, sounds are ideal in the real world, including those produced through electronic synthesis. With modern technology it is difficult to produce, for example, a pure sinusoidal waveform with no impurities or a complex wave with absolutely perfect integer relationships between all the partials. But here we have the distinction between the ideal and the reality of existence. In the development of Western musical theory, this distinction is important. Theoretically, one can demonstrate within the harmonic structure of an ideal complex wave all the basic interval ratios that form the foundation of ideal Western melody and harmony, but the existing musical uses of melody and harmony are far from ideal in practice. They reflect the personal style of the composer.

Logically, the relationship between musical harmony and the acoustical content of an ideal complex waveform looks quite simple and persuasive. For example, a fundamental repetition rate of 100 Hz has ideal partials, or harmonics, at 2 times, 3 times, 4 times, 5 times, 6 times, to n times this basic rate; that is, 200 Hz, 300 Hz, 400 Hz, 500 Hz, 600 Hz, to n times 100 Hz. The ratio between the 2nd partial and the fundamental (200 : 100) is 2 : 1, an octave; that between the 3rd and 2nd partial is 3 : 2 (300 : 200), a fifth; that between the 4th and

3rd is 4 : 3 (400 : 300), a fourth; and so on. These are the same ratios as those of Western melody and harmony as described above. Thus, although it was possible only in modern times to break down a complex wave into its ideal sinusoidal components, the ideal melodic intervals formed by these ideal ratios were in use long before. This lends a certain aura to these musical intervals and suggests that they may well be musically universal, or musically ideal, or even musically more correct than any others. It also seems to imply that cultures using other melodic intervals based upon different systems or even upon arbitrary ratios are using musical sounds that do not have the validity of those of the West. Indeed, this is precisely what was thought in the West until recently, and for precisely those reasons.

In a world such as today's, where communication is so far-reaching and instantaneous, it becomes imperative to address the issue of "perfectness," or universality, in music, particularly the universality of the Western intervals described above. Intuition—inaccurate, subjective, and biased as it is—tells one that, considering the enormous diversity of musical sounds across the world now readily accessible, it seems neither sensible nor justifiable, ethnologically, to claim that the basic intervals of the Western tradition, or any other for that matter, are universal, more intrinsically musical, or possessed of more nomothetic properties than intervals from any other musical tradition. We do not need elaborate electronic equipment to tell us that some music from different traditions can be as attractive and meaningful as our own, nor that notions of perfection are not uniform across the globe. But in addition to these observations, and particularly considering the origins of Western musical culture, there is cause for more than a suspicion that the interval ratios in Western music are revered because of cultural beliefs concerning their musical relevance, appropriateness, or universality, beliefs that are little different in motivation or veracity from those of any other culture. Further, I suggest that the entire development of Western music, as with any other musical culture, has been due as much to cultural beliefs as to its supposed derivation from scientific truths, even though Western musical theory has often been presented as scientifically based.

THE ORIGINS OF WESTERN MUSICAL THEORY IN
PYTHAGOREAN PROPORTIONAL THEORY

The existence of a sophisticated and well-established theory of musical pitch, melody, and harmony, one that contains scientific, philosophical, and musical elements, leads one to accept that Western musical sounds are products of more than mere cultural belief. The assumption is that a belief is not a product of scientifically and logically derived laws; the products of such laws must, therefore, be more universally applicable than those of what might be characterized as random effects of culturally developed habits, such as, for example, the extraordinary practice of throat singing found uniquely among the Inuit of northern Canada.

The theory, or the so-called scientific basis, of Western melody and harmony goes back in time at least 3,000 years to ancient China and Mesopotamia. But a direct link can be traced from Pythagoras (ca. 570–500 .B.C.) and the teachings of his secret society in Crotona (southern Italy, or Great Greece as it was then known) right up to the present day. It is known that Pythagoras spent many years studying in Babylon and Egypt, and possibly even farther East, before settling in Crotona to found his society and propagate his knowledge of the cosmic significance of number. Although we have no writings of Pythagoras himself, a great deal about his ideas exists in the writings of others who followed him and his school of thinking. He was clearly the most important of the pre-Socratic philosophers, although he was more interested in mysticism and numerology than in syllogistic thinking. He saw number as the essence of all things, as a sort of mystical and magical force. Without doubt he was introduced to such ideas during his time in Babylon, which had a history of mathematically based mysticism going back at least to the third millennium B.C.

Pythagoras and his followers were responsible for providing a well-developed theoretical framework for the marvels of number relationships, arguing that the essence of all things derives from these relationships, including the planets and such basic matter as air, fire, water, and earth. Thoroughly versed in the mathematical thinking of both the Babylonian and Egyptian traditions as Pythagoras was, it is almost certain that from them he acquired the prototypes for his theory that the physical and intellectual harmony affecting humans, the world, and the cosmos—the mysterious force that binds them all together, keeps things in their place and working at their most efficient state—is expressible in number. Thus number, and proportionism, became an important part of all Greek philosophical discourse in the succeeding centuries.

The beginnings of mathematics were doubtless connected with everyday needs in counting property, family, or material goods. But as humans became fascinated by the mystery of the world and the sky above them, they also came to marvel at the wonders of number. It was as much a mystery to them that certain numbers were not divisible (for example, the primes of 2, 3, 5, and 7) as that the stars shone in the sky at night. Inevitably connections were made between numbers and the heavens. There were only seven planets visible, for example, so the number 7, a prime, had special significance. There were four corners of the earth, information obtainable from observations made with the aid of the Pole Star, and so the number 4 had special significance. Thus mathematics and religion grew in tandem; priests were those who had mathematical knowledge and could relate it to the cosmos. Mathematics became the key to all knowledge, the oracle, the source of divine truth.

Cuneiform writings containing complex number series and a kind of algebraic formulae in use in ancient Sumeria and dating back to at least 2100 B.C. are in the world's museums today (Eves, 1964). A form of algebra existed then, enabling people to calculate areas of rectangles, various types of triangles, and many other shapes, a well as to divide the circle into 360 equal parts. The so-called Pythagorean theorem (the square of the hypotenuse of a right triangle equals the sum of the squares of the other two sides) was also known to the ancient Sumerians more than 1,500 years before Pythagoras lived. In fact, the type of rhetorical algebra employed by the ancient Sumerians included quadratic and cubic equations that enabled them to perform complex feats of engineering. Similarly, the Egyptians employed a form of algebra in their constructional work (Gillings, 1962).

There is ample evidence of an equally well developed use of algebra in ancient China and India during these times, more than 4,000 years ago. Mathematical knowledge in China during the reign of the Emperor You (2357–2258 B.C.) was at least as advanced as that of the Sumerians and the Greeks 1,500 years later (Boyer, 1968; Bunt, Jones, & Bedient, 1976; Scott, 1960).

It is in this context of at least 2,000 years of prior development in mathematical knowledge that we can place Pythagoras and his times in the sixth century B.C. He traveled across the ancient world of the Near and Middle East obtaining an education in the science and mysticism of the times.

Pythagoras was concerned to find the essence of matter, the single force or center from which all life and matter sprang. Commensurate with all knowledge in the ancient world, he saw number as the source, the essence, the wellspring of all truth. He argued that the number 1, the monad, must be unity, and therefore the smallest unit and the essence he sought. The number 2 comprises opposites, like male and female, and 3 completes a series: in 1 + 2 = 3, 1 is a beginning and 3 is an ending, with 2 in the middle, exactly halfway, and also being the arithmetic mean of the beginning and ending [i.e., $(1 + 3) \div 2$ = 2]. The number 4 completes the perfect sequence of numbers, being perfect and complete for several reasons. There are four corners of the earth, considered a flat disc by the Sumerians and divided into quadrants by means of divisions obtained using the Pole Star as reference. Thus the number 4 had ancient significance. Arithmetically, 4 equals the sum of the beginning and the ending (1 and 3) and is also the square of the mean of these two numbers (2). Of even greater significance, as far as Pythagoras' scheme of things is concerned, is the fact that the sum of these first four integers equals 10, the decad. This was considered to be the perfect number and thus to define the limits of the universe.

There were thought to be nine heavenly bodies in the sky, including the earth and the moon. To make ten, and so enable conformity to the notion of the perfection of the number 10, the Pythagoreans postulated that there must be a tenth planet hidden behind the sun that was never visible to earth. Hence, the ten planets mark the limit of the universe. Consequently, all developments in the universe can be derived from the tetrad 1, 2, 3, 4. These numbers were thought to contain the secrets of all life and matter as well as divine truth. Pythagoreans swore an oath to the tetrad—"I swear by him who bequeathed to our soul the tetractys, source containing the root of everlasting nature." They named the number 10 the *tetractys*, the sum of the first four numbers.

This does not make much sense to us nowadays, with our more conceptually highly developed science. But to an individual more than 2,500 years ago, this was the most secret and powerful source available for developing understanding. The use of whole numbers in this way was "the ontological basis for the being and intelligibility of the world" (Hyland, 1973, p. 131). However, the Pythagoreans were greatly puzzled by the challenge to this ontological basis posed by Pythagoras' supposed discovery of incommensurable numbers, that is, numbers that have no common measure, or divisor, either integral or fraction, save unity. Pythagoras noted the incommensurability of the diagonal of a square to its sides, for example. The puzzle for Pythagoreans arose from the realization that "if incommensurables really exist, then the claim that the world is through and through rational, that everything is related by a determinable mathematical relation, is made utterly precarious" (Hyland, 1973, p. 131). Nonetheless, the tetractys became clothed in mysticism and divinity. It became associated with the four basic elements: air, water, earth, and fire. Use of these numbers in deriving proportions was considered by Pythagoras, and by Plato and Aristotle after him, to be the prerequisite for developing true wisdom. There were four disciplines thought essential for mastery of true knowledge in Pythagoras' scheme of things. These were relayed through time to medieval Europe by various writers who referred to them as the quadrivium: arithmetic, music, geometry, and astronomy. The problem of incommensurables, however, remained throughout to disturb more thoughtful minds.

Pythagoreans believed that arithmetic dealt in number, which is pure form, "uncreated and unchanging, nonphysical and atemporal" (Heninger, 1974, p. 71). As number is transformed from the intellectual to the physical realm in the shape of geometric objects, such as the triangle (having three points) or the pyramid (having four points), so it becomes a perceptual physical extension for the senses. Its true nature, however, remains in its pure form as an abstract intellectual entity, a number. Music, for the Pythagoreans, was the science that dealt with relationships between whole numbers expressed as ratios, or proportions. It was regarded by them as the physical manifestation of the perfectness of ideal numerical relationships, or proportions. It is relative quantity, whereas arithmetic is absolute quantity. But the sounds of such music were considered ideal rather than actual as far as the scheme of knowledge was concerned. The sounds do not need to exist as physical entities; they are relative to proportions derived from the perfect series of numbers, 1, 2, 3, 4.

These numbers can be derived from basic geometric forms used in the ancient world: 1 is the point, 2 is the straight line, 3 is the triangle, and 4 is the pyramid, providing the third dimension. Thus these basic geometric forms and the number series derived from them were thought to provide the key to understanding all things. For example, a cube has six faces, eight vertices, and twelve edges, thus providing the number series 6, 8, 12. Using the basic numerical series 1, 2, 3, 4 as the source of ideal proportions, we find that if the number 9 is added to produce the series 6, 8, 9, 12, there is a set of proportional relationships to be derived as follows:

$$12 : 6 = 2 : 1$$
$$12 : 8 = 3 : 2$$
$$9 : 6 = 3 : 2$$
$$12 : 9 = 4 : 3$$
$$8 : 6 = 4 : 3$$

There are other important properties of these four numbers in terms of various mathematical means or averages. The arithmetic mean of 6 and 12 is 9. The harmonic mean of 6 and 12 is 8. The harmonic mean, as derived by the Pythagoreans, was a number whose differences from the first and last numbers in the series formed a proportion equal to the proportion of the first and last numbers themselves; that is, the difference between 8 and 12 is 4, and the difference between 8 and 6 is 2. The numbers 4 and 2 relate to the numbers 12 and 6 in that both pairs reduce to the proportion 2 : 1. (Using modern mathematical techniques, the harmonic mean is calculated as the reciprocal of the arithmetic mean of the reciprocals of the series.)

Because of these unique properties in this series (the numbers 6, 8, 9, 12), the ancient Greek monochord was divided into these proportions, which gave the intervals of the octave, fifth, and fourth. Thus, starting with a string of a given length, a string half that length (6 units being half of 12) yields the octave; two-thirds that length (i.e., 8 : 12 or 6 : 9), a fifth; and three-quarters that length (9 : 12 or 6 : 8), a fourth. Since the numbers can be derived from the parameters of a cube, the cube was described by Pythagoras as a harmonic body. These numbers relating to the cube were certainly known in Babylon, Egypt, and China well before the time of Pythagoras. Special properties were bestowed by the ancient Babylonians, Egyptians, and Chinese upon all objects that could be defined by the mathematical proportions in the manner explained. Pythagoras described them as harmonic in the sense that their configuration matches the way objects, particularly the planets, are naturally related to one another in the cosmos. Thus the intervals of the octave, fifth, and fourth are harmonic because of their mathematical perfection, as demonstrated by proportional relationships, and they were thought to provide the clue to the mysteries of how the planets move about the sky without falling or crashing into one another.

Pythagoras not only assumed the existence of a tenth planet, a counter-earth, but also theorized that the planets must move around the heavens in some sort of perfectly harmonious order and relationship. He argued that since moving bodies on earth, like a vibrating string, make sounds, so must the planets. Since they must be harmonically related, such relationships must be in the "divine" proportions related to the tetrad. Thus the music of the spheres is the sound of the planets expressed in the proportions of 1 : 2 : 3 : 4, or, musically speaking, the intervals of the octave, fifth, and fourth. He argued that they sound continually, thus preventing humans from hearing them, and that only if they were to stop, which they never do, could the heavenly music be discerned. By extrapolation, the most perfect music on earth would be that relating to these heavenly sounds. From this theory came the notion of the harmony of the spheres, which has lived on to inspire poets, artists, and musicians up to the present time. And this relationship between number and musical perfection, exemplified in the manner in which ratios can be used to calculate melodic intervals, developed into a powerful artistic as well as mystical and religious theory, even dogma. But its origins predate the time of Pythagoras.

Although the theory known as "harmonics" is normally associated with the name Pythagoras, there is little doubt, as indicated above, that the essence of the theory was known many centuries before Pythagoras lived, and not only in cultures in the Middle East. The ancient Chinese used the *lu* tonal system, which was essentially the same, four centuries earlier. This system was in use during the period of the Early, or Western, Chou (1122–770 B.C.). Basically, the system enabled musicians to divide the octave into twelve semitones by means of twelve consecutive steps of equal fifths. The system even included an awareness of the "Pythagorean comma," the extra interval left over after going through the cycle of fifths and expecting to arrive back where one started.

The twelve semitones were called *lu*s. The word *lu* has several possible meanings, including rule, regulation, tube, pitch, and pipe (Kuttner, 1965). Furthermore, each of the twelve tones of the equally divided octave had names that relate both to the acoustical nature of the tone, within the context of the interval it formed with the tonic, and to its cosmic significance. Kuttner points out that some of the names indicate the presence of a highly developed scientific and technical culture. Additionally, the tones were each labelled "yin" or "yang" ("male" or "female"). Thus a complex system of tonal organization, based on acoustical laws and linked to cosmic influences, was already in existence and well established hundreds of years before the time of Pythagoras.

Nevertheless, a number of ancient Greek and Roman sources, including Plato and Aristotle, purport to explain how Pythagoras "discovered" these harmonies, or intervallic relationships formed by proportional relationships, as he was passing a blacksmith's forge. Iamblichus, an important source from the fourth century A.D. who quoted earlier writers, described how Pythagoras, in passing a blacksmith's forge, heard the sounds of the hammers in "perfect harmony," that is, sounding the intervals of the octave, fourth, and fifth. He went into the smithy and asked to examine the hammers. He asked the men to exchange hammers in order to eliminate any effect caused by differences in the force with which each blacksmith wielded the hammer. He found, however, that the hammers, not the smiths, were responsible for the different sounds, and that their weights were in the ratio $12 : 9 : 8 : 6$. In some accounts there was a fifth hammer that did not have a weight within these ratios. When this was left out, the musical effect increased. Pythagoras went home, tried the proportions on his monochord, and found the same beautiful musical effect.

Clearly this cannot be taken seriously. It is not the weight of a hammer striking some object that is the cause of that object's pitch; it is the nature of the object itself. For example, if one strikes a cymbal with a light wooden mallet, some harmonics but not others will sound. If the strike is made with a felt beater in an appropriate place, a fuller set of harmonics will be heard, but the pitch will not alter. The relationship between the type or weight of the beater and the pitch elicited is not a functional one, since pitch is derived from our perception of the disturbance pattern formed by a vibrating object; it can be obtained from any two or three adjacent harmonics in the resultant waveform irrespective of the method used for setting the object into vibration. Nevertheless, the myth of how Pythagoras discovered the ideal musical proportions lived on until modern times. For example, Handel wrote a set of variations on a theme known as "The Harmonious Blacksmith"; the origins of the title are obscure, but it very likely indicates the myth's presence in eighteenth-century musical thought. Almost every music theory book published from the sixteenth century onwards mentions this myth.

All this is testimony to the power of the mythical and mystical aspects of Pythagorean reasoning about music and its pervasiveness throughout the development of Western culture. The Pythagoreans insisted upon the mathematical purity of music. Plutarch (A.D. ca.50–ca.125), a most important writer of the Roman period, was a Platonist and an important source of information on the ancient world. In *Parallel Lives, Platonic Issues*, and *Moral Essays* he provided details and philosophical arguments from the Greek and Egyptian civilizations. In *Moral Essays* he explained that "Pythagoras . . . reproved all judgement of music which is by the ear. . . . Music was not to be judged in by hearing but by proportional harmony," by which he meant ratios that were shown to be theoretically perfect (quoted in Heninger, 1974, p. 91).

This is very much like saying that the only true music is that which is not heard, that which is the product of pure intellect. In fact, Keats alludes to this in his "Ode on a Grecian Urn":

Heard melodies are sweet, but those unheard
Are sweeter; therefore, ye soft pipes, play on;
Not to the sensual ear, but, more endear'd,
Pipe to the spirit ditties of no tone.

That the ideas of Pythagoras were still extant in early nineteenth-century thought is both remarkable and pertinent to our endeavour in trying to understand the cultural belief system underlying Western music. It is also testimony to the enormous influence throughout Western civilization of Pythagorean aesthetics. To the Pythagoreans the ideal music was an intellectual form conceived through number and had little to do with the senses. In spite of this, the proportional theory of the Pythagoreans provided the motivation for the development of Western musical theory right up to the present day through theorists such as Zarlino and Rameau, the latter of whom did make the link with our sensory processes.

THE PYTHAGOREAN THEORY OF HARMONICS
AND MUSICAL PRACTICE

The Pythagorean system produces some problems of tuning—that is, of fixing the pitch of various notes of a scale—that in turn create difficulties in practical music-making. Principally, the issue concerns two things: the so-called Pythagorean comma and the unpleasant aural effects of Pythagorean thirds (ratio 81 : 64) when sounding against the natural harmonics in the sounds of musical instruments that contain differently proportioned thirds (e.g., "just" thirds, whose ratio is 5 : 4, or 386 cents).

The Pythagorean comma can best be explained using the modern system of dividing up an octave into cents. One cent equals the 1200th root of 2. The complete octave comprises 1200 cents; if divided into twelve equal parts, as in the tuning system we call "equal temperament," each semitone will comprise 100 cents and each tone, 200 cents. Thus the perfect fifth will be 700 cents. This system of tuning all semitones to the same number of cents (100) is now the established norm with keyboard instruments, especially the range of electronic keyboards and various sound modules in the sphere of sound synthesis. The problem with this is that the natural fifth, that produced by the 3rd partial, or 2nd harmonic above the fundamental repetition rate of a periodic vibration, is actually 702 cents. This is produced by a ratio of 3 : 2, whereas the equal fifth, 700 cents, requires a ratio of

433 : 289. Cent values for any interval can be calculated by using logarithms to base 10. The logarithm for the ratio of an interval is divided by the logarithm for 1 cent. Thus the natural fifth has a ratio 3 : 2 = 1.5, and the logarithm for this is 0.1760913. This is divided by the logarithm of 1 cent (log 2 ÷ 1200), which is 0.0002508. [One cent is arrived at by taking the 12th root of 2 (1.0595), to give a semitone, and then the 100th root of this, which equals 1.000578.] In other words, this process divides the octave into twelve equal parts, and each of these equal parts is divided into 100 equal parts to give 1 cent.

As far as we know, the equal fifth did not in fact exist, even in theory, until modern times. And although theoretically there was a consciousness of the need for an equal division of the octave as far back as ancient Greece and China in the Early Chou period, it was scientifically beyond the capabilities of those times to produce a workable system of dividing up the octave. In other words, the only fifth known in these earlier times was the natural one, which equals 702 cents using the proportion 3 : 2.

The system of tuning and therefore of building scales used by the ancient Chinese of 3,000 years ago, other civilizations in between, and then the Pythagoreans and subsequent ancient Greek theorists was based upon the so-called cycle of natural fifths. Using modern staff notational names and the system of cents, it can best be understood by imagining middle C to be 0 cents, in which case G above middle C will be 702 cents higher. Moving up to the next pitch, another fifth higher, will produce 1,404 cents. Subtract 1,200 cents (the size of the octave), and the remaining 204 cents higher than middle C is the pitch for D, one tone higher. A fifth above D is A; arithmetically, this pitch is arrived at by multiplying 702 by 3 (the third step above C using the rising fifth as each step) to give 2,106 cents. Subtract 1,200 cents for the octave, and the pitch for A equals 906 cents above C. Table 3.1 shows the rising cycle of natural fifths expressed in cents calculated in the manner explained above. In Table 3.2, these calculated values, expressed in cents, are presented in ascending pitch order to give a twelve-note scale above middle C.

It can be seen from Table 3.1 that the calculation in cents for F, a perfect fourth above C, is different from that for the natural fourth. The natural fourth is related to the note below it in the ratio of 4 : 3 (the 4th natural harmonic), which produces a pitch interval of 498 cents. However, using the upward natural fifth as a basis for calculation, a pitch interval of 522 cents results. The difference between these two is 24 cents, which has been termed the "Pythagorean (or ditonic) comma"—the amount left over when the true or natural

TABLE 3.1 The cycle of natural fifths, in cents

Step Number	Staff Letter Name	Distance in cents above middle C	
12	C	1200	(an octave higher)
11	F	522	(natural fourth = 498 cents; the 24 cents difference equals the Pythagorean comma)
10	$A^{\#}$ or B^{b}	1020	
9	$D^{\#}$ or E^{b}	318	
8	$G^{\#}$ or A^{b}	816	
7	$C^{\#}$ or D^{b}	114	
6	$F^{\#}$ or G^{b}	612	
5	B	1110	
4	E	480	
3	A	906	
2	D	204	
1	G	702	
0	middle C	0	

TABLE 3.2 The cycle of natural fifths in ascending pitch order, producing a 12-note scale expressed in cents

Note	Cents
C	1200
B	1110
B^{b} ($A^{\#}$)	1020
A	906
A^{b} ($G^{\#}$)	816
G	702
G^{b} ($F^{\#}$)	612
F	522
E	408
E^{b} ($D^{\#}$)	318
D	204
D^{b} ($C^{\#}$)	114
Middle C	0

fourth is subtracted from the calculated one. The ditonic comma is also the interval between six whole tones and the pure octave, whose ratio, as given in Helmholtz (1885/1954), is 531441 : 524288 (approximately 74 : 73), but modern calculations are more accurate at 1671 : 1648, which also equals 24 cents. Ideally the octave should equal six whole tones, but in the same way that the cycle of fifths produces a pitch for the interval of the fourth different from that of the natural harmonics, the addition of six tones falls short of the pure octave (ratio 2 : 1) by 24 cents. The ordinary, or syntonic, comma, mentioned as part of Pythagorean theory by Didymus and Ptolemy, is the difference between the "just" major third, using the fifth harmonic of the natural harmonic series (ratio 5 : 4), and the Pythagorean ditone, or major third (with a ratio of 81 : 64). This ratio is obtained by adding the ratio for two whole tones (9 : 8 + 9 : 8 = 81 : 64), remembering that to add ratios you multiply.

The Pythagoreans of the time of Plato and Aristotle used proportional methods of calculating intervals based on the musical tetractys. The musical tetractys comprises the numbers 6, 8, 9, and 12, whose proportional relationships yield the intervals shown in Figure 3.1.

Since a fourth equals two whole tones plus a semitone, this was expressed mathematically as 256 : 243 + 9 : 8 + 9 : 8. The ratio for the semitone (256 : 243) is obtained from the difference between the perfect fourth (4 : 3) and the major third (81 : 64). This sequence is recorded by many writers, including Aristoxenus and Ptolemy; the latter stated that it was the sequence of tuning ratios employed by the string players of his day. This was referred to as the "tense" diatonic of Aristoxenus. Didymus and Ptolemy described a minor tone as a ratio of 10 : 9. Thus there were two types of tone, each with its own proportion—9 : 8 and 10 : 9—and a semitone whose proportion (256 : 243) was not exactly half of either of the two tones, but was regarded as the difference between the fourth (the tetrachord) and the sum of two tones.

Without going into the labyrinthine matters of ancient proportional theory any further, it can be appreciated how difficult it was to reach agreement on how to divide up the octave satisfactorily for everyone's needs, as well as how heterogeneous, complex, and contradictory the system actually was. The ancient Greeks based their scales on the tetrachord, or C–F using modern notation, and they employed three basic variations, the diatonic, enharmonic, and chromatic, each of which had several variants with their own proportions. These terms did not, of course, have the same meanings in ancient Greek music as they enjoy in modern musical theory. The tetrachord

FIGURE 3.1 The Musical Tetractys, showing proportions and their respective musical intervals

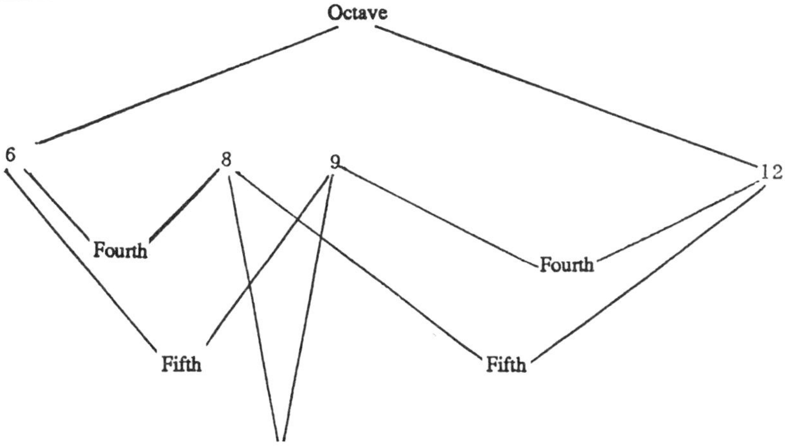

Whole tone—the difference between 3:2 and 4:3 = 9:8
(i.e., the difference between the fourth and the fifth)

Note: With proportions one must multiply to add and divide to subtract. This means that 3:2 - 4:3 = 3/4 : 2/3 = 9:8.

comprised four notes within the interval of the perfect fourth (ratio 4 : 3). In modern musical theory this amounts to two whole tones and a semitone. In the application of ancient proportional theory to each of these three forms of the tetrachord, varied fractional tones were employed in the many variants of each of the three, including intervals of less than a semitone and more than a tone. Some examples are: "soft" chromatic, $1/3$ tone–$1/3$ tone–$1\frac{5}{6}$ tones; "hemiolic" chromatic, $3/8$ tone–$3/8$ tone–$1\frac{3}{4}$ tones; and "tonal" chromatic, $1/2$ tone–$1/2$ tone–$1\frac{1}{2}$ tones. The basic enharmonic was $1/4$ tone–$1/4$ tone–2 tones, and there were many variants of this sequence. From these few examples it can be seen how great was the variation possible, as some tones were stretched to produce intervals larger than a tone while others were diminished to produce fractions of a tone. Ancient Greek proportional theory enabled musicians to calculate many different ways of dividing up the basic proportion of the tetrachord—4 : 3—provided the three resulting proportions added up to this overall interval. Here, again, it must be remembered that proportions are added by multiplying them and subtracted by dividing them: e.g., 3 : 2 (the fifth) + 4 : 3 (the fourth) = 12 : 6 = 2 : 1 (the octave). All such proportions were available to performing musicians through appropriately placed marks dividing up the fingerboards under strings or the position of holes in wind instruments.

Many different systems were employed to divide up the tetrachord at various times in the ancient Greek and Roman eras. Often they were associated with some great theorist. The diatonic of Archytas was 28 : 27–8 : 7–9 : 8. This was described as the most common diatonic of the day by Ptolemy. The so-called septimal tone (8 : 7) was employed in Greek music from the fourth century B.C. to the second century A.D. (Winnington-Ingram, 1980). The chromatic divisions of the tetrachord included a "soft" chromatic of Ptolemy (28 : 27–15 : 14–6 : 5) and a "tense" chromatic (22 : 21–12 : 11–7 : 6), again of Ptolemy, a well as many others.

The profusion of forms for the tetrachord created the enormous, expressive variety of Greek monody, which the Romans took over and developed. By the time of Boethius (A.D. 480–524), many scholars were trying to piece together the theories of ancient Greece and Rome by translating the works of earlier scholars and adding their own commentary in some cases. From his own time until the sixteenth century, Boethius was Europe's most important single source of information concerning the proportional theories of ancient Greece and Rome. In *De institutione musica*, he described in detail the Pythagorean system of harmonics, and it was this which formed the main focus of study for medieval scholars as far as music was concerned. Thus Pythagorean harmonics became the most important influence on the development of Western music until the sixteenth century, when other ancient sources became available to many people through the growth of printing and the enthusiasm for translating old Greek or Latin texts into modern languages.

In its original form, Pythagorean proportional arithmetic was more than just a means of dividing up musical intervals so as to form scales. It constituted the most important basis of modern mathematics until the work of Euclid. In the historical development of mathematics, Euclidian geometry replaced Pythagorean proportionism and set mathematical scholars on the path that eventually led to Newton and Einstein. By contrast, in the historical development of musical theory based on mathematics, Pythagoreanism remained the most important source of theoretical speculation until very recently. So although the basis of musical theory became mathematically archaic, even obsolete, quite early on, it nonetheless lived on to influence acoustical theory in music. The historical transmission of Pythagorean cosmic connections among music, mathematics, and related ancient proportional theories can be traced through a number of authors, as shown in Table 3.3.

Writers such as Plutarch, Dio Cassius, and Athenaeus provide important information about the social context of music and the relationship among music, religion, politics, and social class. Plutarch and Dio Cassius (A.D. 155–229) reported a great deal on beliefs in ancient Egypt, and it is clear that the mathematics of music, as well as the links between music and the planets, formed an important part of music's function in the courtly life of ancient Egypt. Athenaeus reported on similar matters pertaining to ancient Roman life.

Purely in terms of the historical line of transmission of Pythagorean harmonics, there are several ancient treatises that are central or crucial, Barbera (1980) lists five: the *Sectio canonis* (author unknown but attributed to Euclid, doubtfully); Nicomachus, *Enchiridion*; Theon, *Expositio*; Gaudentius, *Harmonica*; and Boethius, *De institutione musica*. In the first four works can be seen the originals upon

TABLE 3.3 Principal authors responsible for the transmission of ancient theories about music, in chronological order

Author	Time of Writing	Writing
Pythagoras	6th century B.C.	no writings left
Hippasus	5th century B.C.	no writings left
Philolaus	5th century B.C.	fragments, description
Achytas	4th century B.C.	fragments, description
Plato	4th century B.C.	*Republic, Laws, Timaeus, Epinomis, Theaetetus*
Aristotle	4th century B.C.	*Politics, Poetics, Metaphysics*
Speusippus	4th century B.C.	*On Pythagorean Numbers*
Xenocrates	4th century B.C.	*Things Pythagorean*
Eculid	4th century B.C.	*Elements*
anonymous	4th century B.C.	*Sectio canonis*
Eratmosthenes	3rd century B.C.	*Platonicus*
Plutarch	1st to 2nd century A.D.	*De musica* (?), *Isis and Osiris*
Dio Cassius	1st to 2nd century A.D.	fragments, description
Nicomachus	2nd century A.D.	*Introductio Arithmetica; Enchiridion Harmonices*
Theon	2nd century A.D.	*Expositio*
Ptolemy	2nd century A.D.	*Harmonica*
Athenaeus	2nd century A.D.	*The Deipnosophists*
Gaudentius	3rd century A.D.	*Harmonica*
Iamblichus	4th century A.D.	*De communis mathematica*
Boethius	6th century A.D.	*De institutione musica*

which Boethius based his treatise. Here it must be stressed that a distinction is being drawn between the authors who supplied the most potent and valuable treatises on Pythagorean harmonics and the channels through which this knowledge was transmitted through medieval European scholarship up to modern times. In the former regard, the *Sectio canonis* and the works of Nicomachus, Theon, Ptolemy, and Iamblichus are of paramount importance (Barbera, 1980). In the latter, it was Boethius who became the source of knowledge, even though he was merely expounding the ideas of these earlier authors, particularly Nicomachus. Ptolemy became a most important source only for Renaissance musical theorists, composers, and scholars, but by this time the works of many of the great scholars of antiquity were becoming available in translation.

The influence of Pythagorean harmonic theory can seen in scores derived from medieval neums. In Davison and Apel (1964), examples of early polyphony from *Scholia enchiriadis* (c. A.D. 850) show organum whose parts move in parallel octaves, fourths, and fifths. Further developments in' composition reflecting the influence of contemporary theory can be seen in the music of France in particular, culminating in the adventurous works of Léonin and Perotin le Grand of twelfth-century Paris. Each took theory as a basis but composed music in free and imaginative style influenced by secular models from troubadours as well as sacred plainsong.

THE EXPANSION OF MUSICAL HARMONIC THEORY IN THE RENAISSANCE

All musical theoretical works from the fifteenth century onwards explained in great detail the musical tetractys, using the proportions derived from the series 6, 8, 9, 12. Ancient Pythagoreanism was expounded as it related to the basic musical intervals of the fourth, fifth, and octave, but there was a great deal of speculation about whether other intervals could be termed consonant or dissonant. The major and minor thirds and sixths were particularly interesting from this point of view. The most important aspect of the theoretical argument had its roots in proportional theory. It was considered that only superparticular ratios could be consonant. The superparticular ratio is one where the two numbers are related in such a manner that the second number divides into the first once, leaving one part of itself as a remainder. Thus 3 : 2, 4 : 3, 5 : 4, 6 : 5 qualify as superparticular ratios in that, for example, 2 divides into 3 once with 1 left over. So, theoretically, the major and minor thirds (5 : 4 and 6 : 5, respectively) could be classed as consonances. They had not been admitted as consonances in ancient Greek and Roman times because they included numbers outside the tetrad (i.e., 5 and 6). Only with the development of proportional theory and the widespread use of the proportions 6 : 8 : 9 : 12 was it possible to make such arguments for consonance. It was this kind of theoretical argument that occupied a great deal of the time and intellectual energy of medieval monks and early Renaissance theorists.

From the fifteenth century onwards, the modern influence of Pythagorean harmonics can be seen on the development of modern harmony. One of the most important early figures in this regard was Bartolomé Ramos de Pareja (born A.D. 1440). At one point he lectured on Boethius at Salamanca, one of Italy's oldest universities. In 1482 he published *Musica practica* in Bologna. This was a revolutionary work for its day and caused a storm of controversy. He advocated replacing the old Guidonian solmization based on the hexachord (ut, re, me, fa, sol, la) with a set of syllables (psal-li-tur, per voc-es is-tas) based purely on the eight notes of the octave to form the major or minor scale. He declared major and minor thirds consonant, and while remaining within the framework of the Pythagorean theory of tuning, he approached "just" intonation in his revision of the older system, so that ratios of 5 : 4 and 6 : 5 were used for the major and minor thirds, respectively. These ratios were not part of the Pythagorean system. The Pythagorean major third, comprising the addition of two whole tones, was generally regarded as harsh because of its wider interval ratio of 9 : 8 + 9 : 8 = 81 : 64.

As time went on, the widespread use of harmony eventually made it necessary to "temper" the Pythagorean third by flattening it to avoid the acoustic problem of beats when it was combined with certain other notes. Similarly, the Pythagorean minor third was flatter than the natural, or "just," minor third. The former has a ratio of 32 : 27, and the latter of 6 : 5. In practice these intervals also produced sounds unsatisfactory to the ear, and performing musicians were "tempering" their tuning to make the musical sounds conform more to their artistic expectations. The same began to happen with the interval of the fifth. The natural fifth of 702 cents (ratio 3 : 2) caused similar problems for musical performance as musical harmony became more sophisticated and a greater pitch range came into use with the introduction of new instruments.

To some extent Ramos was merely attempting to set out in theory what musicians were actually doing in practice. He went so far as to suggest a twelve-note scale that, in view of the needs of chromatic keyboards (which were then becoming fashionable) and the demands of tuning lutes and other similar string instruments, is highly significant in the development of modern tunings. In fact, Barbour (1953) explains how many lute tunings approached equal temperament during the sixteenth century. A cursory glance through early sixteenth-century lute music shows widespread use of chromaticism. For example, the Spanish lutenist Luis de Narváez, in a set of variations for lute, included all twelve notes of the chromatic scale within the first nineteen bars (Davison & Apel, 1964). Ramos' theories, however, enraged some of his contemporaries. Burzio, in his *Musices opusculum* of 1487, bitterly attacked Ramos, accusing him of insulting the revered name of Guido d'Arezzo, the eleventh-century monk who set down the practices of his time and established the hexachord and solmization as the basis for melody. But it was Ramos' advocacy of what became known as "just" tuning ratios that most concerns us here. These "just" ratios are based upon the "natural" intervals formed by the harmonic series. Although the composition of a complex wave in terms of its sinusoidal components was not fully understood until the nineteenth century, proportional relationships between the partials (that is, $6:5$, $5:4$, $4:3$, $3:2$, $2:1$) were suspected, and by the seventeenth century it was a fact accepted by such scientists as Marin Mersenne. Renaissance musicians arrived at these simple ratios through Pythagorean harmonics, however, not through knowledge of the harmonic spectrum of a vibrating string or column of air.

Ptolemy and Didymus advocated the use of the simpler ratios of $6:5$ and $5:4$ for the minor and major thirds, respectively, in place of the more complex Pythagorean ratios. Boethius mentioned both authors in *De musica* but failed to go into detail concerning their theories. He merely expounded the Pythagorean proportional theories without providing alternative or later theoretical calculations. Since Boethius was the most important source for medieval scholars of musical theory, and since the work of Ptolemy and others was suppressed during the so-called Dark Ages, the simpler ratios of "just" tuning were not widely disseminated until the fifteenth and sixteenth centuries.

They were known, however. Walter Odington, a thirteenth-century English scholar of Oxford, mentioned them in *De speculatione musices*, written around the turn of the thirteenth and fourteenth centuries, during which time he was lodged in Merton College, Oxford. He stated that consonant thirds had ratios of $5:4$ and $6:5$ and that singers intuitively used these ratios instead of those given by the

Pythagorean monochord (Barbour, 1953). Davison and Apel (1964) quote a twelfth-century hymn to St. Magnus from Britain that uses parallel thirds throughout; thus Odington would certainly have heard singers using the "forbidden" thirds profusely. Moreover, they could also be heard in the music of the Notre Dame School of twelfth- and thirteenth-century Paris. Ptolemy and Didymus reasoned that tuning was correct only if superparticular ratios were used, and all their tunings used these ratios. They argued that music sounded best when the ear and the ratio are in agreement, rather than simply when the theoretical argument of proportional theory has been satisfied. In this they echoed the extensive writings of Aristoxenus on this matter and foreshadowed the bitter arguments between musicians and theorists that have characterized the entire development of Western musical theory up to the present times, particularly those concerning a supposed affinity between the workings of the inner ear and Pythagorean harmonic theory.

Another important Renaissance theorist was Don Nicola Vicentino (1511–1572). He was interested in "saving music from the old-fashioned excesses of contrapuntal polyphony" (quoted in Lang, 1978, p. 295) and helping music return to that of the ancients, namely, the music of ancient Greece. His *L'Antica Musica Ridotta alla Moderna Prattica*, published in 1555, principally advocated the use of more expressive tunings in the enharmonic and chromatic proportions of ancient Greece, together with the discontinuation of the "old diatonic," which, he said, should be relegated to the antiquarian. What this meant in practice was that adventurous musicians began to use chromatic modifications to notes in order to give greater expressiveness, which they imagined was a quality of ancient Greek music. This, of course, led to the use of all twelve notes contained in an octave within the course of a single piece of music. Such an application of ancient Greek enharmonic and chromatic ways of dividing up the tetrachord was inaccurate in terms of its origins, but, however historically inaccurate it was, the idea provided a stimulus for modern music to experiment with the expressive use of chromatic melody and harmony—something that characterizes the most modern developments of Western musical art.

Without doubt a most important influence in the course of modern Western musical theory is Gioseffo Zarlino (1517–1590), a fellow pupil of Willaert's with Vicentino. Zarlino was primarily a music theorist as seen through the eyes of history, but he held the post of first *maestro di cappella* at St. Marks, Venice, and as such he had to compose liturgical music. He wrote three treatises: *Istitutione har-*

moniche, 1558; *Dimostratione harmoniche*, 1571; and *Sopplimenti musicali*, 1588. The first, the *Istitutione harmoniche*, was extremely influential. It was translated into French, German, and Dutch during the sixteenth century, thus spreading the influence of Zarlino across the most important musical centers of Europe. The treatise is divided into four books, the first being a discourse on the excellence of music, the second expounding the Ptolemaic system of dividing up the strings of the monochord, the third setting out the laws of counterpoint, and the fourth explaining the system of modes that we now call "ecclesiastical" and that has survived until the present. The most controversial was the second book, rejecting Pythagorean division of the tetrachord in favor of that of Ptolemy into the "greater tone" (major tone, ratio 9 : 8), the "lesser tone" (minor tone, ratio 10 : 9), and the diatonic semitone (ratio 16 : 15). The ratios of these intervals are all superparticular, and are, therefore, more musically correct according to Ptolemy's arguments concerning the quality of superparticular proportions. This gained favor with composers who preferred the great contrapuntal traditions emanating from Willaert and his predecessors. However, Zarlino upset many people with such views, not only the committed Pythagoreans. There were those who supported a system that enabled the octave to be divided up into twelve equal semitones, favoring a more strongly chromatic content to music. While there was not a satisfactory proportional theory to support a fully chromatic tuning, equal across the octave, it was clear that not only was the notion put forward in ancient Greece—by Aristoxenus, for example—but it was attempted in practice in the tunings of musicians playing various string instruments. Although brief, this discussion should indicate the wealth of musical styles and controversies surrounding the most important element of music, the division of the octave into constituent parts, during the sixteenth and subsequent centuries.

Zarlino accepted uncritically the belief handed down by the medieval and earlier Renaissance authors that music is the harmonizing agent of the universe. In the first part of the *Istitutione*, citing Boethius, he explained the function of different types of music. *Musica mundana*, or universal music, coordinates the spheres of the heavens, holds together the four elements—fire, air, water, and earth—and organizes time and the seasons. *Musica humana*, or human music, is the force that binds together the various parts of the body and helps maintain the harmony of the soul and body. He explained in some detail how this harmony is achieved in both types of music. For example, the primary elements of air and water are ideally mixed in the ratio of 3 : 2, but the same proportion of water to earth produces frigidity. He set out a complete system of contraries and concordances involving the elements that produce the unheard music which he labeled *musica animastica.* Contrasting with such music is *musica organistica,* or organic music. This has two classes, harmonic or natural (*harmonica o naturale*), which is vocal music and *musica artificiata,* or instrumental music. The common source of these types of music is number and proportion, and in particular the number 6, or "numero senario." He argued that 6 is the first perfect number because it is the sum of all the numbers of which it is also the multiple: $1 + 2 + 3 = 6 = 1 \times 2 \times 3$. He also cited the six planets in the sky; many examples from Plato of six elements of various things, ranging from hymns to celebrate six generations to the six species of movement to the six types of logic; and the fact that the world was created in six days. For musical proportions, the important point for Zarlino was that all the primary consonances of his day could be expressed as superparticular ratios using only the numbers from 1 to 6.

This is similar to the claim of the Pythagoreans concerning the numbers 1 to 4, but Zarlino included the intervals of the major and minor thirds and sixths in his full scheme of harmony, whereas the Pythagoreans did not. Most important for the development of modern harmony, Zarlino differentiated between the major and minor third on the basis of proportional theory and described the musical and affective character of each as an extrapolation of this theory.

He described the major third as a harmonic proportion, the highest accolade, while considering the minor third as merely an arithmetic proportion. This meant that the major interval had qualities of perfectness, excellence, brightness, optimism, and happiness, whereas the minor had sadness and a sense of imperfectness about it. This provided impetus for composers to use major chords, keys, and melodies for representing any positive type of situation and their minor forms for any negative or unhappy situations. According to proportional theory, Zarlino demonstrated his proof in the following divisions of the tetrachord:

C	D	E	F	G	A
180	160	144	135	120	108
	9 : 8	10 : 9	16 : 15	9 : 8	10 : 9

In the interval C–G, E (144) represents the harmonic mean between C (180) and G (120) [i.e. $180 : 120 = 3 : 2$ and $(180 - 144) : (144 - 120) = 36 : 24$, which also equals $3 : 2$], a relationship consid-

ered more "perfect" than a simple arithmetic mean. In the interval D–
A, F (135) represents the arithmetic mean between D (160) and A
(108). Actually, it should be 134, since $160 + 108 \div 2 = 134$, but the
problem of the Pythagorean comma intrudes here.

In effect, Zarlino rejected the Pythagorean division of the monochord that had been traditional in all medieval and early Renaissance
treatises. The syntonic diatonic tuning proposed by Ptolemy seemed
to fit the needs of Zarlino's harmonic requirements perfectly. This is
where the middle (or meson) tetrachord is divided up as follows:

432		480		540		576	
A		G		F		E	
	9 : 10		8 : 9		15 : 16		
	Lesser		Greater		Diatonic		(Just)
	Tone		Tone		Semitone		

With this system of tuning, most of the fifths and thirds have "pure"
or natural tuning within the octave. Fretted and keyboard instruments
could only approximate to this tuning, and musicians had to temper
their tunings accordingly. Zarlino explained in great detail how to
employ many systems to achieve suitable tempering of tones.

Vincenzo Galilei attacked the views of Zarlino, as they appeared
in *Istitutione*, in his treatises *Dialogo della musica antica e della
moderna* (in 1581) and *Discorso intorno alle opere di messer Gioseffo Zarlino di Chioggia* (in 1589). Basically, Galilei was a committed
Pythagorean who favored the division of the tetrachord into two
greater tones and a limma (i.e., two tones of proportion 9 : 8, and a
limma of proportion 256 : 243).

Finding mathematical solutions for various ways of dividing up
the octave and the tetrachord was a major feature of musical theory
and practice from the sixteenth to the nineteenth centuries. This was a
crucial development, since without a solution to the problems of
beats, commas, and "wolf" intervals, the development of modern
harmony would have been impossible. Composers would have been
unable to combine certain different pitches satisfactorily without producing sounds acoustically unacceptable to Western ears. By the eighteenth century the various attempts to reconcile the needs of composers who wrote for and played chromatic keyboard instruments had
yielded an enormous variety of solutions. Barbour (1953) cites many
examples of situations in which composers were confronted by a be-
wildering variety of tunings on different organs, other keyboard in-

struments, and the various fretted instruments still in use, not to mention the growing dominance of string instruments in the violin class whose players were expected to stop strings according to one system or other of tuning. Table 3.4 compares some of the effects of different tuning systems.

Theoretical controversies tended to fuel a desire for experimentation in some composition and performance. In the latter, the practice of modifying pitches chromatically was known as *musica ficta*, which eventually found its way into notational form. The fifth became a serious problem as time went on. The natural fifth caused all sorts of difficulties as the range of pitches used in musical composition increased. Some kind of tempering of the interval by diminishing it slightly became imperative. In his *Istitutione*, Zarlino suggested reducing the fifth by two-sevenths of a comma to produce a meantone system of tuning, and he intended this to be used on chromatic key-

TABLE 3.4 Comparison of different tuning systems, showing pitch and cent values

Interval from Concert A (440 Hz)	Proportion	Note above (Hz)	Note below (Hz)
Whole tone		B	G
Equal	449:400	493.9	391.982
Pythagorean	9:8	495	391.11
Mean	180:161	491.93	393.55
Just	10:9	488.88	396
Minor third		C	F#
Equal	44:37	523.24	370
Pythagorean	32:27	521.48	371.25
Just	6:5	528	366.67
Major third		C#	F
Equal	63:50	554.4	349.206
Pythagorean	81:64	556.87	347.654
Just	5:4	550	352
Perfect fourth		D	E
Equal	303:227	587.313	329.636
Pythagorean/Just	4:3	586.667	330
Perfect fifth		E	D
Equal	433:289	659.239	293.67
Pythagorean/Just	2:3	660	293.44

Note: The above discrepancies become more acute with compound intervals.

board instruments. However, Zarlino's system was inferior to many others that were being developed. It reduced many other intervals in size by one-seventh of a comma, or 3 cents, which caused additional problems.

One of the first modern attempts at equal tuning of the 12 semitones was that of Giovanni Maria Lanfranco, who published his *Scintille de musica* in 1533 in Brescia, where he was organist and master of the choristers at the cathedral. He advocated that "5ths are to be tuned so flat that the ear is pleased with them, and 3rds as sharp as can be endured" (Barbour, 1953, p. 45). This implied a tempering of the Pythagorean tunings by a judicious flattening of both fifths and thirds. A most important point is his advocacy of equivalence for F# and G♭ and C# and D♭ in their tunings, thus suggesting the equal temperament that now holds sway on keyboards.

Many sources in the sixteenth century indicate that equal tuning was actually practiced, particularly by lute players. The idea of using the mean, or average, between two notes as a method of tuning the tetrachord was advocated by some. For example, Aron's 1523 *Toscanello* was an early treatise supporting what became known as "meantone" temperament. Put very simply, a tone is calculated as the mean of a pure third. This means that the ratio of the tone will be the square root of 5 : 4. Applying Aron's scheme across the octave results in the fifth being reduced from 702 cents to 696.6 cents. Another system, based upon Ptolemy, employs simple ratios relating to the harmonic series. This was called "just" tuning. In this system the proportions are similar to those advocated by Zarlino using the "perfect" number 6. The problem with all these and their variants is simply that over a pitch range of more than two octaves the proportions do not add up; there are fractions left over at the octave. Even the ideal of equal tuning has its own problems; the fifths and thirds do not give the same aesthetic pleasure as those of unequal systems to ears unaccustomed to older tuning ratios.

In *Sopplimenti musicali* Zarlino had provided three methods for dividing the octave into twelve equal parts. In 1636, Marin Mersenne, in *Harmonie universelle*, examined a number of ways to divide the octave into twelve equal parts. In particular he dealt with the problem of the comma and how to distribute it equally across all intervals of the octave. He discussed at some length the relative merits of each tuning system from an aesthetic viewpoint, one of which was concerned with the effects on the ear of different ways of tuning the main intervals of the third, fourth, and fifth. Many other mathematicians and musicians in the following 200 years supplied ingenious solutions to the problem as well as a wealth of argument praising the merits of one system above another. Among the most prominent were Andreas Werckmeister, who published *Musicalische temperatur* in 1691 in Frankfurt and Leipzig, and Johann George Neidhardt, who published *Sectio canonis harmonici* in 1724 in Königsberg. Nowadays we can regard the problem of dividing up the octave into twelve equal parts as a simple matter of calculating the twelfth root of 2.

It should be borne in mind, however, that historically the influence of Pythagoras was so complete that it was impossible merely to sweep away more than 2,000 years of such influence in order to overcome the problems of the comma presented by Pythagorean tuning. More important, musicians and theorists held strong views about the aesthetic purpose and value of pure intervals, even if they did tend to produce beats and other undesirable acoustic effects over wide pitch ranges. Belief in the special musical power of intervals designed in antiquity held a powerful place in the minds of musicians during the entire Renaissance. Of particular interest is the presence at this early stage in modern musical history of the seeds of the destruction of the major/minor diatonic system—seeds that were also responsible for its development. Just tuning contributed to its establishment, and equal temperament led eventually to its dissolution by its facilitation of increasing use of chromaticism.

THE SURVIVAL OF PYTHAGOREANISM
THROUGH RAMEAU AND BEYOND

Musicians and theorists tended to work from within the constraints of theory almost reverentially, even though they were obliged to try to solve the virtually insoluble problems presented by the ancient laws of proportionism. Be that as it may, by the eighteenth century equal temperament had become the central and most important new issue in musical theory. Many earlier attempts to tune semitones equally had sounded equal to most ears, even though mathematically they were not. They did not produce precisely 100 cents for each semitone, but as far as the human ear is concerned they are sufficiently near to sound equal. As explained in Chapter 2, modern research into categorical perception in language and music has shown how we classify stimuli into categories, often placing a set of mathematically discrete pitches into a single pitch class (Siegel & Siegel, 1977a). Thus it can be said that the human ear had accepted equal temperament from a number of very close approximations long before it became a mathematically simple procedure to use the twelfth root of 2. Without doubt, some of the attempts of the sixteenth century produced tunings very close to equal temperament as far as human auditory perception is concerned, particularly those used on the lute. Moreover, there were some empiricists who questioned the musical superiority of the ancient interval ratios, based as they are upon small whole numbers rather than ratios involving roots of 2.

Simon Stevin (1548–1620), a Flemish mathematician and engineer, attempted to calculate the intervals of equal temperament and advocated their use in a manuscript, written around 1608, entitled *Vande Spiegheling der Singconst*. He argued that there was no compelling reason why musical intervals calculated using small integers should sound any better to the ear than those calculated using roots of 2. The controversy was not entirely mathematical; it was also aesthetic in that ancient beliefs in the perfectness of Pythagorean and other ancient proportions were very strong in the minds of musicians and musical scholars, who tended to reject such empiricism and objectivity as "unmusical."

The gradual acceptance of equal tuning for the twelve notes of the octave was a significant factor in enabling the theoretical writings of Rameau to assume such monumental significance in the development of Western musical theory, even though they were not a product of original thinking. Equal temperament was finally accepted in most countries of continental Europe by the middle of the nineteenth century, though England did not accept it until late in the century. Rameau's theories concerning functional harmony did not reach their full potential until the same time in Europe, but without equal temperament this potential could not have been realized. It is Rameau who provided the last and most important link in the chain of dissemination of tonal harmonic theory in music that had begun in Western culture with Pythagoras in the 6th century B.C. The twentieth century has, however, witnessed the breakup of tonal harmony and the virtual abandonment of ancient Pythagorean notions linking musical and cosmic harmony. The ultimate stage, and nemesis for the great Pythagorean tradition, involved the increasing use of chromatic harmony in the late nineteenth century, which evolved into the use of so-called twelve-note serialism in the music of Schoenberg and his pupils in the early years of this century.

Jean Philippe Rameau was born in Dijon in 1683 and died in Paris in 1764. During his life he became a most important influence on contemporary French music. His influence on music theory generally lasted until the beginnings of the twentieth century and beyond. He propounded the notion of what is often called "functional harmony," that is, harmonic progression defined in terms of progressions by the root of a chord rather than by the actual bass note. Although it is generally believed that Rameau made musicians think differently about harmony, he was not the first to describe harmony in terms of triads, whereby the root of the chord becomes its most important signifier. Rivera (1978) points out the sixteenth-century origins of such ideas in the work of Avianus, in 1581, and others. However, it was the written work of Rameau that became the focus from the eighteenth century onwards. As a composer, Rameau practiced his theory first in his keyboard pieces and later in his operas.

Instead of treating the bass note as the most important line in harmony, irrespective of whether it was the root, third, or fifth of a chord, Rameau suggested that chords should be recognized in terms of their root, that is, the bass note upon which the triad is built. Chords should be regarded as being in root position, first inversion, or second inversion, and so on. Chord progressions could be better understood as progressions of fundamental bass notes, and harmonic movement could thus be better codified. Furthermore, chords could assume functions such as pivot chords in modulations and could be extended to include sevenths, ninths, elevenths, and thirteenths, all relating to the bass note as the root.

It took some time before composers began to understand how Rameau's revolutionary ideas had opened up a whole new world of harmony. For many years following the publication of Rameau's theories, musicians continued to use the figured bass as the approach to harmony and composition. It was not until the nineteenth century that the true potential and ultimate application of this theory was realized in the richly chromatic and modulatory compositions of Liszt, Chopin, Wagner, Schumann, Brahms, Mahler, Richard Strauss, and others.

Of particular interest, however, is the reasoning Rameau gave for his theoretical description of chords. He claimed that his theory had scientific underpinning in that it was derived from the natural order of things, in this case the *corps sonore*, or the natural components of a vibrating string—the harmonic series. He pointed out that it was an observable fact that the components of the major triad could be found in the pitches of the partials of a vibrating string. He was quoting from the work of a number of mathematicians who had identified the nature of the harmonic content of a complex wave formed by a vibrating string. In particular Joseph Sauveur had established both the term *acoustics* and the doctrine of linking the proportional theory of intervals with acoustical overtones in his *Principes d'acoustique de musique* of 1701. However, much earlier Mersenne had been aware of the existence of harmonics and overtones, and many musicians claimed to be able to hear them. Rameau employed the help of some contemporary mathematicians, notably Mairan and de Gamaches, in the formulation of his thesis that functional harmony is derived from the natural harmonics of a vibrating string.

The essence of Rameau's theory is that since the upward harmonic series produces both the complete dominant chord and the major triad on the tonic within the first thirteen overtones, these chords are intended by nature to be the most pleasing. They naturally form the pillars upon which musical harmonic progression should be built, he argued. Further, he cited the possibility of exciting vibrations sympathetic to those of the natural harmonic series in the cochlea, thus linking the natural vibrations of a string with the natural proclivities of the human ear. He was aware of the physical possibility of undertones as well, and by extrapolation he suggested that another harmonic series could be derived below the fundamental vibration rate of the string to give another chord of great importance, that on the subdominant root. By calculating the harmonic series below the tonic C in the same fashion as above, the notes F, A, and C can be derived, as can the notes of a minor triad. In this way, he argued, they balance the major modality of the upper harmonic series. Rameau placed the three most powerful chords in a key—the tonic, dominant, and subdominant—firmly in the natural components of a vibrating object. He proclaimed these three chords therefore to be the basis of all keys and the linchpin of harmony from which all harmonies spring. By adding up the notes of these three triads, all the notes of a major scale can be obtained. He suggested that since these triads are built in thirds, with major and minor thirds stacked on top of each other, additional chords could be built by stacking thirds to produce the dissonances of the seventh, ninth, and eleventh chords. Moreover, modulations to other key centers could best be understood and utilized through understanding of the power of the fundamental bass. He argued that since all these chords can be derived from the vibrating string and its partials above and below, the fundamental base note is the true generator of harmony, just as the fundamental rate of vibration of a string is the true generator of the upper and lower partials.

It was a powerfully seductive theory, even if it had flaws that Rameau's contemporaries were quick to point out. But this was no hindrance as far as musicians of the nineteenth century were concerned. To them, Rameau's articulation of the importance of the fundamental bass and the functional harmonic relationships between chords built above a bass note gave a freedom that was exploited to the full. Harmony, dissonance, and chromatic inflections became components of musical language as powerful as melody, and equally articulate in expression. Rameau's theory was without doubt a major contributory factor in this.

The first, and most important, of Rameau's theoretical works appeared in 1722. Its title, *Traite de l'harmonie reduite à ses principes naturels*, indicated the main thrust of Rameau's thesis—that the laws of harmony he propounded were based upon natural laws, the laws of the physics of sound. Leaving aside for the moment Rameau's case in citing natural laws of physics, his theory of harmony codified for future generations the extremely important principle of a hierarchy of functions for chords within the tonal system of the major and minor scales. Composers had for some time, however, been intuitively writing hierarchically in their harmonies. There was consensus concerning the importance of the dominant and the tonic chords, for example, as well as the secondary role of other chords within a particular key, as is evident in many seventeenth-century works. But there was no clearly understood harmonic function for chords. Composers still tended to think in intervals above a bass note, rather than in chord progressions, until Rameau provided the impetus to regard harmony as functional in vertical terms rather than as a result of intervallic superimposition upon a bass line. The existing theoretical texts from which composers learned their craft in the early eighteenth century taught them to think in intervals rather than in chord progressions. In contrast, Rameau's theories enabled composers to think in chords, and later treatises on musical theory adapted and developed them.

This is not to say that many composers did not write harmony—as though it never occurred to them to regard it as functional—before Rameau's theories were known. They did. But just as it took Schoenberg, two centuries later, to codify into a written theory (the so-called 12-note theory) the extensive chromaticism that had been in widespread use by most composers, so it took Rameau's theories to establish the notion of functional harmony that was already occurring in musical practice. It must be said, however, that composers were not consciously changing their perception of the function of the bass line as the reference point for intervallic descriptions of harmony above the figured bass, even though their music appeared to be doing precisely that. Rameau, however, made his theory into a musically logical system that eventually became a part of the basis of musical education right up to today.

A member of the Académie des Sciences in Paris, Jean Le Rond d'Alembert, wrote in Volume 1 of the 1751 *Encyclopédie* that what distinguishes Rameau "is that he has reflected with much success on the theory of [music]; that he has found in the fundamental bass the principal of harmony and of melody; that by this means he has reduced to simpler and more certain laws a science confined before him to arbitrary rules, or [rules] dictated by blind experiment" (quoted in Bernard, 1980, p. 38). However, an extensive and bitter controversy developed involving Rousseau, d'Alembert, and Rameau, initially concerning Rousseau's criticisms of Rameau's theories. There were political overtones to the controversy in that d'Alembert, Diderot, Rousseau, and the Encyclopedists in general were suspected of being antichurch and anti-France, and their attacks on Rameau were seen as attacks on French music and French culture.

D'Alembert, by all accounts, did not wish the argument with Rameau to escalate for these reasons. Rameau was seen as a pillar of French culture, whereas his opponents were not. D'Alembert did not succeed in preventing Rameau from escalating the controversy. His sharp rebuke to Rameau in Volume 6 of the *Encyclopédie* only served to rile Rameau further. At stake for d'Alembert was the survival of the Académie and the Encyclopedists, who were being watched by their powerful Jesuit enemies at the French court. Rameau, however, had another agenda: he wanted to become a member of the Académie, and he was somewhat enraged by the way d'Alembert tended to dismiss his theories of sound. Rameau accused him of being unmusical and too academic, and he even cast doubts on d'Alembert's intellectual capacity. Rameau failed in his bid to be elected to the Academie, and the scientific basis of his musical theory remained suspect.

The dispute became heated and degenerated to the level of insult. However, there were some substantive issues at stake. These concerned the relevance of mathematics to music and the place of music among the sciences. Rameau claimed, in true Pythagorean fashion (although he intended to demystify Pythagorean harmonics), that the laws of music existed in nature before human reason could gain access to them. He argued that the sciences contained the source, that is, the true proportions, of harmony within the overtone structure of a vibrating string and that there was a natural response to the effects of these proportions in music because of their sympathy with the workings of the inner ear. Rameau eventually shifted his ground during the bitter dispute; he moved from using the vibrating string as the source of his scientific proof to citing Pythagoras and his proportional theory. Rameau suggested that Pythagoras had made contributions to arithmetic that, in turn, made geometry possible and had also discovered the numerical ratios that describe the sizes of the intervals in the major and minor chords, In his 1761 *Suite de la reponse de M. d'Alembert* . . . Rameau wrote:

> Is not geometry based on arithmetic, and arithmetic upon proportions? Scarcely has a sonorous body sounded, when the ear is struck by a delightful proportion. Soon after we discover there the proportions upon which alone all of geometry are based. (quoted in Bernard, 1980, p. 41)

This earned a particularly scathing attack from the Encyclopedists, who ridiculed Rameau's naive attribution to Pythagorean proportional theory not only the harmonies of music but all geometry. To Rameau, however, the old Pythagorean myth, which claimed that the true proportions of harmony existed waiting to be discovered, had credence. He resorted to Pythagorean doctrine in suggesting that the sounds produced from the Pythagorean proportions using the tetrad (numbers 1–4) affected the listener by virtue of their perfectness, a perfectness that was rooted in the mathematical proportions of lengths of strings and interval ratios. Rameau argued that the harmonic series produced by the *corps sonore* is directly given by nature and that everything in music arises from this phenomenon, just as the Pythagoreans had argued that their proportional theory has a supposed relationship to the music of the spheres.

D'Alembert retorted, correctly, that the *corps sonore* cannot by itself give rise to the musical system based on the perfect, natural triad, because in practice musicians employ temperament to alter the natural fifth and third. He pointed out that not only do musicians temper intervals, using ones that are different from those naturally occurring in harmonic contents, but that the harmonic contents cited by Rameau are as ideal and remote from reality as are the harmonies of the spheres quoted by the Pythagoreans. Rousseau (1749/1966), in his *Essay on the Origin of Languages*, was opposed to any notion of utilizing mathematics in the cause of musical expression: "Even if one spent a thousand years calculating the relations of sounds and the laws of harmony, how would one ever make of that art an imitative art?" (p. 57). In the following chapter, Rousseau explicated the relationship between the sound and the impact it has on the hearer, emphasizing that meaning is implicit not in the sound but in the intention of the hearer: "The sounds of a melody do not affect us merely as sounds, but as signs of our affections, or our feelings" (p. 59). He described the recognition of expression in music by a mind capable of such recognition as the "moral" effect of music. Even animals display this effect, he maintained, since a dog barking will attract another; but when the dog imitates a cat mewing, the cat becomes disinterested on discovering it is only imitation. Further on he condemned the whole notion of applying science to music:

> See how everything continually takes us back to the moral effects of which I spoke, and how far from understanding the power of their art are those many musicians who think of the potency of sounds only in terms of air pressure and string vibration. The more they assimilate it to purely physical impressions, the farther they get from its source and the more they deprive it of its primitive energy . . . with all its accord and all its harmony it will have no more effect on us. (p. 65)

The growing gulf between the discoveries of physics and the traditional theory of musical harmony became embarrassing by the beginning of the nineteenth century. Musical theory ignores the fact that vibrating strings have inharmonic partials as well as harmonic ones because of such physical factors as degree of stiffness, placement of the bridge, and method of securing the string for tightening. Piano strings, for example, tend to produce out-of-tune partials. They become inharmonic to the extent that by the 15th partial they are so sharp that the 15th is near the ideal pitch of the 16th partial. Strings on fretted and other string instruments display peculiar characteristics in their harmonic content that are dependent upon the physical nature of the instrument. Brass instruments tend to produce flat harmonics, and the vibrational behavior of a simple tube, like that of a simple string, is considerably modified in musical practices, both in performance and manufacture of instruments, to overcome the problems of inharmonic partials. Brass tubes have bell-shaped ends fixed with specially shaped metal to control the harmonic partials, for example. Some of this was known to the Encyclopedists, which only served to increase their scorn for notions such as those of Rameau. The emerging Industrial Revolution and its scientific underpinnings were already producing instruments that overcame the physical defects inherent in using certain shapes and materials for producing musical sound. Brass instruments, for example, began to use valves, making it easier to play more notes "in tune." In essence, science was becoming interested in producing the perfect instrument in order to realize in music the myth of acoustic perfection implicit in Western musical theory.

Basically, the argument hinged on misconceptions about the relationship between physics and the intuitive, artistic practices that had grown up over thousands of years in the realm of music. The natural physical content of a sound is not used in music without a great deal of alteration and manipulation. The ideal ratios of the harmonic series use small integers. Thus we get 2 : 1 between the 2nd partial and the fundamental, 3 : 2 between the 3rd and 2nd, and so on. As Rousseau and d'Alembert correctly pointed out, the use of these ratios is not satisfactory in musical practice, since many theorists had spent their lives attempting to find solutions to the problems of the comma. Moreover, equal temperament was the compromise solution that eventually became universally adopted a century or more later. Equal temperament did not use the natural proportions to which Rameau referred, yet, ironically, his harmonic system could not work properly without it. But this fact became obvious only in the nineteenth century and later, by which time the immensely valuable artistic rewards from Rameau's system of classifying harmony were obvious.

The Encyclopedists did not agree with Rameau's notion of a generative explanation for harmony. Rousseau, in particular, was scathing in his dismissal of Rameau's attempts to show how all the laws of harmony were generated by the properties of the vibrating string. He cited not only scientific flaws but also musical ones. He correctly saw harmony as something subject to human invention, something that may or may not be influenced by the laws of physics. He did not see that musical harmony could or should be limited to the chord system proposed by Rameau, and he flatly rejected the notion of a generative principle that could explain all musical harmony. D'Alembert supported Rousseau in this, stating that "we should conclude that the systems, or rather the dreams of the philosophers on most metaphysical questions deserve no place in a work exclusively intended to contain the real knowledge acquired by the human mind" (quoted in Bernard, 1980, p. 43).

Further, he challenged Rameau to explain how it was that "persons born with natural ability can compose songs even without having the least knowledge of harmony" (quoted in Bernard, 1980, p. 43) if, as Rameau maintained, all melody was derived from harmony, which, in turn, was derived from knowledge of the natural laws of vibrating objects. Since Rameau suggested that the natural laws of music were already in existence waiting to be found by human minds, it would have to follow that those who produced melodies not conforming to the natural laws were musically defective. The problem of accounting for music performed by those ignorant of such laws was never addressed by Rameau. This was pointed out by the Encyclopedists, and it remains one of the questions unanswered by many who seek to reduce the art of music to restricting laws rather than accept the significance of the role of the inventiveness of the human mind.

Rameau was upset by such attacks, since he was especially proud of the supposed scientific basis for his theory. D'Alembert, on the other hand, found Rameau's theories extremely valuable for music but rejected both the argument for their scientific origin and the value of such a position. He felt that all such attempts to "discover ultimate causes were doomed to failure" (quoted in Bernard, 1980, p. 43). Rameau felt the need to impose some kind of Cartesian order on music (he was a friend of Descartes), whereas for d'Alembert, a philosopher of the Enlightenment, the formulation of the principle was not the first step, as it was with Rameau. The principle that Rameau was anxious to prove was, as far as d'Alembert was concerned, unprovable and irrelevant to music, for "perhaps," said d'Alembert, "harmony is governed by another unknown principle, more general than that of the sonorous body" (quoted in Bernard, 1980, p. 43). However, d'Alembert made no attempt to define this unknown possible principle.

Despite this bitter dispute, the contribution of Rameau to musical theory is indisputable. Although his case for finding the source of harmony in the natural harmonic series is flawed, his musical arguments are powerful. His idea that two different bass notes can in fact be part of the same chord when the chord is positioned differently, while not entirely new, was, nevertheless, a crucial distinction for music—crucial in the sense that it provided greater clarity in defining and describing harmony and harmonic progression than the old figured bass was able to do.

The final stage of Pythagorean proportionism was heralded by Rameau's harmonic theories, bringing the influence of Pythagoras right into modern music. Whether the case is spurious for building a harmonic system on proportional theory in the belief that it represents a natural order of things, as the Encyclopedists argued it was, is somewhat academic: a harmonic system had been established in music. The main point is that Pythagoreanism had survived to become something for Rameau to fall back on when his other arguments were under attack, that Pythagorean proportions remained the basis of Western melody and harmony throughout the development of Western culture. This is a truly remarkable situation, considering the origins, antiquity, and modes of transmission through time, through epochs, and through the rise of modern rationalism and empiricism. It surely puts music into a different category of human activity than that of scientific discovery, where new laws destroy the veracity and scientific usefulness of old ones. The continued belief in the significance of Pythagoreanism over a period of more than 2,500 years of scientific and technological advance in the West justifies the notion that Western music is built on belief masquerading as science. It is particularly instructive to see how Rameau began by using the mathematics and physics of his time as scientific proof for his theories. In his earlier works, the *Traite de l'harmonie . . .* of 1722, the *Generation harmonique* of 1737, and the *Demonstration du principe de l'harmonie* of 1750, he relied upon the work of Sauveur for the scientific basis for his theory. In 1761, when the flaws inherent in attempting to lean on contemporary science became apparent, he reverted to Pythagorean proportionism itself in his replies to the attacks of d'Alembert.

In 1863, just over a century after Rameau's acrimonious public quarrel with the Encyclopedists, Herman Helmholtz published the first edition of his monumental tome, *On the Sensations of Tone*. He began this work with a review of the history of musical acoustics, mentioning that "even Pythagoras knew that when strings of different lengths but of the same make, and subjected to the same tension, were used to give the perfect consonances of the octave, fifth and fourth their lengths must be in the ratios of $1 : 2$, $2 : 3$, or $3 : 4$ respectively" (1885/1954, p. 1). He went on to explain how Pythagoras got this from Egypt and how

> later physics has extended the law of Pythagoras by passing from the lengths of strings to the number of vibrations, and thus making it applicable to the tones of all musical instruments, and the numerical relations $4 : 5$ and $5 : 6$ have been added to the above for the less perfect consonances of the major and minor thirds. (p. 1)

He added a note of caution, however, by saying that he was "not aware that any real step was ever made towards answering the question: What have musical consonances to do with the ratios of the first six numbers?" It is notable that a great scientist like Helmholtz suggested how modern physics had extended the Pythagorean laws rather than rendered them obsolete, thus displaying a desire to fuse musical and scientific theory into a coherent and connected body of knowledge. The views of Rousseau and d'Alembert still present a formidable obstacle to such attempts and, indeed, still adumbrate the basic arguments today in musical aesthetics, a field intimately connected with this whole debate. Aspects of Helmholtz's monumental work became significant in the development of some revolutionary ideas in music. These were the scientific chapters dealing with the nature of musical sounds and the workings of the human ear. As well as the references to music of traditions other than those of the West. One of the composers most affected was Edgard Varèse, who envisaged a complete assimilation between music and science. At any rate, the outcome was the decisive rejection of Pythagorean harmonics and the diatonic key system, leaving the musical field open to individual preference in matters of scales and tunings based on contemporary scientific capabilities. However, there are still some vestiges of support for the proportions of Pythagoras. Patterson (1986) postulates an analogy between computers using digital-analogue conversion techniques and the workings of the human ear. He suggests that once the input has gone beyond the analogue stage to reach the cochlea and the basilar membrane, the information is translated into a digital code. He postulates that at this point the neural firing rates within the cochlea and along the eighth cranial nerve may well react sympathetically to the "natural" proportions of 2 : 1, 3 : 2, and 4 : 3 or, musically, the octave, the fifth, and the fourth. The issue is still unresolved. We still do not know whether Pythagorean proportionism relates to something in nature. But despite the fact that for more than two millennia scientists have consistently failed to produce any convincing evidence in support of this relation—and seem no more likely to do so now—the quest has not been abandoned.

CHAPTER 4

Belief in Music's Power as an Expressive Symbol

One of the most highly developed and universally acknowledged attributes of Western music is its capacity to represent in sound various moods, emotions, or dramatic events. In the popular entertainment media, use of evocative musical sounds as a background is taken for granted. We expect, for example, a passionate sweep of melody on massed violins to accompany a romantic love scene or a sudden crescendo for full orchestra to frame a traumatic or dangerous dramatic incident. In fact, almost any situation in drama, advertising, or even newscasts is expected to be accompanied, preceded, or followed by suitable music, suitable meaning the use of musical sounds appropriate to the mood, atmosphere, character, or nature of events being presented. So ubiquitous is this expectation that one might suspect the existence of systematic rules or laws of semiotics in music. In fact, in the pragmatic and practical traditions of music in entertainment, workable lists of suitable musical representations to be used in all manner of situations have long been in use.

In the 1920s there were many such musical publications, ranging from piano arrangements for home use to professional scores for the theater. Titles such as "Sinister Presto," or "Dramatic Tension in Russian Atmosphere," or "In an Opium Den" betray the intent of the music. Apart from this, many theater and cinema pianists and organists regarded improvisation of suitable "mood" music as part of their professional work, and, later, as sound came to movies, composers and arrangers were required to provide background music chosen specifically for its evocative powers. The first movie with sound—*The Jazz Singer*, released in 1927—included as background music passages from Tchaikovsky's overture-fantasy *Romeo and Juliet* as well as many other examples either plagiarized from or imitative of nineteenth-century musical "affect." One of the most important movies of the 1940s, *Gone with the Wind,* released in 1939, used music as an integral and crucial part of the drama. The score, composed by Max Steiner, was symphonic in style and borrowed musical ideas freely from nineteenth- and early twentieth-century symphonic and operatic masters to enhance the emotional impact of the visual scenes and dialogue. It included a most memorable main theme representing the main dramatic theme of the movie—loyalty to the family house and estate. It was all very much in the spirit of the nineteenth-century romantic composers of tone poems.

An important point about this development in movies generally is that it popularized, and perhaps trivialized, this most important element in Western musical culture—its power to represent moods, create atmosphere, or heighten dramatic tension. Large segments of the populace, while unable to receive a classical education, were exposed to popularizations of this most profound aspect of Western musical art through the cinema.

The validity of the idea that musical elements contain extramusical meaning has long been subjected to scholarly inquiry. Some expressed doubts about its verisimilitude, perceptually; others, convinced of the effectiveness of musical representations of the extramusical, suggested systems or catalogues based on the works of composers. For example, Cooke (1959) suggested the systematic use of musical elements matched with extramusical meanings in the works of composers of the seventeenth to nineteenth centuries. He cited many examples, but where these originated is an epistemological issue that requires attention. Suppose that the first instance of a certain use of musical representation is identified in the works of a particular composer; let us choose as an example Monteverdi and the particular sounds he used to depict the underworld in his opera *La favola d'Orfeo*—low-pitched, menacing, reedy instrumental sounds, acoustically rich in harmonic content, and now well established in Western consciousness as signs of the unknown, of terror and dread. Why did he select such sounds? And why should they have become, nearly 400 years later, the *sine qua non* for depicting horror? According to Cooke's thesis, the answer to the latter question is their continual usage by successive composers following Monteverdi's invention. The answer to the first question is much more problematic, and, as a corollary, we might well ask where the *idea* of musical representation came from.

The origins of such ideas, as far as Western musical art is concerned, are to be found in the writings of Plato and Aristotle. This might suggest that musical representation is entirely contrived in that the aim of Western musical art from its very beginnings has been to invent musical sounds for such uses. Applying this line of thought, we might say that Monteverdi invented the representational meaning of the particular musical passages depicting the underworld in *Orfeo* and that, as such, their significance is entirely artificial and contrived. In one sense, therefore, it might be said that Monteverdi invented the relationship, in that he had no catalogue to refer to; he had merely his artistic sensibilities. But these sensibilities are susceptible to more general influences, as suggested by Marks (1978) in his explication of the theory concerning a certain basic unity of the senses. According to this theory, it might be postulated that Monteverdi, in reaching intuitively for a musical representation for the underworld and all the concepts of terror associated with it, utilized a basic store of experiences derived from different sensory modes.

Humans have, according to Marks, a proclivity for relating information across the sense modalities. Marks shows experimentally how we readily match intensity of light with high-pitched sounds, for example. And in relating how poets use verbal imagery, which betrays a similar cross-modal transfer, or matching of information, he provides some examples from Swinburne:

Sounds lovelier than the light,
And light more sweet than song from night's own bird;

and

Like fire are the notes of the trumpets
that flash through the darkness of sound.

He points out that such cross-modal comparisons are "implicit in Plato's psychophysical doctrine" as well as being "explicit in Aristotelean doctrine" (Marks, 1978, p. 64).

In such a context it might be possible to explain Monteverdi's choice of sound. The sight of the underworld—dark, forbidding, full of images of terror and the unknown—as depicted in paintings Monteverdi had seen, perhaps, and the poetic descriptions he had read describing the underworld similarly, were matched cross-modally with sounds that relate to these in some basic perceptual manner. This might be explained as resulting from a basic functional unity of our sensory and cognitive apparatus, as Marks implies, that enables us to match sensory input in color, shape, sound, and so forth with affective responses and verbal concepts in such a manner that they easily become associated. Thus dark, large, unfamiliar shapes might naturally be associated with loud, deep, complex sounds, which in turn are associated with fear, terror, and dread of the unknown.

Some might argue that the idea of such value-laden cross-modal comparisons and matchings must have started with someone, perhaps Plato or some earlier figure, and that continual revisiting of the idea as Western culture evolved ensured its survival. Others might reply that this is a natural way for humans to respond to their environment and that Plato merely made an astute observation of the existence of this response. This chicken-and-egg puzzle is probably unsolvable, unless it can be shown that other cultures without a Plato either have or have not concerned themselves with such cross-modal transfer and matching in their artistic activities.

One further issue concerns whether the meaning or value applied to the associations is also part of any natural proclivity toward a unity of the senses or whether such meaning is merely a product of Western culture. Can we exhibit some basic unity of the senses without exhibiting some basic unity of meaning as well? Can we display a natural proclivity to match low-pitched, frightening musical sounds with concepts of terror associated with the underworld of ancient mythology without also believing that the underworld is full of terror and dread?

If cultural interpretations of spiritual existence beyond our worldly one differ, then so must any value or meaning applied to the cross-modal matchings. If such is the case, we are left with the proclivity for such matchings as possibly being universal, but not their substance. A similar but related question concerns whether musical sounds contain in themselves the essence of character, or *ethos*, of a person, a nation, or a situation. It was this latter notion that was central to the artistic theories of ancient Greece and has remained so throughout the development of Western musical art. Quite clearly the theory fueled the activity of musicians, and it is possible to trace its development and evolution as a central notion in musical composition. The theory of musical representation comprises a substantial part of Western musical theory, and it is difficult to imagine how composers could write music in ignorance of a theory that formed an important part of their education and musical training. I argue, in fact, that the basic unity of the senses referred to is inextricable from meanings and that meaning is entirely culturally derived.

The theory, then, has existed for at least 2,000 years, and, not surprisingly, the effect of such ideas has been that composers have traditionally attempted to make music into a language in order to exploit, artistically, this supposed link across modalities. But what sort of a language is Western music? Has Western musical art produced sounds that are inevitably associated with particular extramusical events, moods, or feelings by virtue of some inexorable and intuitive link between the two? Or are such associations arbitrary, left to the whim of the composer, who only needs sufficient exposure of his or her musical inventions to make them work? Both of these aspects of expression, the contrivance of a musical language and the nature of the semantic properties of this language, are dealt with in the writings of Plato and Aristotle, and both suggested that musical sounds do contain intrinsic semantic properties.

Discussion about how music represents extramusical things, or whether music signifies nothing but itself, and which composers best exemplify such capabilities in their music, constitute the main problems of musical aesthetics in the Western traditions. Scientists have sought answers through empirical investigation, and musical controversies have divided communities, even nations, over these issues. But, irrespective of its foundation and veracity, so characteristic of musical art in the West has the notion of representation now become that it is often regarded by Westerners, *a priori*, as an attribute of musical sound in all cultures. Until fairly recently it was generally assumed in the West that music in other cultures, by utilizing some related system of musical semantic code, also attempted to represent emotions or symbolize events through imitating their affective nature. In the popular Western consciousness it is acceptable to listen for representations of sadness or happiness, or some other human state, in the music of aboriginals, for example.

REPRESENTATION BY MUSIC IN WESTERN CULTURE

The whole notion of music and representation is rooted in the traditions of Platonism, primarily in the theory of *ethos*, which originated in the work of Damon of Athens but received notable exegesis in the writings of Plato, in particular in *The Republic*. In *The Politics* and *The Poetics* of Aristotle, similar ideas are found but presented within the context of Aristotle's cosmology. Although these ideas were given a somewhat different emphasis, they had many points in common where the arts (including music), education, and politics were concerned. The works of Plato and Aristotle were read, plagiarized, and rewritten in translation from the Roman period through the beginnings of modern Europe right up to the time of the great intellectual changes wrought by the Renaissance of the fourteenth to sixteenth centuries and beyond, and they have continued to be the focus of debate in musical aesthetics up to modern times. In particular, most of the musical furors since the sixteenth century have been concerned in some way with opposing views of the true meaning of Plato or Aristotle in their statements about the relationships between music and poetry; specifically, these debates have had to do with the notion of mimesis and the ways in which music can reflect the meaning inherent in texts and with the theory of rhetoric in its applications to music in the form of what has become known in music as "word painting." In musical theory a term has long been in use to signal the central importance of the links between music and poetry—*musica poetica*.

The nineteenth century witnessed an aesthetic debate, at times most bitter, concerning whether music could represent specific feelings or the general nature of feelings in ways more meaningful than words. This controversy occurred despite certain eighteenth-century skeptical and empiricist views questioning whether music could represent such things at all! Composers, writers, philosophers, and music lovers took sides, and composers such as Tchaikovsky, Liszt, Wagner, and Berlioz were pitted against nonrepresentational composers such as Brahms, whom some felt wrote "pure" music: music which is thought to be exclusively a structural, classical expression relying on intrinsic musical qualities such as counterpoint, melody, harmony, and formal structure. But Brahms, seemingly oblivious to the debate raging around him, never asserted that his music either did or did not represent feelings. He labeled practically all his purely instrumental works numerically only, except for one or two tantalizingly evocative exceptions such as the *Tragic Overture*. He was also a great friend and admirer of Robert Schumann, one of the most ardent proponents of the representational "camp."

The overtly representational composers of the nineteenth century were often the object of bitter criticism and hostility in artistic circles, and in all European countries there were contemporary music critics who allied themselves on one side or the other. In Germany one critic described Tchaikovsky's music as "musical madness," and Berlioz's music was ridiculed by Cherubini as grotesque, vulgar, and lacking in compositional skill. Liszt's piano music was described in England as an attempt to smash perfectly good pianos and in Germany as an invitation to stamping and hissing from the audience (Sitwell, 1967). In England, it must be said, there was a prevalent view, in direct contradiction of Plato and Aristotle, that music should be removed from the list of imitative arts.

At the root of this controversy were a number of related issues. The craft of composition, developed over centuries into a highly sophisticated set of formal procedures, was held up against what some considered to be the destructive effects of more abstract notions of achieving an important goal of Western musical art—the representation of humanity's inner mental life and the exemplification of mental and spiritual perfection through music. Such effects were considered destructive because they often called for abandoning or modifying well-established formal musical procedures of composition. Some have tended to regard the act of composition as essentially musical, having nothing, or very little, to do with things outside of music: the composer invents music using musical elements and constructs a musical edifice that is independent of nonmusical matters. But epistemologically this notion rests on shaky ground. The influence of principles of construction in language, drawn essentially from the art and science of rhetoric, has been practically absolute and complete in the development of musical forms and the craft of musical composition in Western culture.

Composers could hardly ignore the problems of relationships between music and poetry, which, in turn, yielded more sophisticated examples of *musica poetica*. Some, convinced that music was an independent and complete mode of expression in itself, scorned what they saw as the dilution of music by applications from spoken language. Historically, the connection between poetry and music has been unequivocal; yet, paradoxically, in a purely musical sense the art of music in the West has developed into an independent and self-contained mode of expression in terms of musical form. In this latter sense the art of music has become at times mere form without substance in the view of some, a fate only too easily arising from such a growth of musical theory.

The art of composition is elucidated in many theoretical treatises from the sixteenth century onwards. Initially, the influence of Pythagorean harmonics and Aristotle's *Rhetoric* dominated such works. Early theoreticians were trying to establish basic principles that founded musical practices on both numbers and the ancient and well-known principles of rhetoric. Modern harmony and laws of chord progressions and modulations from one tonal center to another had their origins in Pythagorean harmonics, while formal contrapuntal structures, such as fugue, canon, and fantasia, and later tonal structures, such as those of sonata form, had their origins in Aristotle's *Rhetoric* and *Poetics*.

The ancient original frameworks were gradually abandoned, and music theory, by the nineteenth century, had lost its references to harmonics and rhetoric. It became a theory complete unto itself in its descriptions of purely musical elements and their configurations within the formal principles of musical composition; to many, music became an abstract art of sound. This had the effect of producing a great deal of bland music that owed its existence merely to principles of structure and that had lost its lifeblood, as it were, by abandoning its allegiance to rhetoric and expressiveness. In reaction, the nineteenth-century romantic composers, who sought to infuse into musical composition its original intent as propounded by Aristotle and Plato, criticized what they saw as arid, inhuman exercises in musical form, while at the same time demonstrating a new affective role for music in their works. The stage was set for an aesthetic battle between the notion of music as formal structure and music as affective communication.

This was an old controversy. In Plato's *Phaedrus* (ca. 370 B.C.), Socrates disparaged the place of ethics in rhetoric. He saw rhetoric as a mechanical technique distinct from its content (Kennedy, 1980). Aristotle viewed it somewhat differently in his *Rhetoric* (ca. 330 B.C.), and Cicero (106–43 B.C.) and Quintilian (A.D. 40–95) took up Aristotle's views on the relationship between form and substance, which were passed on to the Middle Ages and beyond. This particular issue continues to flare up today as opponents of some new development in music make accusations about either lack of content or lack of formal discipline.

Certain of the musical wars that have raged over the last four centuries have actually been about the maintenance of standards in the craft of composition and resistance to new ideas that were seen as unskilled, even if such arguments have been clothed in political terms by some. They have also been concerned with attempts to resolve the issue of whether music or poetry is the predominant artform, whether music serves poetry or vice versa. To understand more fully the nature of the debate and the causes supported by various groups or individual composers throughout the course of Western musical development, it is necessary to go back to the origins of such ideas and trace their musical evolution.

THE ORIGINS OF THE BELIEF IN MUSIC'S REPRESENTATIONAL POWERS

In ancient Greek culture the unity of the visual and performing arts was an accepted fact. In all discussions on the arts it was tacitly assumed that the term included what we know as music, painting, poetry, drama, and dance. Both Plato and Aristotle wrote about the distinct and various ways in which the different arts all "imitate action," and even though they might concentrate their attentions during discussion on one form, usually poetry, it was clear that they included all the arts. The main principle expounded in both Plato and Aristotle concerns a notion of art as representing or imitating the inner human spirit—the *ethos*, or character.

One of the earliest written explanations of the power of music to evoke, represent, or imitate behaviors, emotions, or events occurs in Plato's *Republic*. In this work, Plato (428–348 B.C.) was describing an ideal state and all its components. *Mousike* (literally, the business of the Muses, who were the goddesses of poetic inspiration) was presented more as a tool of the state in achieving a perfect society than simply as an aesthetic activity, a notion that had particular appeal in the nineteenth century following the political and social turmoil caused by the Industrial and French Revolutions. In such a context it is interesting to note that he did not argue whether or not music has such powers; he assumed it does and issued the following warning:

> We'll consult with Damon about which [rhythms] are appropriate to illiberality and insolence or madness and the rest of vice, and which rhythms must be left for their opposites. . . .
>
> But are you about to determine that grace and gracelessness accompany rhythm and lack of it? Of course . . . inharmoniousness [is] akin to bad speech and bad disposition, while their opposites are akin to, and imitations of, the opposite—moderate and good disposition. (Bloom, trans., 1968, bk. III, 400)

Thus Plato seemed convinced that rhythm has powers to influence behavior because it contains elements in the sound that are associated in a powerful manner with thoughts and behaviors. He even advocated censorship:

> Must we, then, supervise the poets and compel them to impress the image of the good disposition on their poems or not to make them among us? Or must we also supervise the other craftsmen and prevent them from impressing this bad disposition, a licentious, illiberal, and graceless one . . . so that our guardians won't be reared on images of vice?
>
> In this way they'd have by far the finest rearing. (Bloom, trans., 1968, bk. III, 401a–d)

Earlier he talked about sung melody and the ideal ways in which it should reflect the *ethos*, or character, or the words being sung, having first, of course, selected the appropriate *ethos* to imitate in melody. Socrates asks Glaucon whether

> you are, in the first place capable of saying that melody is composed of three things—speech, harmonic mode, and rhythm? . . . and what is speech in it surely does not differ from the speech that isn't sung insofar as it must be spoken according to the same models? . . . And, further, that harmonic mode and the rhythm must follow the speech? (Bloom, trans., 1968, bk. III, 398d)

The dialogue then goes on to discuss the various modes and their suitability for the *ethos* that might be suggested in poetry in a passage frequently quoted by Renaissance musical theorists, particularly in Italy during the sixteenth century. It implies that modes, or scales, have intrinsic properties that enable them to represent character, or *ethos*. Many did not read on to find that "there'll be no need of many-toned or panharmonic instruments for our songs and melodies . . . then we'll not support the craftsmen who make lutes, harps, and all the instruments that are many stringed and play many modes" (Bloom, trans., 1968, bk. III, 399c). The preference is clearly for simple modes that merely reflect accurately the "accents of a man who is courageous . . . or performs a peaceful deed" (Bloom, trans., 1968, bk. III, 399a). This is known as the theory of *ethos*, or character.

In the sixteenth century the argument turned on whether the imitation was sufficient if musicians chose the appropriate mode, or scale, for the whole composition, or whether it was necessary to choose a different phrase (or melodic fragment) or chord for each different situation being "painted" in music. The more traditionally minded preferred the former.

It must be remembered that Plato was concerned about the demise of what he considered to be the highest values of Athenian life prior to the destructive effects of the Peloponnesian war and the subsequent decline of Athens. In *The Republic* he was suggesting a kind of blue-print for an ideal state that would recapture some of the moral great-ness he felt Athens had lost. The importance he gave to music, and to the arts in general, in contributing both to the formation of good character and behavior in citizens and to the growth of an ideal politi-cal state by virtue of its educative function in developing the leaders of society, has had repercussions throughout Western civilization, partic-ularly in the field of education. For musicians of modern times the inextricable link between music and poetry was firmly established in these ancient writings.

Plato's pupil Aristotle (384–322 B.C.) echoed these sentiments in *The Politics*, where he explained that music was introduced into education because it "is useful for the rational enjoyment of leisure" (Welldon, trans., 1883, p. 227). He went on to discuss whether it is necessary actually to take part in performance in order to learn about the importance of a right use of leisure. Listeners can benefit just as much as performers. He suggested how music can produce certain conditions of character. Citing the compositions of Olympus, he stated that they "can make our souls enthusiastic, and enthusiasm is a condition of the soul . . . when we listen to imitations, we all acquire a sympathy with the feelings imitated . . . for it is in rhythms and melodies that we have the realistic imitations of anger and mildness as well as of courage, temperance and all their opposites and of moral qualities in general" (Welldon, trans., 1883, p. 228).

Like Plato, Aristotle, in *The Politics*, was concerned with the political uses of music. To this end he agreed with Plato that music should be used in the development of the young because of its powers of representing desirable behaviors and of inculcating these in the minds of listeners. In *The Poetics*, however, Aristotle was concerned with the elements of music and their aesthetic juxtapositions. Here he intimated that, although music has the kinds of powers he specified in *The Politics*, a proper study of music should include a study of the elements that make up rhythms and melodies. It is clear that Aristotle felt it appropriate to label and classify musical elements in similar manner to the classifications of oratory, which formed the beginnings of the art of rhetoric. In his cosmology he took delight in the inventiveness and variety observable in all things, including both naturally occurring phenomena and the human inventions, such as speech, poetry, and musical sounds.

In *The Poetics*, written in the fourth century B.C., Aristotle stated at the beginning:

> Epic poetry, tragedy, comedy, dithyrambics, as also, for the most part, the music of the flute and of the lyre—all these are, in the most general view of them, imitations; differing, however, from each other in three respects, according to the different means, the different objects, or the different manner of their imitation. (Twining, trans., 1789/1934, p. 5)

He did not simply mean imitation in the modern sense of using the word to describe someone mimicking, say, the bark of a dog. He meant representation by art—mimesis. To Aristotle, the nature and origin of poetry (and all the arts) comes from two instincts in human nature itself: the instinct for imitation and the instinct for harmony (melody in our modern sense) and rhythm. Imitation is concerned with the intellectual and moral content of art; harmony and rhythm refer to the "pleasures of form we usually consider purely aesthetic" (Fergusson, ed., 1961, p. 5), by which he meant the properties of the sung melodic and rhythmic modes or scales. Thus Aristotle recognized both form and content and linked the two in the sense that both reflect human instincts that are essential components in artistic activity: art should represent the highest moral values as exemplified in imitative fashion in the modes, or scales, utilized by performers.

From these precepts arises a profound difficulty. Music cannot represent nonmusical things in the ways that poetry and drama can. A word has signification value by convention, as do musical sounds, but there is a difference. Words have clearly defined meanings and relate to concrete objects or abstract ideas in such a fashion that they can be used in logical discourse and propositional language. Musical sounds, in contrast, are vague and cannot be used in either sense in the way that words can. What Aristotle was referring to was not so much an attempt to make music like words but to ascribe the same intent for music as for words. This is quite different from simply equating music with poetry, as though they had identical and equal capacity to imitate and serve as a vehicle for discourse about the human condition. Clearly, Aristotle indicated that each artform operated differently according to the character and limitations of its own medium. Yet, despite this, musicians and theorists wrote what became known as *musica poetica* and set out its constructional principles in the most systematic manner, as though music was like verbal language in its semantic properties.

From the very beginnings, music was seen as capable of representing national characteristics, emotions, and feelings. In Aristotle, this idea was extended because of his belief in the instinctive origins of imitation and the ability of melody to incorporate imitation of what he termed *praxis*, or action. By this he meant the moral and rational purposes that lie behind a particular activity, the motives for doing something as much as the activity itself. Thus the employment of "harmony" in imitation (mimesis) would require the utilization of melody that contains imitations of suitable moral and rational aims and objectives. He did not suggest in *The Poetics* a systematic set of relationships between melody and moral purposes so much as a *modus operandi* for music and the arts. But in the sixteenth and seventeenth centuries this is precisely what theorists did with music. They interpreted and applied the principles of the art of rhetoric as the source for the details in drawing up laws for the construction of musical forms.

In contrast to Pythagorean harmonics, Aristoxenus (born at Tarentum ca. 370 B.C. and a pupil of Aristotle) suggested a more empirical approach to music theory. In *Harmonics* he suggested that the principles of music theory "must be recognized by sensory perception as primary truths of harmonics" (quoted in Barbera, 1980, p. 129). Since the Pythagoreans generally did not rely on the senses to arrive at musical "truths," but instead held up proportional theory as the path to such truths, this was a distinctly different approach to musical theory and practice. Aristoxenus suggested that a musician "requires more than a knowledge of harmonics and that the sciences of rhythm, meter and instruments all play roles in describing music. All these sciences plus poetry yield music" (quoted in Barbera, 1980, p. 132). His approach was, therefore, much more all-embracing than that of harmonic theory alone.

Aristoxenus described a mental process he called *synesis*, an intuitive mental response to music. He defined the "musical intuition" displayed by those who write and perform music and those who listen as some "inherent mental capacity comprising one's implicit musical knowledge" (quoted in Levin, 1972, p. 213). He tended to dismiss all theorizing about music as meaningless, advocating instead that we rely entirely on our ears and intuitive judgments. He warned that "we shall be sure to miss the truth unless we place the supreme and ultimate, not in the thing determined, but in the activity that determines" (quoted in Levin, 1972, p. 213). Aristoxenus conceived of *synesis* as essentially an activity of the mind in responding in accordance with its musical intuition and, as such, inaccessible to "the probings of science or empiricism" (Levin, 1972, p. 213).

In fact, Aristotle suggested something similar: "All art is concerned with creation, and to practice an art is to contemplate how to create something that admits of existence or non-existence, and the efficient cause of which is in the maker but not the thing made" (quoted in Levin, 1972, p. 213). But this brings us to a central question of Western aesthetics: Does the art created contain representations of the inner being of the person who made it, of the person who is observing it, or of some universal human sentiment? The *ethos* theory holds that all are involved, that humankind intuitively aims for the good, the ideal, the perfect, both in artistic acts and sensory perception of these acts.

THE TRANSMISSION OF THEORIES ABOUT MUSIC
THROUGHOUT WESTERN CULTURE

Clericism and the God-Centered View of Musical Expression

Between the age of Plato and Aristotle and the European Renaissance it is possible to trace the path along which their ideas traveled through time. The Romans wrote extensively about the powers of music. Plutarch, in his commentary on the *Timaeus* of Plato, stated that the Chaldeans connected musical intervals with the seasons: "the perfect fourth = Autumn; the fifth = Winter; the octave = Summer; the tonic, or unison = Spring. . . . This was a cornerstone in the doctrine of ethos" (Henderson, 1969, p. 253). Plutarch also referred to the ancient Egyptian links between the four jingling bars on the sistrum, a sacred instrument, and the four elements. As these bars were shaken by the priest, they "immediately became active forces," since "all things are subject to motion" (Farmer, 1969, p. 259).

Ptolemy (second century A.D.) presented what he saw as two extremist views of music: those of the latter-day Pythagoreans as opposed to those of the followers of Aristoxenus. "Ear and reason are the judges of harmony" according to Ptolemy (quoted in Winnington-Ingram, 1980). Athenaeus (ca. A.D. 200), who lived in Rome most of his life, referred to nearly 800 writers on many matters connected with everyday life. In mentioning the Pythagorean Cleinius, Athenaeus explained that Cleinius calmed himself down when angry by playing the cithera (Strunk, 1950, p. 48). He explained further that music "appeases surliness . . . produces good temper and gladness . . . and the drunkard becomes a gentleman" (in Strunk, 1950, p. 52). He reported Theophrastus as claiming that playing a Phrygian melody on the aulos over the affected body part would cure sciatica, and described certain specific qualities contained in certain types of music. The melodies and rhythms of the Dorians, for example, exhibit qualities of manly vigor, magnificence of bearing, and sobriety, whereas those of the Aeolians contain elements of ostentation and turgidity, even conceit. The Ionians produced music that was "well adapted to tragedy because of their seriousness" (in Strunk, 1950, p. 49), and so on. This is a clear reference to the Platonic theory of *ethos*.

Many writers in medieval times referred to Plato, Aristotle, and such later writers as Athenaeus in their reiteration of these ideas. One of the most important of the Roman references for later writers was Augustine (born A.D. 354). In *The Confessions*, under the heading "the pleasures taken in hearing," he explained that he was greatly troubled by the pleasure he felt at the sound of the singer's voice when the psalms were sung during the divine office. He clearly acknowledged the power of music to affect the listener in various ways that followed the ideas of Aristotle in *The Politics*, but he introduced a specifically Christian element into the debate.

For Augustine, purity of heart was infinitely more important than links between knowledge and the "good." To this extent he was less interested in either the classification of musical elements and the objects of their representational powers or the Platonic and Aristotelean notions of music as linking knowledge and the attainment of an ideal state of "goodness." He was, however, interested in the power of music to exert influence on the minds of intellectually "weaker brethren" who might not be able to attain the highest levels of spirituality through the power of intellect alone. In this context he was prepared to approve the use of music as a means of helping such people attain spiritual goals.

Generally, though, Augustine was deeply concerned about the sensuous appeal of music. In *The Confessions* (Chapter 32, Book 10) he explained his own personal problem in this regard:

> The delights of the ear drew and held me much more powerfully, but thou didst unbind me and liberate me. In those melodies which thy words inspire when sung with a sweet and trained voice, I still find repose; yet not so as to cling to them, but always so as to be able to free myself as I wish (Outler, ed., 1955, p. 230).

Augustine went into some detail about his personal battle with the sensuous qualities of music and the ways in which melodies can enhance the meaning of the words. He seemed less concerned with arguments about the nature of music's power to evoke the meanings of the words than with its undoubted power to seduce the listener by virtue of its sensuous qualities. In particular, he was concerned about the fact that he sometimes "seems to attribute more respect unto those airs than is fitting" (Outler, ed., 1955, p. 230), and he admitted that "our minds are far more devoutly and earnestly inflamed in piety by the holy words when they are sung than when they are not" (Outler, ed., 1955, p. 230). Yet he clearly regarded the auditory pleasure provided by musical sound as a sin.

One of the most significant influences on Western thought during the whole medieval period, Augustine was a powerful influence in the intellectual movement known as medieval clericism—a force which provided political stability as well as a certain artistic sterility during the thousand years of medieval European life. It was under the influ-

ence of Augustine's powerful intellect that the growth of compositional craftsmanship, exemplified in the rise of polyphony, was kept
within the confines of a God-centered universe. Musical composition
was likened to imitations of God's creation, after Aristotle, and linger-
ing notions of Pythagorean cosmic proportionism were transmuted
into a specifically Christian, God-centered cosmology.

One of the most influential figures of the late Roman period was
Boethius, who was mentioned in Chapter 3 in connection with his
role in disseminating proportional theory throughout medieval times.
His work was similarly important for aesthetic theory. His writings on
music, notably *De institutione musica*, became the basis of medieval
musical aesthetics. He attempted a consensus of classical philosophy,
regarding music as a branch of mathematics but unlike the others in
that it was perceptible aurally. He postulated three types of music:
musica mundana, or cosmic music, the order and harmony of the
universe as derived from ancient Pythagoreanism; *musica humana*,
or human music reflecting the harmony of the universe in the healthy
body and soul; and *musica instrumentalis*, the audible music humans
make.

During this time, however, the influence of Aristotle was never
completely extinguished. Despite papal bans, centers such as Paris,
where a university was founded in the twelfth century, defied the
pope's authority and instituted courses in Aristotle's philosophical
writings. But it was the rise of humanism during the fourteenth to
sixteenth centuries that provided the main driving force for a shift
away from the spiritual role of music advocated by Augustine toward
the idea of linking music and poetry in what was believed to be the
authentic ancient Greek manner. During the sixteenth century in particular, the influence of Plato and the *ethos* theory can be seen in the
music of all European countries, but particularly that of Italy. And
musical art became concerned with the mental life of man rather than
with expression of the ineffable and infinite majesty of a Christian
God and universe.

Music and Rhetoric

It was at the beginning of the sixteenth century that the Venetian
printer Aldus Manutius (1450–1515) began to print copies of many
Greek and Latin classical writings, including Plato's *Republic* and Aristotle's *Poetics*. Before then, Plato's dialogues had been translated by
Ficini in 1477, and Aristotle's *Rhetoric* had appeared in a Latin translation by George of Trebozond in 1478 (Kennedy, 1980). Soon after, the

Italian madrigal developed into a powerful model for attempting fusion between the arts of music and poetry. Composers were increasingly concerned with Platonic notions of making the music represent the meaning of the words set. Their work showed some highly expressive uses of harmony, melody, and rhythm as they strove to find appropriate musical elements with which to match the expressiveness of poetry.

In sixteenth-century Italy the work of the greatest poets was allied with the music of the greatest musicians in order to achieve this union of the two arts. The works of Petrarch and Boccaccio were popular choices for setting to music. One passage from Dante's *Inferno* describing the shrieks of the damned was set to music by at least seven composers because it obviously evoked musical word painting (Lang, 1978). Marenzio's favorite poet was Sannazaro, and Tasso attracted many musicians of the time eager to use the new style of word painting in their compositions. The movement, which eventually became characterized as a new style of musical composition, was compared unfavorably by some to the old style, with its scholasticism and deliberate focus on compositional technique. Even so, this "old style" was not utterly devoid of expressiveness or word painting.

There is little doubt that musical practices had never entirely lost their origins in their reliance on words as the source of expressiveness, however cloaked by prevailing constraints of authority. The difference between the old and new styles was essentially one of shifting emphasis in the early stages, but the culmination of all this was the birth of modern opera and an entirely new expressive style of music. This occurred partly because of a desire to find the perfect artistic vehicle for recreating the *mousike* of ancient Greece and partly because of the increasingly restrictive stance toward musical expression taken by the Catholic Church in its fight against the Reformation. The older polyphonic craftsmanship was preferred by the Church not for musical reasons but because it was more readily associated, in view of its historical origins and associations, with the notion of a God-centered universe. In contrast, the humanistic applications to music of rediscovered Aristotelean principles of rhetoric, oratorical skills, and the general idea of mimesis in the arts were considered to be part of the problem the Reformation posed to the Catholic Church. In view of this, the Counter-Reformation was launched as much against the new music as against the rhetoric of Martin Luther.

The development of modern opera, beginning initially in the work of a group in Florence in the late sixteenth century known as the *Camerata*, became a vehicle for the secular flowering of the notion that music imitates or paints in sound the meanings found in words. But it was Monteverdi who provided the first examples of modern opera generally regarded as worthy of performance as operas. The first is generally accepted to be Monteverdi's *La favola d'Orfeo*, commissioned by the two sons of the Duke of Mantua and set to a libretto by the duke's secretary of state, Alessandro Stiggio. This was first performed in 1607 in Mantua. It contains some of the most dramatic musical representations of events and emotions found in music up to that time. It also signified a radical departure from some of the more destructive ideas of the *Camerata*, whose members wanted to abandon all established musical tradition in favor of a re-creation of the simple monody of ancient Greek music as characterized by Plato in *The Republic*.

None of the group, it must be stated, had any idea of what Greek music actually sounded like. In contrast, Monteverdi gave the new style a remarkable quality through fusion with the great compositional craftsmanship of the past, thus bringing opera into the mainstream of musical thought. He also led the way in establishing the artistic viability of applying rhetorical principles of construction to music despite the resultant abandonment of many established rules of composition.

It has already been mentioned that at the crux of the new style lay a conscious and well-informed intention to apply systematically the laws of rhetoric to music. There were a number of reasons that this occurred. The dissemination of the ideas of Plato and Aristotle, first in secondary sources such as Quintilian, then via translations, contributed to the formation of a more humanistic view of the world. Inevitably, music was affected. Secular education became established, and the *trivium* was expanded to include music. This brought music into the same educational arena as dialectic, grammar, and rhetoric.

The influence of rhetoric on the arts in general was considerable and in music became of great consequence. This is witnessed in the appearance of numerous theoretical works in Germany, France, and England as well as Italy, although the major contribution as time went on came from Germany. It must also be remembered that the predominant compositional style at this time was polyphonic, based on points of imitation derived from plainsong or even secular songs. The development of fugue was one of the great artistic achievements of the period. In essence theorists adapted to fugal composition the classical principles of rhetoric: invention, disposition, elocution, memorization, and pronunciation. Of these, elocution, the decoration and embellishment of ideas from the invention, was most important in the Renaissance applications to music.

By the late seventeenth century such approaches to musical composition were, in any case, routine among musicians, particularly in Germany. In England, there appeared a number of treatises. In 1636 Charles Butler produced *The Principles of Music*, in which he set out in general the notion of music being linked with poetry in its function. On the opening page he stated: "Music is [the] Art of modulating notes in voice or instrument. [These] having a great power over [the] affections of [the] mind, by its various Moods produces in [the] hearers various effect" (Butler, 1636/1970, p. 1). He went on to list and describe some of these effects and how to obtain them using various elements of music.

There is, however, no evidence of any systematic and uniform method or format being universally adopted all over Europe; it was merely that the general notion of applying the principles of rhetoric to music was widespread and well established at this time. Such was the product of nearly two centuries of theoretical exegesis and practical application.

One of the first German theorists of what became known as *musica poetica* was Gallus Dressler (1533–ca. 1585), a church composer in Magdeburg and a teacher at the Magdeburg gymnasium. In his treatise on *musica poetica* (*Praecepta musicae poeticae*, 1564) he remarked that "in musica poetica nothing is more worthy for insertion [in a composition] than *fugae*. Indeed, they embellish music and they result in music constructed according to nature and art" (quoted in Butler, 1977, p. 50). The reference to fugue is particularly important, since the development of fugue as a form is almost entirely due to the application of the laws of rhetoric to music. By *fugae*, Dressler meant the translation to music of rhetorical devices in the construction of polyphonic compositions. Even earlier, Joannes Stomius (1502–1564), in his 1537 *Prima ad musicen instructio*, wrote about "things ingenious, which are called *Mimesis* or *fugae*, where a single voice is sung in consequence but with certain intervals of time intervening" (Augsberg, 1537). This, as Butler (1977) points out, equates "fuga, meaning in this case canon, with a specific rhetorical figure, mimesis" (p. 51). Stomius went on to apply other terms from rhetorical rules to the construction of a fugal piece.

A more extensive work applying such rules to music was a treatise entitled *De musica* (ca. 1559) by Anonymous of Besançon (Butler, 1977). According to Butler, this treatise is unique among the early ones applying rhetorical principles to music because of the large number of figures cited in order to delineate clearly the rhetorical concept underlying the art of fugue.

Following these came the work of Joachim Burmeister (ca. 1566–1629), a most important figure in this field. He made extensive use of the terminology of rhetoric in his descriptions of the construction of fugue. He suggested that the exposition of a fugue should use the standard rhetorical procedure of *confirmatio*; each entry would be part of a logical series, the logic being musically arid yet employing interval and key relationships. Burmeister included descriptions of various psychological effects to be expected of the musical elements in fugal exposition, in the manner of elocution in rhetoric. As each successive entry comes in, "this diverts the listener's attention suddenly from the previous simultaneously concluding entry" (quoted in Butler, 1977, p. 57). He defined a variety of fugal techniques in rhetorical terms: for example, double fugue—*metalepsis*; counterfugue—*hypallage*. This had ramifications for the later concept of fugue in the seventeenth and eighteenth centuries (Butler, 1977), resulting in the equating of fugal structure with syllogistic reasoning.

A number of later theorists took up this notion, explaining in great detail how fugues are examples of musical logic based on the principles of logical reasoning. For example, in 1802 Johann Nikolaus Forkel attributed precisely this approach to musical composition to the works of J. S. Bach in his biography of the most famous cantor of St. Thomas Church in Leipzig. Another leading German theorist was Johann Mattheson (1681–1764). He set out the main principles of fugal writing based upon rhetoric, particularly its development from a focus on elocution in the Renaissance to the more formal, logical structures of the baroque period.

Mattheson, a composer, was a friend and contemporary of Handel in their youthful days and a most influential musician throughout Germany and other parts of Europe. In *Der volkommene Capellmeister*, in 1739, he set out a comprehensive format involving presenting arguments in the manner of verbal display, but in musical fashion, using musical elements instead of words. It must be remembered that young musicians of this time learned their craft from treatises such as Mattheson's; they grew up, therefore, accepting without question the application of laws of rhetoric to music—in effect, the equating of musical and verbal expression with little qualification. It was in this way that the belief system surrounding musical expression and its inexorable link with words (poetry) was nurtured and fostered in successive generations. Young people were educated in both rhetoric and music as part of their formal education. The connection between the two became, therefore, obvious and simple to understand. To see this more fully it is necessary to examine some rhetorical principles in applications to musical composition. Some examples from Mattheson's treatise are sufficient to indicate the nature of this educational edifice through which young musicians had to pass.

In part 2 of Mattheson's treatise, concerning the disposition, elaboration, and decoration of melodies, he stated that "invention itself is not enough though it may solve half the problem, for there must be invention to begin with" (quoted in Lennenberg, 1958, p. 193). The format included *inventio*—the invention of a musical idea or theme; *dispositio*—the arrangement of the idea or theme in a composition; *decoratio*—development or decoration of the theme; and *pronunciato*—the performance or delivery of the work. He likened musical composition to a building plan used in constructing a house, except that the building plan for music is taken from rhetoric: "musical disposition differs from rhetoric only in its medium" (quoted in Lennenberg, 1958, p. 194), a reference to Aristotle's *Poetics*. He advocated a careful examination of good speeches in order to understand how rhetoric enables one to construct the best types of communication. Musical disposition, he maintained, must observe the same six parts as does the speaker: "introduction, narration, proposition, confirmation, argument, and close [i.e.] *exordium, narratio, propositio, confirmatio, confutatio,* at *peroratio*" (quoted in Lennenberg, 1958, p. 194).

His explanations of the function of each of these parts are worth looking at as further indications of the processes for applying rhetoric to music that seventeenth- and eighteenth-century musicians learned in their training. He explained that:

> *Exordium* is the introduction and beginning of a melody in which its purpose and intention are shown in order to prepare the listener and to arouse his attention. In a movement without instruments, for voice and bass only, the introduction is very often contained in the prelude of the thorough bass. . . . [Otherwise] it can be found in the *ritornello*. . . .
>
> *Narratio* is, as it were, a report, a tale in which the meaning and nature of delivery is suggested. It is found at the entrance of the vocal part or the outstanding *concertato*-part and is related to the preceding *exordium* by means of a clever connection.
>
> *The Propositio,* the proposition itself, briefly contains the meaning and purpose of musical speech. It is of two kinds, simple and compound. . . . [They] have their place immediately following the first paragraph of the melody. . . . The subject [is presented] briefly and simply. Thereupon

the vocal part begins its *propositio variata*, unites with the bass, and thus creates a compound proposition. . . .
Confutatio is the resolution of objections. In music it may be expressed by means of ties or by the citation and refutation of . . . foreign passages. Such contrasts, carefully used, are a special source of aural pleasure. Everything that goes against the proposition is resolved and settled. . . .
Peroratio, finally, is the end or conclusion of our musical oration and must, above all else, be especially moving. The conclusion . . . is . . . most often found in the postlude. . . . It is customary that the aria concludes with the same material with which it began. This, consequently, serves as *peroratio* as well as *exordium*. (quoted in Lennenberg, 1958, pp. 194–195)

He went on to examine an aria by Benedetto Marcello (1686–1739), a famous Italian composer and singer who wrote instrumental concertos, oratorios, operas, cantatas, and numerous other genres of the day. The aria is typically imitative in the early-eighteenth-century musical sense, and Mattheson examined every theme entry, modulation, rhythmic variation, *tessitura*—in fact, every musical aspect of the composition—citing them as illustration of the rules referred to above. The detail is exhaustive, and the didactic tone of the treatise compelling and intimidating. Clearly, in writings such as this, which were common at the time, the links between musical constructions and verbal orations were systematic and unambiguous—systematic in the sense that each writer found his own parallels and illustrated them, not in the sense that a uniform principle linking musical and verbal constructions was apparent all over a particular country or the continent of Europe. The effect on musical composition was to provide some basis and structure for the construction of music. It induced a sense that musical composition was a rational and logical activity and that musical works were to be judged according to principles of construction. Essentially, the establishment of coherent musical forms was the product, even if the effect, in the opinion of some, was to make it as easy to write a fugue as to write a letter—a triumph of style over substance and a move away from ethical considerations.

ARTISTIC CONTROVERSY SURROUNDING
THE *ETHOS* THEORY AND MUSIC

At the beginning of the seventeenth century the furor surrounding Monteverdi's so-called Second Practice took the form of a series of written treatises and letters. The debate was ostensibly musical, but underlying it was a philosophical issue: Monteverdi showed in his music the influence of Plato's *ethos* theory, with its essentially human-centered motivations; arrayed against him were those who were fighting to preserve the older, God-centered craftsmanship exemplified in polyphonic compositional skills. Giovanni Maria Artusi attacked Monteverdi's apparent abandonment of the old, well-established principles of composition in a treatise published in 1600 (*L'Artusi, ovvera Delle imperfettione della musica moderna*), where he ridiculed the new style as exemplified in some of Monteverdi's madrigals. He had obtained manuscript copies, and, removing the words and the identity of the composer, he proceeded to analyze the content in the light of practices of composition established in Italy by the great Flemish masters of the fifteenth and early sixteenth centuries, in particular Artusi's teacher, Willaert. These practices, which demanded rigid standards of skill in the craft of composition, were founded on the contrapuntal writings of Jan van Ockeghem (1430–1495) and Josquin Desprez (1450–1521) and carried on by the French and the Italians who developed them through to the times of Zarlino and Palestrina. All this was founded on much older principles of construction taken from the art of rhetoric.

Monteverdi eventually answered Artusi in the form of the now famous letter that appeared as a preface to his *Fifth Book of Madrigals*, published in 1605. The letter is not as explicit, however, as the *Declaration* issued by Claudio Monteverdi's brother, Giulio Cesare, in 1607. The essence of the latter's case concerns the preeminence of the word over music supposedly advocated in Plato's exegesis of the *ethos* theory in *The Republic*. G. C. Monteverdi maintained that Plato said: "The song is composed of three things: the words, harmony, and the rhythm . . . and so of the apt and the unapt, if the rhythm follow the words, and not the words these . . . do not the manner of the diction and the words follow and conform to the disposition of the soul?" (in Strunk, 1950, p. 407). He was quoting from Ficini's Latin translation of Plato, which did not provide the accuracy and clarity of later translations. As we have seen above, the context of this passage is within a much larger dialogue about the nature of the *ethos* theory.

Artusi and Zarlino assumed that Plato was saying the mode, or scale, not a particular melodic fragment based on a scale, must be chosen for its imitative qualities. They upheld the importance of the whole mode and its imitative powers and, consequently, were attacked by Galilei for advocating what he called the "tyranny of the mode." Monteverdi, a highly trained and expert musician in the traditional sense, intuitively realized that the kind of expression he desired could not be achieved by confining his compositions to one mode throughout, as Artusi implied should be done. Also, by virtue of his training, Monteverdi was certainly influenced by the art of rhetoric in his musical composition. Many later theorists—after the fact, it must be admitted—noted this in their frequent quotations from Monteverdi's music in exemplification of their particular explanation of the applications of rhetoric to music.

With a conglomeration of ideas taken from Plato, from the practices of rhetoric, and from the older traditions of word painting derived from Aristotle, Monteverdi forged a new expressive style in music. It mattered little to musicians that Plato was advocating the use of only those modes that contained a *suitable ethos*. Plato suggested that, ideally, other modes reflecting an unsuitable *ethos* should not be used for music because of their corrupting effects on the listener. Monteverdi did not act upon this. He interpreted the theory to mean that music should imitate the *ethos*, irrespective of its ethical or moral desirability. The new expressiveness in music, as far as Monteverdi was concerned, had no didactic or political intentions; he was concerned solely with artistic goals.

In one sense the controversy was a matter of an older generation, represented by Artusi, accusing a younger, led by Monteverdi, not just of abandoning the old standards but of being ignorant of them and uneducated in their tenets. This is a familiar situation in any age, but here the main argument concerned interpretation of Plato's comments in *The Republic* about the ideal relationships between music and words. Monteverdi was captivated by the spirit of his age in its attempts to re-create the artistic glories of ancient Greece. The idea of re-creating Greek drama was especially attractive and exciting, and inevitably the focus of argument became disagreement as to what Plato actually said and what he meant about the relationship between music and words.

Monteverdi was by no means the first composer to be attracted by the wealth of artistic ideas found in Plato and Aristotle, nor the first to use them to his own artistic ends. Earlier in the sixteenth century, the Italian madrigal composers were practicing what became known as the *stile espressivo*: an attempt to make music match the moods suggested by the words. Composers such as Cipriano de Rore, Luca Marenzio, and, later, Don Carlo Gesualdo were developing a dynamic pictorial style of composing. The music was intended to provide a metaphor in sound of the meanings expressed in the words.

Images, moods, and affect were translated into musical terms in this lyric approach to composition. Richly chromatic chords were used expressively, as were contrasting tempi, harmonic texture, and melodic phrases. These applications constituted the first stages in, as it were, a literal art of word painting in music, which, in turn, provided material for musical embellishment. There followed the application of rhetorical principles of logical discourse to create musical form, which provided a *modus operandi* for composers to create large-scale works. Thus a style of musical composition evolved that was influenced by constructional applications taken from rhetoric together with various interpretations of the theory of *ethos* and the notion of mimesis.

There were, naturally, problems in such a bold synthesis and extrapolation. Some were philosophically based, others were musical; but all sprang from the difficulties inherent in attempts to apply general philosophical theories to the particulars of a creative activity such as music. Principally, the problems centered around aspects of interpretation and application. The artistic activities that Plato and Aristotle knew, and therefore the ones they wrote about, were, to a much larger extent than modern artistic activity enjoys, regarded and practiced as an integrated and unified expression. It was therefore quite reasonable to discuss the *ethos* theory using the plastic arts, poetry, or music because of their belief that the performing and visual arts were all capable of representing the same things and were naturally and intrinsically complementary to each other, even though it was acknowledged that they each used different media.

However, in the following two millennia each artform has become highly specialized, making it difficult to extrapolate from one to the other. Music, for example, uses sounds now that, to the ancient Greeks, would have been inconceivable as well as incomprehensible. Moreover, taken literally, Plato's specification of suitable sounds for inculcating desirable behaviors would preclude most of what we today call, as well as what the world of Monteverdi called, music. It is, therefore, not in the least bit surprising that whatever a composer did would be open to the severest criticism from some contemporaries.

What must be said is that the details provided by Plato and Aristotle in assigning to certain melodies or rhythms a particular character or *ethos* were insufficient for Renaissance composers to use in making similar claims in respect of the music they knew. The acoustical nature of an ancient Greek rhythm or melody was not known, and the composers who applied the theories of Greece to music had no empirical evidence upon which to base their choices of music to fit any mood, feeling, or passion. Some used the traditions of Pythagorean harmonics as a guide; others used intuition. In short, all they had to go on was the theory and the descriptions of applications to a musical tradition that had disappeared almost without trace.

Successive schools of philosophers in more modern times have provided various interpretations of ancient Greek aesthetics and musical practice. These often contradicted one another, thereby tending to provide theoretical support for one musical practice against another and becoming ammunition, as it were, in one or another artistic war. Nevertheless, composers took what they could from the available theory and made musical use of it, and from this philosophical and artistic license grew the complex belief system surrounding the varying practices of expressionism found in modern Western music. What follows is an outline illustrating the nature of the problems inherent in applying modern interpretations of ancient aesthetic theory to music in modern times and the positions taken by some of the main players—both musical and philosophical.

MUSICAL MIMESIS AND AESTHETIC THEORY IN THE ENLIGHTENMENT

It is possible to characterize the progression of ideas concerning music and poetry as moving from the notion of word painting, to an application of formal principles of rhetoric, to the establishment of systematic rules and principles governing musical expression. Such principles were based upon a belief in the existence of an affective character for each of the various musical elements—melody, harmony, and rhythm. By the seventeenth century the debate had turned toward a systematic examination of musical elements in light of beliefs in both the imitative powers of music and the role of mathematics in forming ideal musical scales. This was in response to the new scientific and philosophical tone of the times. In 1649 Descartes produced a powerful and influential argument in favor of establishing scientific principles of musical expression in *Les passions de l'âme*. This argument emanated from a "belief that he had discovered a rational, scientific explanation for the physiological nature of the passions and the objective nature of emotion" (Buelow, 1980, p. 801). As Buelow further points out, this was a common concern regarding all the forms of art at this time.

The development of musical structure as a systematic form of logical argument, expressed through the musical elements of melody and harmony in a compositional procedure known generically as counterpoint, was entirely due to the sophisticated stage that had been reached in the applications of rhetoric to music. Most significant composers of the eighteenth century were greatly influenced by the art of rhetoric applied to music and succumbed to some interpretation of the notion of musical mimesis to some degree or other. By this time however, such applications of rhetoric had resulted in the establishment of clear constructional principles that were purely musical, enabling composers to construct, say, a fugue, a canzona, a ricecare, and, eventually, a full classical sonata form with the same procedural confidence as one used in making logical arguments in language. But even the most classical of composers, Mozart and Haydn, though they became famous for their mastery of purely constructional principles taken from rhetoric, displayed tendencies toward utilizing musical representation in their operas and symphonies.

There is, for example, a clear difference between the music Mozart wrote for comic and tragic scenes in his operas. And one of the most intellectual and constructional of composers, J. S. Bach, used musical representations of nature or of events as described in the words of the text, particularly in works such as the "St. Matthew" Passion and his cantatas, although the influence of rhetoric in his keyboard works is unmistakable. Yet it was quite possible by the eighteenth century to compose a piece of music that was constructionally elegant yet lacking in any *ethos* or representational qualities relating either to Christianity or to aesthetic considerations; the secularization of society was well under way, and there was less pressure on composers to write for the glory of God. It was principally this facility for constructing pure musical form that led to many of the musical controversies in modern times, in which the issues concerned form versus substance.

The elevation of form for its own sake was certainly under severe attack at this time; various sides in the debate had no compunction about linking musical matters with political and aesthetic issues, and sometimes little attempt was made to provide convincing musical specifics. Much of the argument rested on certain assumptions about musical meaning and the relationship between musical elements and expression, assumptions that can be traced back to Platonic or Aristotelean origins. Nowhere was this issue more prevalent than in prerevolutionary France.

The eighteenth century saw a famous operatic war, the "quarrel of the buffoons," waged in France between the respective supporters of Rameau and Pergolesi. The ideas of Diderot and Rousseau (e.g., the latter's "Lettre sur la musique française" of 1753) concerning a return to humanity's true nature found expression in musical practices that called for the use of the most simple and unadorned musical elements. Their ideas, which became known as the doctrine of the affections, were based on a theory about the origin and nature of language: human speech must first have been a chant that expressed thought and feeling simultaneously (Sparshot, 1980).

In his *Essay on the Origin of Languages*, Rousseau (1749/1966) stated that "with the first voices came the first articulations or sounds formed according to the respective passions that dictated them" (p. 51). He went on to argue that "since feelings speak before reason . . . poetry was devised before prose" (p. 51). "At first," he claimed, "there was no music but melody and no other melody than the varied sounds of speech" (p. 51). The two diverged as language concerned itself with thought, leaving music to express feeling. Rousseau held the view that rationalism is artificially imposed, that in their natural state humans are "naively passionate" (p. 51); hence music is nearer to humanity's nature than language. By the same token, the artificial structuring of music into forms is precisely that—artificial. As such it falls below the level of art conceived by Rousseau.

Generally, the followers of Rousseau, while not entirely agreeing with all his views, held that music gives imagination more freedom because of its direct contact with the essentially passionate nature of humanity. Kant, for example, in developing Rousseau's ideas further, suggested that music is the least rational of all the arts. All this signaled an attack on the Germanic view of music as pure construction fashioned on the so-called artifice of rhetoric.

Rousseau himself, in 1752, wrote one of the most popular operas of mid-eighteenth century France: *Le Devin du village*. This work, although obviously the product of a musical amateur, succeeded in spite of its technical shortcomings—some might say because of them, in view of the fact that Rousseau was trying to show how the Italian *opera buffa* style got to the heart of the passions, without the trappings of the ponderously learned rhetorical style of Rameau, which, he maintained, merely obscured the meaning and emphasized artificiality. But there was no reason for Rousseau to assume that Rameau held different views concerning music's expressive powers on one level: that of music's ability to affect the listener. Indeed, Rameau was also of the opinion that music got to the heart of the passions, irrespective of the socioeconomic status of the listener. And as a friend and admirer of Descartes, Rameau would hardly have disagreed with the notion that the simple, natural passions could best be represented by simple, unadorned musical elements. (See Chapter 3 for a discussion of the controversy between Rameau and Rousseau from the perspective of Pythagorean harmonics.)

Rameau wrote for and upheld the traditions of French opera for musical, not political, reasons. He was attacked as much for the association between l'Opéra de Paris and the French monarchy as for anything else. For example, the mandatory inclusion of a ballet in opera was a tradition of the French court and imitated in most other European courts. Its stylized movements and music were criticized for their artificiality by Rousseau and his followers, but in this many musicians privately agreed: they were obliged to include the ballet because of the tastes of those who held the purse strings.

Rousseau, however, was describing such things as artificial after the manner of Plato in *The Republic*—they were considered ethically undesirable in that they imitated undesirable behavior and morals. Rameau, on the other hand, was reflecting more recent musical traditions in holding that music's ability to imitate all behavior was available for opera without qualification or restriction. The distinction between the philosopher's concern with the moral and ethical value of what music imitated as opposed to the musician's use of music to imitate all behavior, irrespective of its value, lay at the root of the growing divergence at this time between aesthetic theory in philosophical traditions and musical theory and practice. It led to the citing of inappropriate music by philosophers in exemplification of their claims—inappropriate musically, that is.

Rousseau wrote his opera after hearing Pergolesi's *La serva padrona* in 1752 when the Italian *opera buffa* first came to Paris. So convinced was Rousseau that Pergolesi's music for *La serva padrona* imitated the *ethos* he espoused that he suggested the composer should be the model for all to follow. Pergolesi was, of course, long dead, having died at the age of 26 in 1736. Rousseau obviously knew little of Pergolesi's output as a whole, in particular his extremely expressive works of a more serious vein—his *opera seria* and his sacred music. He might well have made the same case for some of Pergolesi's more serious music, in view of Pergolesi's unique and direct manner of expressing emotion; but, logically, this would have destroyed Rousseau's case, since he would then have had to admit that some of Rameau's compositions might also be in keeping with his notions. But to recognize this requires a more extensive musical knowledge than Rousseau appears to have possessed. This is an argument of a kind quite different from that concerning Rameau's and Rousseau's views on music and science, as outlined in Chapter 3.

Rousseau's case rested on the notion that the natural passions are the most desirable in Platonic terms, together with the contention that opera should be based on the lives of rustic, simple folk who, because they are untainted by the artificialities of civilization, display such passions. Pergolesi, who was educated at the Naples Conservatory, did not hold such views, as far as is known, and there is no evidence to suggest that he ever read anything remotely like them. He would certainly have held the Italian view, also emanating from Plato, that the music should match the "passion," but, in typical Italian style, with the proviso that it mattered little what the passion was, simple or complex, natural or artificial, moral or immoral.

The Naples Conservatory was strictly for training musicians, not educating them in classical philosophy. Pergolesi entered it at the late age of 16 and graduated at 20. This left him less than six years of work as a composer before he died of a fever. He did, however, deliberately write music that was expressive in the traditional Italian manner, a style whose origins dated back centuries and which was avidly imitated across Europe. Henry Purcell (1659–1695) learned about the Italian and French styles from English musicians who had spent time in those countries. He was clearly influenced by the expressive Italian use of chromaticism and affective melodic and harmony.

Jean-Baptiste Lully (1632–1687), an Italian, brought the Italian expressiveness to France during the seventeenth century, when he became the most celebrated musician in all France, even holding the royal patent on compositional style. Rameau was certainly aware of all this, as his early keyboard works illustrate. Rousseau, on the other hand, was Swiss, as his opponents unfailingly reminded him, and, therefore, he could not be expected to know about the historical traditions of French music. It is certainly interesting to speculate how Rousseau would have justified his choice of Pergolesi as a model had he been more versed in musical style and history!

Rousseau's endorsement of certain aspects of the Italian style cannot, therefore, be seen as a criticism of Rameau in a musical sense. In fact, almost any composer he could have chosen would have been equally inappropriate, so ubiquitous was the influence of Italian expressiveness in the music of these times. Musicians across Europe generally felt that if simple people's passions can best be reflected by simple musical elements, then complex people's passions require complex musical elements. This proposition is quite compatible with certain aspects of Rameau's musical style and theory, entirely appropriate to the Italian use of mimesis in music, and not incompatible with Rousseau's view, except for the point that certain passions, being ethically unacceptable, should not be imitated. Rousseau was, in essence, making a political point but attempting to use music as a metaphor. This did not endear him to musicians. As a result of his musically unsubstantiated attack on the musical integrity of the French opera, he was hanged in effigy by the artists of l'Opéra in 1753. Rousseau's criticism of Rameau and the traditional French style of opera angered the musicians and artists of l'Opéra as much for its artistic arbitrariness as for the fact that its author was Swiss.

Following the Rameau-Pergolesi operatic war, Gluck appeared on the French scene in 1773. His opera *Iphigénie en Aulide* was performed in 1774 in Paris. He strove to establish that music in opera was a perfect vehicle for expressing the meaning of the text. Aware of the operatic war of the 1750s and the views of the Encyclopedists, he advocated operatic reform in both musical form and performance. He criticized the use of melodies designed merely to show off the star singer at the expense of the story line or dramatic action—probably something of a concession to the doctrine of the affections and an acknowledgment of the inherent dangers of applying rhetoric to music without concerns for substance. Yet he was quite happy to state that he "sought to reduce music to its true function, that of seconding the poetry" (Lang, 1978, p. 557). He found the substance he sought in the text and believed that music's function was to enhance the meaning of the text. Naturally, such a position earned criticism from those whose concern was with intrinsically musical style, content, and form rather than musical mimesis.

The interesting point here is that the art of composition had developed to the point where musical form could be elevated to a position of autonomy and independence from language, if need be. The result of this situation was a clear dichotomy in attitudes within the world of music: those who saw music as imitative of the word in its expressive intent, and those who saw music as pure, autonomous musical construction whose only expressive intent was that of melody, harmony, rhythm, or counterpoint. Posterity has, however, tended to favor composers who successfully married the two in their music.

In the now famous dedicatory preface to his 1769 opera *Alceste*, addressed to the Duke of Tuscany, Gluck stated that he wanted to "restrict music to its true office of serving poetry by means of expression and by following the situations of the story without interrupting the action or stifling it with a useless superfluity of ornaments" (quoted in Blom, 1954, p. 679). He explained that the overture to the opera should "apprise the spectators of the nature of the action that is to be represented" (p. 679). Overall, he maintained that "there is no rule [of musical composition] which I have not thought it right to set aside willingly for the sake of the intended effect" (p. 679).

Alceste was an enormous success in Vienna, and Gluck, who saw his opera as a "tragedy recited in music" (p. 679), was simply anxious to repeat his success in Paris. Vienna was Gluck's home and where he had earned his reputation. His appearance in Paris was for him a means of enhancing his career, but for the intellectuals of Paris it became an opportunity to indulge in a favorite pastime: operatic warfare. Thus Gluck became embroiled in the aesthetic and political strife of Paris, finding himself as much a rallying cry for the eighteenth-century operatic and political "right wing" there as had been Rameau some years earlier.

It must be pointed out that Gluck's involvement was entirely fortuitous. It had nothing to do with his views on music and poetry or his understanding of the doctrine of the affections and its application to music. It is not convincing, musically, to claim that the issues surrounding the controversy in which Gluck was involved had to do with compositional applications of theories about rationality and music; with musical structuralism for its own sake being dismissed as artificial; or with the fact that the philosophers of the Enlightenment were all for establishing, as far as music was concerned, the true locations of rationality and human feelings, respectively.

Such issues might well have been on the minds of some protagonists, but their applications to the music of Gluck or Piccinni, the Italian opera composer chosen as his opponent, were very superficial. Neither composer had any real involvement with this peculiarly French activity, any more than had the deceased Pergolesi two decades earlier. The controversy was more a matter of finding a composer who came nearest to the ideals of each side and using him as ammunition. At issue, yet again, was whether the arguments had anything to do with music! In the traditions of philosophy, the works of such as Descartes, Rousseau, and Kant are, of course, of immense significance. Yet to apply their ideas to actual events in the course of musical history is not strictly legitimate, as has already been pointed out. It is extraordinarily difficult to equate such philosophical discourse with any particular music found in France at the time in any but an arbitrary manner. In fact, one of the central problems of musical aesthetics, generally, concerns the identity of any actual music that exemplifies a position taken in aesthetic discourse—a subject discussed below in respect to the English and German traditions in aesthetics and music.

What is important, musically, are the origins and educational backgrounds of composers, for two reasons: (1) composers are, to a great extent, at the mercy of their musical training in their acts of composition; and (2) if they do not understand, or have never encountered, a particular aesthetic theory about music and its expressive powers, it is difficult to imagine how or why they would write music illustrating such a theory. We do know that Gluck was well educated in Bohemia and then stayed in Vienna until his mid-20s, when he went to Italy. On the way he undoubtedly picked up ideas about music and the arts generally, but only as a layman, philosophically. His early musical training was clearly in the Germanic traditions, where rhetorical principles were applied to musical composition. However, his time in Italy was equally important in the formation of his musical style and general approach; for this reason alone, the attacks on him by the opponents of l'Opéra are further demonstration of the lack of musical consistency in their arguments. His music contains the very elements that Rousseau championed in Pergolesi—simpleness of melodic and harmonic style, lack of artificially complex contrapuntal textures, and an expressiveness which has immediate appeal.

The importance for Gluck of the imitative and therefore communicative powers of music, but in respect to the whole gamut of human emotion, can be illustrated by his use of music to portray the real feelings of his characters in their actions in the plot. In other words, the music he wrote attempted to imitate the real motives of the characters, irrespective of their superficial behavior. This notion was more Italian than German; the Italians were especially fond of music that expressed pathos, tragedy, or any powerful emotion. It is also indicative of the growing concern with the inner life of the psyche, the inner driving forces of personality and motives, rather than external appearance—something that became a significant feature in nineteenth-century Germanic traditions in both music and philosophy as well as in the new field of psychology.

The more general philosophical problem concerning music and meaning revolved around the issue of how, as well as whether, music imitated the meanings inherent in words. Rousseau maintained that the musician "will not directly represent objects, but he will excite in the mind the same movements which it would feel from seeing them . . . music can put the eye into the ear" (quoted in Smith, 1795/1967, p. 162).

Adam Smith (1723–1790), famous for his economic theories, quoted Rousseau in his *Essays on Philosophical Subjects* (written toward the end of his life) but went on to qualify Rousseau's position considerably. Smith stated that "music's meaning is only made clear by words" (1795/1967, p. 150) and, citing Milton, maintained that music can only be imitative when it is "married to immortal verse, or even to any words of any kind which have distinct sense or meaning" (p. 150). He saw vocal music as superior to purely instrumental music in its powers of imitation: instrumental music's "melodious but un-meaning and inarticulate sounds cannot, like the articulations of the human voice, relate distinctly the circumstances of any particular sto-ry . . . or express clearly . . . the various sentiments and passions which are felt from situations" (p. 157). He explained that we need to be told beforehand what instrumental music is meant to convey, citing Handel's 1740 oratorio based on Milton's *L'Allegro* and *Il Penseroso*, which he probably heard at Lincoln's Inn Fields Theatre. This implies that instrumental music can, and does, imitate emotion in certain circumstances—that is, when its intent is described verbally.

Smith explained that instrumental music does not produce effects in the listener by "imitation properly" (p. 161). "It does not imitate a gay or sedate or melancholy person,'"nor does it engender "sympathy of mood as in vocal music" (p. 161). Instead, he argued that "it becomes itself a gay, sedate or melancholy object," but he did not explain the nature of the melancholy that it engenders in the listener. It does not reflect a person's melancholy or sadness, be that person composer, performer, or listener. So the question of the origin and nature of the melancholy, or other emotion, that the music objectifies remains a mystery. With only a few steps further in this argument, Smith would have begun to approach the position of Schopenhauer, who maintained that music cannot imitate specific emotions, but only the essence of such emotions—sadness itself, for example.

In citing musical examples, Smith mentioned Handel, Corelli, and Pergolesi, together with some French operas from earlier in the centu-ry. He did so, however, not so much to argue from a musical position as merely to illustrate in a very general way by allusion to a complete work. He alluded to "the rocking of a cradle which is said to have been imitated in the concerto of Corelli, which is said to have been composed for the Nativity" (Smith, 1795/1967, p. 158). This refers to Corelli's Concerto Grosso in G Minor, opus 6 no. 8 ("Made for Christ-mas Night"). He explained that we need to know beforehand that it is meant to be about Christmas, otherwise we could never guess purely from the sounds. The point he made is that instrumental sound with-out words cannot be imitative; it has as its purpose and semantic content nothing more than melody, harmony, and rhythm. And in this Smith took issue with his contemporary Charles Avison, who, in his

1752 *Essay in Musical Expression*, maintained that in the case of instrumental music "the complete merit of a piece of music is composed of three distinct arts or merits, that of melody, that of harmony, and that of expression" (quoted in Smith, 1795/1967, p. 170). Good melody and harmony do not lead to expression, argued Smith, anymore than good painting technique and color lead to expression.

A note of confusion is apparent in Smith's argument. He implied that instrumental music can imitate feelings when we are told those feelings beforehand but he stated that it cannot imitate feelings because it is itself a "feeling" object. It is difficult to see how both can be applicable, since they appear to be mutually exclusive. Moreover, an object does not need to imitate itself, and it is difficult to see how an object can assume imitative powers—when we are told it cannot imitate because it is an object—merely by the supplying of verbal descriptions. Smith went on to say that "instrumental music cannot imitate moods, even though it can excite them," since there are "no two things in nature more perfectly disparate than sound and sentiment" (Smith, 1795/1967, p. 162):

Here he seems to be saying that instrumental music is intrinsically inimical to human sentiment, which would appear to rule out both imitation and objectification. It is difficult to see how on the one hand music can excite moods because it becomes itself a gay or melancholy object and yet on the other hand cannot imitate moods at all. Smith claimed that music itself cannot be gay or melancholy in view of the fact that it expresses only the elements of music—melody, harmony, and rhythm. Instrumental music could only imitate feelings, in this case, if the elements of music themselves imitate feelings, as Plato suggested. On the other hand, instrumental music cannot express such things at all, because it is only capable of expressing its own elements, which themselves do not contain any extramusical meaning, as Smith seems to conclude!

From a purely musical standpoint, Smith's views can be seen not only as confused but also as a dismissal of years of belief in the imitative powers of instrumental music on the part of the musicians and theorists of the seventeenth and early eighteenth centuries. The German tradition of applying rules of rhetoric to music had resulted in an instrumental style that clearly accepted the imitative powers of purely instrumental music in the very terms described by Smith in regard to vocal music. But in England there had long been a tradition of instrumental music imitating emotions, or moods, by a systematic application of various musical elements thought to express such things.

Morley, in his *Plain and Easy Introduction to Practical Music*

(1597/1952), explained, in the section dealing with compositional technique, how the various musical elements—chords, melody, rhythm, combination of contrapuntal lines—"may serve to express those effects of cruelty, tyranny, bitterness, and such others, and . . . may fitly express the passions of grief, weeping, sighs, sorrows, sobs, and such like" (p. 290). Although these ideas emanated from the Italian expressive style, and particularly in view of the fact that the music of Italian madrigal composers such as Marenzio was being printed in England at this time, it had long been an English musical trait to attempt to match the "passions" with musical elements in composition. Since there is no reference to such traditions in Smith's writings, it must be assumed that he was unaware of them.

The issue, though, hinges around whether Smith is correct irrespective of whether he knew the intentions of the composer. In all human communication, one might even say all communication among living things, intention is a crucial aspect. To say, as Smith did, that music cannot imitate emotion, by which he meant it cannot communicate it without some attendant verbal explanation, is to deny the role of acculturation.

Someone well versed in the English, Italian, or German musical traditions has little difficulty in ascribing emotional significance to certain chords, melodic shapes, or rhythms in purely instrumental pieces. Such people would recognize "passion" in certain passages of, say, Byrd's motet *Ave Verum Corpus*, or Purcell's String Fantasias, or his full anthem "Hear My Prayer, O Lord," even if they were played only instrumentally.

In fact, during the sixteenth and early seventeenth centuries it was common for composers to write "apt for voices or viols" at the head of their compositions, indicating that it mattered little whether such music was sung or played on instruments—it would still achieve its effect on the listener. To deny semantic content to music by ignoring the traditions it arises from is hardly helpful in any quest to understand music.

Smith was not alone in his views, however. In any essay entitled "On poetry and Music as they affect the mind," James Beattie (1735–1803) declared that music should be removed from the list of imitative arts on the grounds that the power of music lies not in its representational powers but in its ability to affect the listener (Baker & Scruton, 1980; Beattie, 1790/1974). Earlier, John Locke (1632–1704), in "Some Thoughts Concerning Education" had said that "music . . . wastes so much of a young man's time to gain but a moderate skill in it: and engages in such odd company, that many think it better spared

. . . among all those things that ever came into the list of accomplishments, I think I may give it last place" (quoted in Rainbow, 1967, p. 25). And the extremely influential Lord Chesterfield wrote a letter to his son, published in the *Times*, telling him he was "emphatically not to participate himself in performing music"—although he could "go to concerts, opera and pay the fiddler"—in order that he might not "put himself into a highly frivolous and contemptible light" (quoted in Rainbow, 1967, p. 25).

It is not difficult to assess the effect of such views on English musical life when it is realized that England failed to produce a single indigenous composer of international stature between the death of Henry Purcell in 1695 and the birth of Edward Elgar in 1857. Paradoxically, the views of Adam Smith were only a short distance away from those of Schopenhauer in that both agreed that music's expressive powers lie in a different realm from those of language and that music is a more powerful medium of expression. It was Schopenhauer who enlightened and revitalized Wagner to such a degree that the composer remained fired with ideas of the power of music for three decades after reading him. Unfortunately there was no Wagner in England, and Smith's ideas merely tended to pour cold water on a musical climate already made somewhat sterile by the philistine views of such leaders of society as Lord Chesterfield.

The problem of defining the imitative and expressive nature of the arts remains very much with us today. Wollheim (1968) suggests that we "read off" an expression of emotion from a work of art; we do not experience it directly—a reference to the vicariousness of artistic expression and experience, as well as to the assumption that there is some emotion or symbol of it present in the work to be read off. A work of art cannot produce a genuine emotional situation; it can only produce an imitation of one. Our reaction cannot, therefore, be the same as when we experience the real thing. If this is the case, it is not entirely satisfactory simply to maintain that the observer extrapolates his or her own emotions from a work of art.

Vicarious experience from art need not be based on any previous real or genuine emotional experience. We do not need to have experienced murder directly, as Wollheim suggests, in order to feel the vicarious horror of it, whether it is represented in music, as in opera or a tone poem, or in drama, as in the theater and film, or, more concretely, in the plastic arts. Art does not exist in real-life situations; for obvious reasons it cannot! Conversely, as Plato and Aristotle intimated, we do not watch real murder in an opera or a play; we watch an artistic imitation of it. Thus when the issue turns on the so-called naturalness of artistic expression, presumably what is meant by this is not genuineness or absolute authenticity but more effective imitation or more convincing vicariousness.

The issue that remains unresolved, however, concerns whether meaning is intrinsic in musical sound or is merely the product of learned associations. The suggestion here is that it is the latter, which are themselves based upon acquired beliefs. But if music contains an imitation, whether through belief or intrinsic properties, what, precisely, does the work of art contain? If it is an imitation, what is being imitated? Is murder being imitated in Gluck's classical operas, or do they merely present clearer, more effective vicarious experiences of murder? Plato suggested that something quite potent and related to the subject being imitated is contained in the various elements of the artform, even to the extent of influencing behavior for good or ill. This is, of course, inadequate in explaining how it is that we can be entertained by the vicariousness of, say, murder in the context of an opera rather than compelled to go out and commit a murder.

Experiencing the attempted murder in Verdi's *Rigoletto* is entertaining, but it certainly does not make anyone want to go out and commit the real thing unless they are homicidal to start with: Millions of people have seen *Rigoletto* over the years, and even though Gilda ends up actually murdered, these events do not induce the audience to murder someone as a result. The point concerns the effect on the audience and the vicariousness of artistic experience. Any suggested link between musical expression and behavior that rests purely on some supposed intrinsic properties in musical sounds that embody such meanings is not easily demonstrated empirically, and it is this supposed link that is at the heart of the controversy surrounding the nature of aesthetic experience in the arts generally. Precisely what the artistic elements used in any medium convey, and the nature of the experience they provide, are questions central to our understanding of artistic activity.

The nineteenth-century philosophers and musicians took up the challenge. They revisited Plato and went to the heart of the matter by means of a further interpretation of the *ethos* theory. In particular, they wrestled with the notion that music can enable us to communicate with the essence of feelings, where essence is equated with the Platonic notion of ideal *ethos*, or character; this can be done not through greater realism but through greater abstraction to the level of the spirit, the soul of our being—the realm of transcendentalism. It was to this solution that some nineteenth-century philosophers and musicians turned.

MUSIC AS A TRANSCENDENTAL EXPRESSION OF FEELING

In the nineteenth century one of the influential figures in English poetry was Coleridge. He was deeply affected by Schelling's theories, particularly as propounded in *The System of Transcendental Idealism*, first published in 1804, and he possessed an edition of Schelling's *Philosophical Writings*, published in 1809, which contained an essay entitled "On the Relation of the Plastic Arts to Nature." The ideas formulated by Schelling are central to the general theories of expression on which romantic music of the nineteenth century was founded. In England such ideas did not gain much weight with musicians.

Schelling set out some basic principles of the new "transcendental" approach to art. He was talking principally about visual art, but his ideas were becoming commonplace among artists of all kinds in Germany. In the essay mentioned above he stated that

> art, according to the most ancient definition, is wordless poetry. Without doubt, the author of this statement meant to imply that, like those spiritual thoughts, it should express ideas whose source is the soul, not, however, by means of speech, but, like silent nature, by configuration, by form, by sensuous works which are independent of it . . . art, therefore, manifestly occupies the position of an active link between the soul and nature, and can only be comprehended in the living centre between the two of them. (quoted in Read, 1967, p. 324)

By nature, Schelling meant the "world's holy, eternally creating primal energy, which engenders and actively brings forth all things out of itself" (quoted in Read, 1968, p. 325). We imitate beauty and perfection, he maintained, but using nature as our source. The highest purpose of art is to produce an ideal "more noble than reality, together with the expression of spiritual ideas" (p. 327). He went on to discuss the ways for linking body and soul, which is the same artistically as linking forms of beauty with the ideals of the soul. He insisted, however, that we must go beyond mere form. Form proceeds from the "intuitive experience of the artist," and in "every work of art there is a reconcilement of the external with the internal" (p. 18)—of the conscious with the subconscious, of the realm of human existence with the realm of perfection. This, essentially, is the transcendentalist view of the purpose and function of art.

The fact that Schelling, along with some other philosophers of the period, based his ideas on the visual arts, feeling more comfortable in dealing with poetry or visual art than with music, is an indication of a growing awareness that somehow music was different from the other artforms. There were two basic reasons for this. One concerned the generally more abstract nature of musical elements; the other had to do with the complexity of music theory and its relative inaccessibility to those not educated in its tenets. Philosophers who were not trained musicians could not really take any sensible examples from music to fit their theories. Those few who were so educated and did, therefore, provide some musical examples suggested correspondence between elements of melody, harmony, and rhythm and their theoretical constructs in the manner of Plato and Aristotle. This was little different, however, from relating basic elements of language, such as verbs, adjectives, and nouns, with aspects of aesthetic theory. It ignored the deep structure of meaning that emanates more from the ways in which a particular musical tradition employs such elements than from the elements themselves.

In fact, the single most obdurate obstacle to the whole field of musical aesthetics is the elusive quality of the elements of music and their resistance to any meaningful categorization in terms of general aesthetic theory if they are presented devoid of their stylistic context. Musical theory can, and does, supply such details, but they have relevance only within the context of a musical tradition or a composer's style—the same elements are frequently used by different composers to diametrically opposed aesthetic ends.

Schopenhauer's admiration for the music of Rossini, his inability to recognize it as a sophisticated and witty development of Italian *opera buffa*—something quite remote from his lofty ideals—and his dismissal of Haydn—a composer whose music was much nearer to those ideals—is evidence enough of the weakness inherent in ignoring scholarly knowledge of musical style and tradition. It is similar to Rousseau's not recognizing the profound influence on Rameau's style of the expressive Italian style because of his ignorance of musical history. Thus it provides another illustration why aesthetic theory has tended to become remote and distant from what musicians actually do.

Notwithstanding these problems, the theory of Schopenhauer did inspire the composer of some of Western music's finest operas, Richard Wagner. Wagner, however, found Schopenhauer's theory descriptive rather than prescriptive of existing music. He had, in fact, already written a great deal of music to which Schopenhauer's theory applied.

In general, composers wishing to adapt to new ideas did so by making the elements of music respond as they believed they should in their resultant compositional acts. They have always tended to treat the elements of music as flexible semantic objects rather than as icons with fixed and immutable meanings. Philosophers, naive in the craft of musical composition, produce theories of aesthetic function and struggle to fit existing use of musical elements into their frameworks. Conversely, composers, equally naive philosophically, are often taken with an aesthetic idea and readily supply their own application of musical elements, as they were trained and crafted to do, to fit the theory. Yet despite these obvious shortcomings in the ongoing relationship between aesthetic theory and music, there were some overall trends in both fields that did coincide, even if in a somewhat bizarre and irrational manner, and that contributed to the development and production of some of the greatest music in Western culture.

The ideas of Schelling were doubtless read by many composers of the early nineteenth century, particularly in Germany. Mendelssohn's (1842/1956) famous dictum that music contains meanings too precise for words reflects the growing feeling at that time that music has greater powers of transporting the consciousness to other realms of awareness in a more direct and compelling manner than either words or visual art do. Many composers were writing music that overtly invited listeners to dream, to use their imaginations more potently—to do more than merely listen to a good tune or a rousing climax. Berlioz, from the 1830s onwards, wrote works demanding that the audience study their literary allusions before listening to their performance. In particular, *The Fantastic Symphony, Faust, The Childhood of Christ, Harold in Italy, Romeo and Juliet*, and *The Trojans* had clear references to literature and relied on it for the music's *raison d'être*.

Liszt, in defense of Berlioz, wrote that "music can reproduce the impression of the soul . . . and presents at one and the same time the intensity and expression of feeling; it is the embodiment and intelligible essence of feeling. . . . [The] supremacy of music lies in pure flames of emotion" (in Strunk, 1950, p. 849). Liszt was concerned with the transcendental qualities of music, particularly for the sympathetic listener who can be borne aloft on "the towering, sounding waves of music . . . to heights that lie beyond the atmosphere of our earth, and shows us cloud landscapes and archipelagos that move in ethereal space like singing swans" (p. 850). He also suggested that music is indeed the greatest art form because of its power to draw us into "regions which alone it can penetrate, where, in the ringing ether, the heart expands, shares in the immaterial, incorporeal, spiritual life" (p. 850).

It was with such thoughts in mind that Liszt asked listeners to hear not only the music of Berlioz, which he was ostensibly writing about, but also his own output, his Sonata in B Minor, for example. He found a somewhat unsympathetic audience in the young Brahms, however. At Schumann's house in the early 1850s, where Brahms was invited, the great Liszt was introduced to the young pianist and aspiring composer. Brahms was reluctant to play his newly composed piano sonatas to Liszt, who promptly sightread them perfectly. Liszt then played to Brahms his own newest composition, the Sonata in B Minor for piano. Part way through Liszt happened to look around, expecting to find a sympathetic look from a "brother" artist, only to find Brahms fast asleep. Whether this was due to Brahms's legendary ability to fall asleep on a pinhead, or whether he intuitively disliked the lack of classical form and structure in Liszt's transcendental sonata, is not known. Certainly Brahms represented in his works the musical antithesis of Liszt's style as far as structure and continuity with the musical past is concerned.

Many writers of the nineteenth century provide further evidence of the romantic, Germanic view of music exemplified in the music of Liszt, Wagner, Schumann, Tchaikovsky, and other similar composers. Jean Paul (J. P. F.) Richter said: "O music! Thou who bringest past and future so near our wounds with their flying flames. . . . Music! Reverberation from a distant world of harmony! Sigh of the angel within us!" (in Strunk, 1950, p. 772). And E. T. A. Hoffmann asked: "Is not music the mysterious language of a far away spirit world whose wondrous accents, echoing within us awaken us to a higher, more intensive life" (in Strunk, 1950, p. 788).

SCHOPENHAUER AND WAGNER— A WATERSHED IN WESTERN MUSICAL AESTHETICS

The early output of Wagner was clearly influenced by his conceptions of Platonic definitions of the relationships among all the arts, in particular between poetry and music. Wagner, of all the composers in modern history, is probably the nearest one can come to a philosopher-composer. In his prose works, such as *The Work of Art of the Future* in 1849, *Opera and Drama* in 1851, and *A Message to my Friends* in 1851, he set out in exhaustive detail his conception of the Platonic ideal of the fusion of all the arts, in particular the importance of the relationship among all the arts. He saw them all—poetry, drama, dress, mime, instrumental music, dance, song—as together constituting the ideal artform, which he termed *Gesamtkunstwerk*. This artform would not only embrace all the arts but would encapsulate all human experience, all human emotions, feelings, and, most important, unconscious desires and impulses. He described music as an equal of the other artforms in a combined artwork wherein each form interacted and influenced the other. His ideas were "Greek," as he himself admitted, and his intention was not just to revive Greek tragedy but to take it to new heights of expression and meaning.

His early operas include *The Fairies* (1834), *The Ban on Love* (1836), *Rienzi* (1840), *The Flying Dutchman* (1841), *Tannhäuser* (1845), and *Lohengrin* (1848), all written as he was formulating his theory of music drama and all meant to exemplify that theory. The idea of music drama was, as Magee (1983) puts it, concerned with the "insides of characters . . . their emotions not their motives . . . what goes on in the heart and soul" (p. 329). As Magee further states, this was the "opposite of existing opera," which, Wagner felt, dealt with what goes on "outside people," specifically, with what "goes on between" people, and, consequently, dramatic development in such artworks is a "chain of cause and effect" (p. 329). Wagner was, therefore, concerned with developing an artform that touched the secret, innermost parts of our being, an artform within which he believed all the arts were equal in status and function.

Newman (1949) points to the importance of Wagner's theory of music drama and emphasizes that "a clear picture of Wagner's mind processes during the conception and realization of a work is only to be obtained by following him step by step through the literature, ancient and modern, out of which it grew" (p. 5). These "mind processes" were involved initially with the notion of *Gesamtkunstwerk* and, in particular, the importance of the relationship between music and poetry. Ostensibly, therefore, Wagner subscribed to the view that poetry and music go hand in hand and would be equal in artistic terms in the new form of music drama. However, as many commentators have pointed out, this is difficult to support from the evidence of Wagner's actual compositional practices during these years. At times the music appears to overwhelm everything. Subconsciously, Wagner did not agree with his own theoretical position, and it was not until he became acquainted with the philosophy of Schopenhauer that he realized this himself!

In 1854, Wagner read for the first time Schopenhauer's (1788–1860) *The World as Will and Idea*. He was 41 years old and had reached the midpoint of his career as a composer. Schopenhauer was 66 years old and, after a lifetime of obscurity, was just entering his period of fame and renown. The effect on Wagner was spectacular. As Thomas Mann put it:

his acquaintance with Schopenhauer was the great event in Wagner's life. No earlier contact . . . approaches it in personal and historical significance. It meant to him the deepest consolation, the highest self-confirmation; it meant release of mind and spirit, it was utterly and entirely the right thing. There is no doubt that it freed his music from bondage and encouraged it to be itself. (quoted in Magee, 1983, p. 336)

In part what Wagner read was Schopenhauer's clear differentiation between music and the other arts and his elevation of music to the highest artform. He stated that music "stands alone, quite cut off from all the other arts" (Schopenhauer, 1818/1964, vol. 1, p. 330) and that the effect of music is "so much more powerful and penetrating than that of the other arts, for they speak only of shadows, but it speaks of the thing itself" (p. 333). Moreover, if "music is too closely united with words, and tries to form itself according to the events, it is striving to speak a language which is not its own" (p. 338). This is clearly a significant departure from the ancient Greek and more modern Renaissance views on the relationship between music and poetry: in these, music either is a servant of the latter or at best its equal.

Schopenhauer went on to state that no composer has come as near to this idea as Rossini—a choice that musicians might regard as bizarre, as already indicated above. While it is surprising that Schopenhauer did not cite Beethoven instead of Rossini, it should be remembered that Beethoven, too, professed his great admiration for Rossini—albeit for different reasons.

Additionally, he cited Pythagorean harmonics in his attempt to argue the merits of his assertion about the relationship between music and the will; he maintained that consonance, as defined by the "rational" relationships of the Pythagorean fourth, fifth, and octave, "easily adapts itself to our apprehension, [and] becomes the type of the satisfaction of the will" (Schopenhauer, 1818/1964, vol. 3, p. 236). This is merely a repetition of the age-old argument that these intervals, since they are founded upon "rational" proportions, relate to the natural workings of the ear and are the harbingers of that mysterious harmony that unites our existence and is pleasing because of its perfectness.

In citing further scientific "proof," Schopenhauer stated that "the musical quality of the notes is in the proportion of the rapidity of their vibrations, but not their relative strength . . . the highest note is followed by the ear, not the loudest . . . this gives the natural right for delivering melody to the soprano" (vol. 3, p. 237). In late-nineteenth-century musical terms this makes little sense, since it had become frequent compositional practice to move the melody to parts other than the soprano or the highest-pitched instrument in order to achieve the kind of expression that best exemplifies Schopenhauer's ideals for music. But again, Schopenhauer, not being a musician, could hardly be expected to know this. In fact, some of the most autonomously musical and affective melodies in nineteenth-century music are those played on the cello or horn, both of which instruments occupy the tenor line in four-part harmony, that is, one part above the bass line.

Were it not for the fact that Wagner took up Schopenhauer's ideas with such inspirational verve and energy, they would have remained of minor significance in the history of music, largely because Schopenhauer had little idea what they meant in actual musical practice, as his citation of Pythagoras and preference for Rossini over Haydn indicate only too clearly. That Wagner leaped upon these ideas is no surprise, considering that Wagner himself had adumbrated something akin to them in his own writings quite independently and uncognizant of Schopenhauer.

The development of opera since the Renaissance had been concerned primarily with the relative importance of its constituent elements—music, poetry, dance, drama—and Schopenhauer's concern about music's role in representing ideas from other artforms, notably poetry, was also a concern never far from composers' minds. None, however, dared be as radical as Schopenhauer, and then Wagner, in proclaiming the superiority of music as an autonomous and more effective artistic means of expression. That Wagner had implicitly reached a similar viewpoint to that of Schopenhauer is not surprising in view of the history of opera and its ancient Greek origins. What is significant is that Schopenhauer's ideas gave Wagner the impetus to pursue his own inner feelings more vigorously.

Schopenhauer suggested that music has only an indirect relation to the object it expresses or imitates. It expresses not the phenomenon itself but its inner nature, the "in-itself of all phenomena, the will itself"; not "this or that particular and definite joy, this or that sorrow or pain, or horror . . . but joy, sorrow, pain, horror . . . peace of mind themselves, to a certain extent in their abstract, their essential nature, without accessories . . . yet we completely understand them in this extracted quintessence" (Schopenhauer, 1818/1964, vol. 1, p. 338).

Like Plato and Aristotle, Schopenhauer, as well as other theorists and philosophers in between and since, provided a glossary of musical elements and the imitations of human feelings they provide: quick melodies are cheerful, and "striking painful dischords, winding back through many bars to the key note are, as analogous to the delayed, hard won satisfaction, sad"; the *allegro maestoso* imitates a "nobler effort to a more distant end and its final attainment"; the *adagio* "speaks of the pain of a great and noble effort which despises all trifling happiness," and so on (Schopenhauer, 1818/1964, vol. 1, p. 337).

The essence of what Schopenhauer explicated was that in music "we do not recognize the copy or repetition of any Idea (Representation) of existence in the world . . . yet its effect on the inmost nature of man is so powerful" (1818/1964, vol. 1, p. 330). He went on to state, with a strong hint of Pythagoreanism, that the

> effect of music is stronger than the other arts . . . yet the respect in which it stands to the world in the relation of a copy or repetition, is very obscure. . . .
>
> All the other arts objectify the Will indirectly only by means of ideas [representations] . . . [but] music is entirely independent of the phenomenal world, ignores it altogether, could exist if there was no world at all, which cannot be said of the other arts. . . .
>
> Music is as direct an objectification and copy of the whole Will as the world itself . . . and music has, therefore, an indirect relation to ideas [representations] . . . unlike the other arts. . . . According to all this we may regard the phenomenal world, or nature, and music as two different expressions of the same thing. . . . Music, if regarded as an expression of the world, is in the highest degree a universal language, which is related indeed to the universality of concepts. (vol. 1, pp. 331, 333, 339)

Schopenhauer likened the innermost level of feelings, the subconscious, to the Will as manifest in humans. It was Schopenhauer's explanation of the riddle of existence. Kant, whose first great disciple Schopenhauer was, provided some general conclusions from which Schopenhauer worked. Kant raised the question of the relationship between science and life. As Wallace (1970) puts it: "that life is more than knowledge is the cardinal faith which descends from Kant to his disciples and which descended to Kant from Rousseau" (p. 117). Kant suggested that

> supremacy or primacy belongs not to the theoretical, but to the practical reason—not to the intellect, but to the will. . . . The things of which science and experience predicate reality . . . are . . . mere appearances, divided from independent and self-subsisting being by a gulf which science, as such, is powerless to cross. . . . The so-called realities . . . are, by Kant, reduced to mere ideas in our mind—or, as we may even say with Schopenhauer, to a "cerebral phantasmagoria." . . . An invincible feeling assures us that behind appearance there is true being. How is it to be discovered? (Wallace, 1970, p. 118)

Schopenhauer's answer concerned the internal feelings we know and experience as ourselves—our Will. "We feel ourselves alive and active, sentient, emotional, passionate . . . we find ourselves neither divided into parts nor suffering the lapses of time, but altogether free from the limitations of time and space" (quoted in Wallace, 1970, p. 119). He was concerned with the distinction between what we feel, the Will, and what is perceived materially. He saw music as enabling us to have direct access to that mystical part of our being, our inner-most self, in a way more penetrating than any other art, since it is unencumbered by concrete objects or concepts.

In commenting to his wife, Cosima, in 1872, during their frequent discussions on the theories of Schopenhauer, Wagner maintained that when he had written *Opera and Drama*, "I didn't dare to say that it was music which produced drama, although inside myself I knew it" (quoted in Magee, 1983, p. 351). In his essay "Beethoven" (1870), Wagner wrote: "The relation of music to poetry is a sheer illusion" (quoted in Magee, 1983, p. 350). In the following year, in *The Destiny of Opera*, he wrote: "I would almost like to call my dramas deeds of music become visible," and, in 1872, in *On the Term Music Drama*, he stated that "the music sounds, and what it sounds you may see on the stage before you" (quoted in Magee, 1983, p. 350). As Magee (1983) suggests, "by now music is seen [by Wagner] as the overwhelming predominantly all creative element" (p. 351). The earlier conception had given way completely to a notion of drama emanating from music.

There is little doubt that one cannot understate the effect of Schopenhauer on Wagner's articulation of the role and function of music in drama from 1854 onwards. Neither is there any doubt that Wagner intended his music to reflect this, or that a significant difference in his musical style and content can be detected from this time on. In the *Ring* cycle of operas, in *Tristan and Isolde*, and in *Parsifal*, Wagner produced music of such abstraction, eloquence, and aesthetic power in Schopenhauer's terms that it completely overwhelms the words being sung: this certainly is true superficially, in that it is difficult to tell what words are being sung most of the time in his later operas; but it is also true substantively, in that Wagner assures the listener that the music will tell all.

Wagner achieved, probably as far as is possible, a successful application of Schopenhauer's notion of the objectification of the Will to music by coincidence as well as by careful analysis of the philosophical arguments—analysis that occurred after the event in the case of much of his output. Wagner was expert in his comments on the practical developments in opera as he had seen them practiced on the operatic stage. He achieved an equally careful, yet inspired, transformation into musical terms of Schopenhauer's ideas following his acquaintance with the writings of Schopenhauer. This was not achieved, as Schopenhauer had envisaged, in the relatively simple terms of melody and its relation to harmony. Wagner employed a sophisticated mixture of continuous and flowing chromatic counterpoint, which contained themes and motives relating to characters, events, and emotional content, together with what modern psychologists might call applications of information theory: the sudden juxtaposition of the unexpected with the familiar. Additionally, however, his conception of the power of sound—overwhelming at times, cajoling, seducing, or frightening—was intended to touch the very subconscious parts of our being that Freud went to great pains to uncover a few decades after Wagner's death.

Since music is regarded in Schopenhauer's, and subsequently Wagner's, scheme as the objectification of the Will itself and the most powerful of the arts in its effect on the observer, Wagner argued that music can penetrate this subconscious level and bring it to the level of consciousness. Some primary forces in the Will that Schopenhauer talked about were morality, as exemplified in compassion, and the sex drive, as exemplified in love.

Wagner exploited these to the full in the *Ring* cycle, *Tristan and Isolde*, and *Parsifal*, where he made music the primary vehicle of information and the text subsidiary. This was indeed a remarkable reversal of the traditional relationship in opera between words and music, and quite contrary to the traditions emanating from ancient Greece. One major effect of all this on musical composition was to drive a wedge into the whole fabric of music in Western culture that led to developments in the twentieth century whereby music became a completely autonomous artform. To this extent the philosophical writings of Schopenhauer and their championing by Wagner, both equally important, together constitute a most remarkable musical force in modern Western music as far as the long-term effects are concerned.

Composers of the late nineteenth century could hardly ignore Wagner; they wrote under his shadow. He had intended to write symphonies in his last years, following the completion of *Parsifal* in 1882. He died, however, in the following year, leaving only speculation as to the possible nature of the music drama as a symphony. There are hints in *Parsifal* as to its nature, for in this opera Wagner intended the music to contain the entire essence of the drama, with the visual spectacle regarded as an expression of the music. It was Mahler, as much as anyone, who initially took up the challenge. Mahler was well read in aesthetics, including the philosophy of Schopenhauer, and was thoroughly conversant with Wagner's ideals. His symphonies are testimony to his commitment to Wagner's notion of music drama as a symphony, wherein musical sound is intended to contain the essence of meaning, to be more penetrating than visual drama or words.

Western musical culture had thus reached a watershed and, in one sense, completed a full circle of evolution. It started as imitation of *ethos*; traveled through various stages, each concerned with the *modus operandi* of composing music that imitated the meaning inherent in words; only to reach the final stage where, it was concluded, music does not imitate words but, in fact, contains a mode of access to the essences that are alluded to in words. As such, music assumes a role superior to that of words; that of an artform which, as Aristotle maintained, had its own special elements and modes of imitation different from those of poetry.

The claims of Aristotle to the effect that music can make our "souls enthusiastic, and enthusiasm is a condition of the soul" (quoted in Strunk, 1950, p. 18)—so that when we listen to imitations we acquire a sympathy with the feelings imitated—would seem to be at the heart of Western aesthetics. After Wagner and such other composers as Mahler, there was nowhere else to take the theory of *ethos* except around the same circle of arguments about the ways in which music can react to it. Wagner and Schopenhauer both pointed in another direction: the autonomy and independence of musical sound.

The twentieth century has seen a radical departure from the tenets of traditional Western musical theory in the work of many avant-garde musicians, most of whom have taken up the notion of the autonomy of sound as a means of expression remote and distinct from any other type of human communication. Schopenhauer's musical applications of Kant's notion of the autonomy of the Will have been the catalyst, through Wagner, that launched the twentieth-century interest in the expressive use of sound for its own sake. The general populace, however, has gradually, through the effects of various popular-entertainment media, been coaxed into accepting the traditional Platonic theory of musical representation, and most people nowadays have little difficulty in recognizing the musical imitations of various sentiments that have become the main semantic function of Western musical activity. It remains for the twentieth-century practices embodying the notion of the autonomy of musical sound to reach the general consciousness in similar fashion. There is little doubt that most people outside the circles of the musicians concerned are unaware of the aesthetic watershed in the development of Western musical art that occurred with the work of Schopenhauer and Wagner.

CHAPTER 5

The Twentieth Century—
From Symbol to Object

By the end of the nineteenth century it was becoming clear that each new generation of Western artists in all fields was asking more and more uncomfortable questions. The debate within music began to turn away from issues arising from applications of harmonics to Platonic *ethos* and Aristotelean mimesis to concerns relating to intrinsic properties of sound. This inevitably called into question the relevance of established musical structures and forms. Questions such as whether music represented specific feelings or feelings in their abstract essential form—and from these even more detailed questions such as what exactly was being represented by musical elements and which elements represented what—gave way to a preoccupation with the structural and sensual properties of individual musical elements, such as vertical combinations of notes, intervals between pitches, single notes, or sound color of instruments. This was an inevitable outcome of the suggested autonomy of music—its independence from all the other arts—found in the works of Wagner. If music is autonomous as an expression, then it needs to look into itself and examine its own properties—that is, the properties of musical sound per se. This attitude was fueled by the contemporary growth of knowledge about the physical properties and propensities of the pressure waves that create sound.

The capability for generating such pressure waves electronically was evident at the beginning of the century with the invention of the electronic valve in 1908. Consequently, there opened up the artistic possibilities inherent in being able to exercise greater controls than ever before over all aspects of sound. The Italian painter and musician Luigi Russolo hailed the new age of machines by composing works containing noises made from machines he built, such as the work *The Meeting of Automobile and Aeroplane*. His concerts, held before the First World War, usually ended in riots, however, so offended were the sensibilities of his fellow citizens.

Aspiring composers, once attracted to careers as creative musicians, are, of course, susceptible to ideas, theories, and theoretical possibilities that offer aesthetic and empathetic inducements. Few such ideas could be more promising to a lively mind than the artistic potential of exercising freedom of imagination and acoustic realization in musical composition. More than anything else at the turn of the century, it was the promise of artistic freedom suggested by new ideas, new objective scientific thought, and new technology that inspired a fresh flowering of musical activity substantively different from that built on Pythagoreanism. Out of this arose new formal procedures and different aesthetic perspectives. Some thought that a musical sound was itself an object incapable of representing anything, that the only meaning inherent in sound was that relating to how its elements moved in temporal space. Belief in music's representational powers was supplanted by artistic interest in the sensate properties of sound itself.

The ideas upon which musicians acted came, however, not so much from within music itself, nor even directly from advances in physical science, but rather from the more adventurous arts of literature, painting, and sculpture. The edifice of musical theory, built upon Pythagorean harmonics and representational possibilities from within the confines of the theory, was so intimidating that musicians were much slower to respond to new ideas than were artists and poets. At the turn of the century in literature and the visual arts other—and, for music, quite fruitful—questions were being asked and acted upon. In the visual arts in particular, questions concerning the meaning of representation by art had produced almost continual revolution in techniques and approaches since the sixteenth century. Many of these were reactions against "academicism," that is, against the stultifying effects of imposing established and reified styles on young and developing artists. Musicians, however, had not been able to respond in such a rebellious manner until this century. Historically, these revolutionary ideas tended to appear first in visual art and literature and, in fact, to precipitate their appearance in music. Even if musicians wished to respond more readily, the constraints of existing instruments and performance techniques were too great to overcome in any but a perfunctory manner. This century promised something different because of what Edgard Varèse called the "liberation of sound" for the musician's use.

This liberation was to arise out of scientific advance. Just as Pythagoreanism, Platonic notions of *ethos*, and Aristotelean ideas of mimesis became the objective, scientific bases upon which Renaissance Western musical theory and practice were built, so did theories in acoustics, psychology, and mathematical logic become the bases upon which much of the new musical praxis of the twentieth century has been built. It is a matter of contention as to whether the new theories constitute a complete repudiation of Platonic *ethos* and Aristotelean mimesis in the way that they do of Pythagoreanism and harmonic theory. In order to explore both the nature of the new theories and the extent of their reaffirmation or rejection of the theoretical positions of Plato and Aristotle, I focus on two strands of development: (1) the French emphasis on exploring sound for its own sake and inventing new structures based on this and (2) the Austro-Germanic emphasis on functional relationships and structure derived painstakingly from the great tradition. Although these may seem like neat and tidy little compartments within which to slot various composers, in reality they are more in the nature of investigative tools. Many composers straddle one or both of these so-called strands in their music. Nevertheless, in the interests of examining the musical beliefs that have motivated composers in this century, such a division might be useful.

SOUND AND ITS INTRINSIC PROPERTIES

The importance of Paris as one of the major cultural centers in the early years of this century can hardly be overstressed. In poetry, music, and the visual arts, some of the most influential and exciting developments of the times emanated from poets, musicians, and artists working there. Moreover, the Parisian interactions among them during the 1890s and 1900s have been of considerable importance in the development of modern music through to our own time. Two composers in particular who were educated in Paris during this time and have exerted enormous influence on later composers are Claude Debussy and Edgard Varèse. Both derived their approach to musical composition from ideas and activities among painters and writers rather than fellow musicians. It is important, therefore, to examine some of the details of artistic and literary activities of the time that inspired the two composers.

Claude Debussy—The First Wagnerite to Show the Way Forward

Among many musicians of the first half of this century, the work of Claude Debussy (1862–1918) is seminal. His early infatuation with the music of Wagner turned to a more intellectual fascination with the implications of Wagner's music and Schopenhauer's ideas for the autonomy of musical expression. It is clear that among contemporary musicians there were few enough who could lead the way forward from Wagner, who could do other than imitate his chromatic style, thereby missing the possible developments that Debussy eventually hit upon.

As an emerging young composer, he preferred to spend his time among progressive artists and poets rather than musicians; in particular, he got to know the poetry of Baudelaire, Mallarmé, and Verlaine. The music of Mussorgsky he found refreshingly un-Germanic, and the Paris Exposition Universelle of 1889 gave him opportunity to hear and see a Javanese gamelan orchestra. Two years later he met Erik Satie, then a café pianist, whose ideas on musical stasis he found challenging and stimulating. But it was the intellectual movements of symbolism in literature and impressionism in visual art that exerted the greatest and most direct influence on Debussy's emerging musical style. It was from the ideas expounded below that Debussy, transferring them from painting and poetry to music, was able to forge his unique response to the crisis in compositional style that Wagner's music and Schopenhauer's ideas had provoked. Awareness of some details from the ideas of painters is necessary in order to see what Debussy actually took from painting and applied to music.

The founding artists of the movement or group of painters who were labeled "impressionists" were Édouard Manet (1832–1883) and Claude Monet (1840–1926). The latter turned out to be the more radical by insisting on abandoning the studio altogether in favor of painting nature in the open air, actually witnessing nature itself. In this way, when painting a river and sky, for example, the subtle changes that continually occurred as water rippled or clouds passed could be captured. On April 15, 1874, the group, following up a suggestion by Monet, mounted an exhibition under the title of "La Société anonyme des artistes, peintres, sculpteurs." Among the exhibitors were Cézanne, Degas, Monet, Pissarro, and Renoir. It was held in a photographic studio and included a painting of a harbor seen through mists entitled *Impression—Sunrise* by Monet. A critic writing in *Charivari*, Louis Leroy, found this and other works visually illiterate because, he felt, they lacked evidence of technique; consequently he ridiculed the painters, coining the derogatory term *impressionist*, a euphemism for saying they could not paint. The term stuck, and although its origins were meant to deride, it actually engendered a certain hubris in those involved.

Explanations of what impressionism was supposed to be about give the clue to the essential nature of the artist's search for a new approach to form and content based upon the effects of light on perception of visual shapes in nature. There was a concern with the processes of visual perception, with how the eye gathered and organized the myriad of colors, shapes, lines, and sizes confronting it, as well as with visual illusions emanating from the differing effects of light falling on these at different angles, intensities, and hues. It implied looking anew at the world and, for the artist, reflecting this new view of visual perception rather than faithfully reproducing stylized forms relating to classical models of beauty and formal structure.

Monet talked of visual harmonies among the elements of a painting, such as color, shape, texture, and line, rather than how these formal elements fit into a predetermined overall design such as one was trained to do in academic painting. A more thoughtful critical reaction than Leroy's appeared in *Le Rappel* on April 9, 1876. The writer, Emile Blémont, suggested that the objective of the impressionists was to

> render with absolute sincerity, without any arrangement or attenuation, by simple process, the impression aroused in them by the various aspects of reality. For them art is not a minute and meticulous imitation of . . . la belle nature . . . [reproducing] people and objects servilely, nor to reconstruct a subject. They do not imitate; they translate, they interpret, they apply themselves to disentangling the admixture of lines and diverse colours which assail the eye when first it looks at a subject. (quoted in Denvir, 1987, p. 102)

Blémont went on to describe them as "synthesists, not analysts" and, most significantly, he asserted that in their techniques "there are no basic laws other than the relationship of things to each other . . . like Diderot they feel that the idea of beauty lies in the perception of these relationships." And in answer to anticipated criticism for allowing too much individual freedom in such a creed, he countered by elevating the artistic merits of individuality as manifest in individual perceptions of objects: "and as there are probably no two men . . . who see exactly the same relationships in the same object, [so] they do not feel it necessary to alter their personal and direct sensations to comply with any particular convention'' (quoted in Denvir, 1987, p. 102).

In literature the symbolist movement presented an equally startling, new, and complex set of relationships between words and meanings. Baudelaire (1821–1867) and Rimbaud (1854–1891) used words for the acoustic expressionism inherent in the sounds of vowels and consonants rather than for their customary semantic significance within linguistic syntax. Baudelaire wrote a sonnet on the vowels, and Rimbaud, in 1873, wrote about an "Alchemy of tones of Speech," according to which he claimed to have discovered the color of speech vowels: *A* is black; *E*, white; *I*, red; *O*, blue; and *U*, green. He went on to explain the invention of a poetry of words that will be accessible to all the senses. This attitude suggests more an autonomy of medium than anything to do with mimesis.

Mallarmé (1842–1898) was an important figure both in the symbolist movement per se and in its transmission to the world of music through his contact with Debussy. He foreshadowed a poetic development known as concrete poetry, whereby the poem is an object in and by itself; it does not need reference, meaning, or representational elements. Sounds of words are considered complete in themselves as acoustic objects to be manipulated by the poet. With Mallarmé, linguistic mechanisms are stressed and technique becomes an end in itself, as the poet strives to release the rhythms and metaphoric actions of words in nonfunctional juxtapositions. Cynics might well label such ideas as merely an extreme swing of the pendulum toward technique—a modern answer to the ancient Greek debate concerning techniques of rhetoric versus ethical content, with technique winning out over the latter. A more perceptive mind, such as Debussy's, saw it as further ammunition in his quest for autonomy of musical expression. It was more than mere exploration of technique for its own sake: it represented a desire to explore the medium of poetry as an expressive end in itself. It would be unfair to criticize such work for lack of ethical content without considering many other factors in the intellectual and social life of the times. There were good reasons to dismiss the sentiment of past ages; many observed how it had produced untold human suffering and deprivation. But there were other additional motivations at work that account for such uses of the sounds of language. These stem from studies in human perception and the growing interest in understanding the complexities of human thought processes. There was more to this perspective than merely a rejection of ethical content.

Debussy was exposed to these powerful artistic and intellectual movements through his friendship with Mallarmé. He met the symbolists and other intellectuals at the regular and famous Tuesday meetings in Mallarmé's Paris flat, known as "les mardis de la Rue de Rome." Debussy, whose music first appeared in the early 1890s, was a prizewinning scholar of the Paris Conservatory and, like Monteverdi 300 years earlier, expert in the traditional techniques of his time. Before he became fully acquainted with the symbolists, he found the fundamental principles of functional harmony, as explicated by Rameau and developed over the succeeding century, with their concomitant musical forms outmoded and incapable of further development.

As a result of the influence of contemporary poets, artists, and intellectuals, he soon crystallized his views by rejecting the notion that music must have a structure whose function is to facilitate continuity and movement—these merely perpetuate the traditional view of music as a servant of poetry or rhetoric. And here it must be stated that Debussy saw no contradiction in using *ideas* from poetry or painting while opposing the subjugation of music to poetry, painting, or rhetoric in its expressive intent and content. Using these ideas, he suggested that individual chords, melodic fragments, or even sections of a piece are complete in themselves and need not depend for their meaning on their place within a key, their relationship with the dominant chord, or their overall symphonic structure based on the sonata principle. This was, for him, the pathway to the autonomy of sound he was seeking. He actively pursued ideas aimed at discontinuity and absence of functional harmony and melody. He viewed diatonic melody, harmony, and sonata form, as well as the functional relationships derived from these over the previous 300 years, as the musical equivalent of faithfully reproducing an object, person, or scene in painting and relying on traditional semantic content in language use. He justified his proclivity for using the sensuous acoustic qualities of instrumental sounds—that is, using various vertical juxtapositions of notes into chords for their own isolated sensuous properties—by extrapolation from the existing work of impressionist painters and symbolist poets.

He paralleled in music the notion in symbolist poetry of using words for their individual metaphoric and linguistic content rather than their structural function within sentences or phrases. He also paralleled in music the developments of the so-called impressionist painters, who deemed visual elements as important for their own sake. Monet's visual harmony was easily translatable into musical terms, as was Rimbaud's "alchemy" of speech tones.

From these few bare facts can be traced Debussy's movement from his student days of high achievement in traditional musical skills to his position as something of a musical revolutionary. From the reception of the Grand Prix de Rome in 1884 at the age of 22, through the first performance ten years later of his first significant work (the *Prelude to "The Afternoon of a Faun"*), and on to his first major musical event of revolutionary import, the composition of the opera *Pelléas and Mélisande*, first produced in 1902 in Paris, he had progressed from brilliant student to a mature and highly individual composer of immense stature and influence in the world of music. From the *Prelude* onwards, Debussy experimented with musical structures that owed little or nothing to the great traditions of previous centuries.

The musical world Debussy grew up in was dominated in France by the Belgian composer César Franck (1822–1890), whose music was transcendental in typical nineteenth-century fashion and, consequently, highly chromatic. It was also structurally based on dominant and tonic harmonic functions and tonality, or key-centeredness. By the 1880s, when Debussy was a student, the theory of harmony had become a highly sophisticated theory of tonal relationships between chords, which could be colored by chromatic addition and alteration but whose function was to define tonal centers. These latter, in turn, defined the structure of the whole piece of music. Mastery of compositional skills involved mastery of chromatic harmony, modulation, and establishment of successive but related key centers, which were seen as the foundation of symphonic structure. The intrinsic problem with key relationships lay in the fact that beyond the functionality, whether of primary or secondary, of the dominant chord, there was really no one logical progression that had more validity than any other. This functionality relied on the notion of key-centeredness. In logical terms, modulations and even chord progressions were no more organized than the random events of nonfunctional harmony: any key could follow any other, as could any chord, provided a clever enough passage was forged through chord progression. Functional harmony in its neutral state, devoid of a composer's special style, was, in essence, no more than a game to be played by music students as they learned the craft of composition. But because it could be managed by a process of musical logic, however sterile, it earned connotations of a grammar, a logical system that was thought to elevate diatonic tonality, however much chromaticized, into a language system. The spuriousness of this was probably intuitively clear to Debussy, as it became to others after him.

Franck, one of Debussy's teachers at the Paris Conservatory, was an undisputed master of such compositional skills. His music is highly expressive and full of pathos in the nineteenth-century spirit, and there is every reason to believe that Debussy had little difficulty in satisfying the demands of his teachers to judge by the number of prizes he won. Yet within a short time of completing his student years he emerged as a musical radical whose music reflected very little of his training.

At the heart of his revolutionary approach lies the role he assigned to harmony. Debussy rejected the notion of harmony as functional and in so doing, rejected the very bedrock of European musical tradition during the previous few centuries. His training would have taught him the use of chromaticism within a functional scheme of tonality and would have enabled him to provide resolutions to highly chromatic chords within a particular scheme of keys or key relationships. Indeed, the apogee of such theoretically based relationships between chromatic chords, as well as the watershed, was Wagner's harmonic writing, in particular such examples as the so-called Tristan chords shown in Figure 5.1. These chords can be described variously in musical theory because of their ambiguity. The second chord can be seen as both a half-diminished supertonic seventh and a French augmented sixth, and the third as both a German augmented sixth and a dominant seventh. Thus the progression can, because of its tonal ambiguity, straddle several tonal areas, or keys. The possibilities inherent in using successive augmented sixth or secondary seventh chords, chromatically decorated in such a way that they could function as either freestanding augmented sixths or dominant sevenths, opened up two avenues to composers: one was the possibility of marvelous harmonic flexibility; the other, the possibility of decadence from within.

FIGURE 5.1 Wagner's "Tristan chords," showing the ambiguity of tonal center

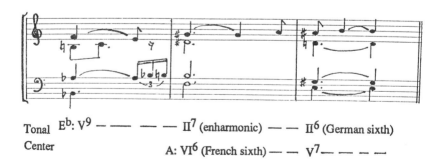

Tonal E^b: V^9 — — — — — II^7 (enharmonic) — — II^6 (German sixth)

Center   A: VI^6 (French sixth) — — V^7 — — — —

The decadence lies in the fact that to modern ears a tonal, key-centered resolution of the Tristan chords is not necessary, since they induce no harmonic tension, so accustomed have we become to both functional and nonfunctional harmony. We can see now that neither is an absolute. Within the context of a clearly focused key center they do require such resolution, but within a nonfunctional context they do not. Such progressions as this, and many similarly ambiguous ones, are to be found in *Parsifal*, showing the extreme flexibility of the theory as well as its decadence. To some, it seemed that only a small step beyond this was needed to justify almost any chromatic progression, and, not surprisingly, the reaction of the musical world to Wagner's extreme chromaticism was diverse. Some puzzled over the tonal implications of the Tristan chords for decades, and their theoretical strivings became the basis of musical education for practically every music student during this century. Others took the bold step of furthering the definition of harmonic function, making chromaticism itself, rather than the diatonic scale, the basic element; this was the approach of Schoenberg and his school. Debussy saw the situation as marking nothing more than an end: the end of functional harmony and of the theory of chromaticism within a diatonic framework of functional key relations.

It must be mentioned, however, that Debussy did not reach his position entirely in a vacuum, without any musical precedents. By the middle to late nineteenth century incipient uses of nonfunctional harmony were appearing in many places. In France itself the music of Gabriel Fauré (1845–1924) contained elements of nonfunctional chording. Fauré was also a professor at the Paris Conservatory before becoming its director from 1902 to 1920. There were even more signs in the music of various Russian composers of the times, including Borodin, Glinka, and Mussorgsky, whose music Debussy would have heard. And in the harmonies of Wagner himself there were many hints of a dissolution of harmonic function that Debussy found particularly interesting and thought-provoking. He attended Bayreuth during the 1880s, and heard *Tristan, Die Meistersinger*, and *Parsifal* there. The last opera in particular contains many examples of harmonic license that borders on the nonfunctional.

Of equal importance was Debussy's experience at the 1889 Paris Exhibition, where he heard the Javanese gamelan playing what seemed like the pentatonic scale based on the black notes of the equally tempered piano. A critical ear such as Debussy's would doubtless have heard far more than this superficial likeness, including the unique and substantively different tempering as well as the subtle and sensitive relationships between harmonic content of the individual gamelan instruments and the melodic fragments that, repeated with equally subtle variations, formed an entirely novel way of structuring a musical event. None of this was lost on Debussy. Both the pentatonic scale played with Western temperament and the whole-tone scale were known to him before this encounter: his teachers at the Paris Conservatory had already introduced him to different scales, including these. Indeed, the uniqueness of Debussy's music came from his ability to seize on already existing ideas and incipient trends and, with help from painters and poets, develop a unique personal style of composition that offered a model to later composers in developing their own styles.

Having rejected the existing structural theory, Debussy filled the void with the musically ingenious yet generally unoriginal notion of discontinuity and completeness for each chord within itself. He saw that chords could be expressive as objects alone, just as vowels and consonants are in symbolist poetry or colors, shapes, and lines are in impressionist painting. They need not progress to another chord by virtue of some outmoded canon of musical theory, and neither need there be a sense of continuity within a piece of music. Musical motion, continuity, and harmonic function within the diatonic key system had been the central goal of composition from at least the early eighteenth century onwards, and it was Rameau, another Frenchman, whose theoretical work had enabled musicians to achieve these goals with the aid of a comprehensive and pervasive musical theory.

If Debussy's time was ripe for such a rejection, his reasons were entirely artistic and aesthetic. The work of several nineteenth-century scientists, including the polymath Hermann Helmholtz, seemed to show that there was scientific support for Rameau's theory of a fundamental bass and functional harmony in the ideal harmonic content of musical sound and the primacy of the fundamental in pitch perception. As we saw in Chapter 2, it was not until the middle of our own century that science was able to refute the notion of a scientific basis for Rameau's theories.

Despite this lack of scientific support, other than through theories of visual perception, it seemed to Debussy quite appropriate that the sounds of music—melodies and harmonies—could be employed as sonic objects complete in themselves rather than as dependent structural elements. Debussy's musical aesthetic theory was not, then, logical in the strict sense of the term. But then, neither was Rameau's, as we have seen. The logical point to be deduced from this is that musicians do not arrive at their artistic intuitions rationally, though they may readily anticipate scientific laws. Rameau anticipated the primacy of the fundamental in nineteenth-century scientific theories of pitch perception in his theory of the fundamental bass, even though it has turned out to be incorrect; and Debussy anticipated the more recent developments in auditory theory, which rely on pattern recognition of the whole waveform, through his abandonment of functional harmony, thus forcing the listener to derive pitch and melody from nonfunctional harmonic underpinning of both.

It is tantalizing to think that the respective scientific theories of auditory perception that Rameau and Debussy anticipated provided support for their musical aesthetic theories, even though the genesis of their intuition is traceable from elsewhere than music. Debussy, lacking any scientific arguments for the application of visual perception theories to auditory perception, relied on more traditional media, those of rhetoric and allegory in literature.

In the early 1900s Debussy published a series of articles in which he expounded his new aesthetic. Under the pseudonym of M. Croche, he discussed the musical irrelevance of theory per se, not just traditional theory: "In all compositions I endeavour to fathom the diverse impulses inspiring them and their inner life. Is not this much more interesting than the game of pulling them to pieces?" (Debussy, 1927/ 1962, p. 5). Further on, he propounded the notion of simplicity, saying he preferred "the simple notes of an Egyptian shepherd's pipe; for he collaborates with the landscape and hears harmonies unknown to your treatises" (p. 7). He went on to denounce theory even more vehemently: "Musicians listen only to the music written by cunning hands, never to that which is in nature's script. To see the sun rise is more profitable than to hear the Pastoral Symphony (Beethoven). What is the use of your almost incomprehensible art?" (p. 7).

It is clear that Debussy was attacking the whole edifice of late-nineteenth-century Western musical theory as much for its aesthetic bankruptcy as for its spurious underpinnings. He was concerned with the artificiality of compositional procedures and the remoteness of their products from what he saw as true aesthetic experience. He became more prescriptive when he talked of how some had tried in poetry and painting to shake off the "ancient dust of tradition," and "with some trepidation" how some had tried it in music, only to be scorned by the attribution of various labels, such as "symbolists" or "impressionists." With some apparent bitterness, he spoke of those musicians who like "poor sheep flock docilely to the slaughterhouses which a discerning fate has prepared for them" (p. 8). "Uniqueness" is the key, rather than being "merely an expression of society" (p. 8).

And, as if in answer to the pedagogues who would doubtless ask questions about uniqueness equaling total license and artistic, expressive chaos, he wrote: "Discipline must be sought in freedom, and not within the formulas of an outworn philosophy only fit for the feebleminded. Give ear to no man's counsel; but listen to the wind which tells in passing the history of world" (p. 8).

The resemblance to discussions about the work of the impressionists during the 1870s and 1880s is unmistakable, but it should not be surprising in view of Debussy's close association with the intellectual circles of Paris in general and with Mallarmé in particular. Debussy did not exactly present a prescription in the general sense of the word, but he did point clearly to a rejection of traditional theory and its replacement by more intuitive motives. Debussy was not, however, advocating total freedom, merely freedom for him to do what his artistic sensibilities dictated, which is similar in essence to the critical appraisal of the work of the impressionist painters by Emile Blémont.

With his background of mastery in traditional techniques, one cannot accuse Debussy of accidental artistic confusion, chaos, or anarchy through ignorance; he had reached some clear directives in his music and sought the intellectual freedom to pursue them, freedom from what he saw as those who could merely quote rules to him rather than attempt to understand what he was doing. If his music was artistically confusing, as some believed, it was not a result of Debussy's design; the confusion was in the mind of those unable to appreciate his artistic products. Criticism could be leveled at his lack of a coherent theory that could explicate his methods and constructions. However, the point he made consistently is that he had no theory, merely his own sensibilities arising from the compositional process. This explanation is one more commonly associated with painters than musicians; but in the traditions of French music, certainly from Debussy on, it is one that assumes great significance during this century. It is particularly applicable to the music of Edgard Varèse.

Edgard Varèse—A Pioneer for the Autonomy of Musical Sound

During the early 1900s Varèse was emerging from his student days in Paris. In many ways he was in the same intellectual mold as Debussy in that he rejected traditional musical theory after having shown a certain mastery of traditional compositional techniques at the Paris Conservatory. From the outset, however, Varèse was much more radical than Debussy, drawing his inspiration from sources in science as well as visual art. Picasso's (1881–1973) 1907 work *Les Demoiselles d'Avignon* showed angular, distorted shapes and reflected a growing interest in primitive sculpture as well as the work of Cézanne. The cubist movement was clearly a major influence on Varèse's thinking about music at this time, and he sought to translate these ideas into music by composing several works. No musical compositions of this period have survived, however. Varèse's other main interest lay in acoustics; in particular, Helmholtz's *On the Sensations of Tone* (1885/ 1954) and Busoni's "Sketch of a New Aesthetic of Music" (1911/1962) were influential for him. From Helmholtz's work Varèse developed a fascination with the nature of complex pressure waves, in particular the way in which they are composed of many sinusoidal waves, each resolvable by the ear, according to Helmholtz. Helmholtz's monumental work contains a comprehensive analysis of all aspects of the pressure waves we call sound. It was in this new science that Varèse saw the future of musical aesthetics. It is equally interesting to note that Debussy found no inspiration in modern science for his musical aesthetic, even though science was later to prove that his nonfunctional harmonies did not fly in the face of any laws of auditory functioning in humans. Debussy appeared to know this intuitively.

From the two sources, cubism and science, Varèse forged the most radical aesthetic theory for music to date. He espoused newness for the sake of newness and rejected traditional notions of beauty perceived through representation of forms of beauty. For him beauty was merely a product of the processes of composition; it was not a conscious attempt to re-create beauty through order, form, or structure, or through deliberately trying to please. The essential artistic activity lay in what the instinct can conceive as the artist manipulates materials and constructs the artistic object. Varèse had assimilated this influence before he left Paris for America in 1915.

Varèse called music an "art-science," recalling medieval times when music was considered a science along with geometry and astronomy. This being the case, Varèse maintained, there is intrinsic value in musical sound per se, not in what it represents. He asked listeners not to "connect my music with anything external or objective" and asked them not to "try to discover a descriptive programme for it. Regard it, please, in the abstract. Think of it as existing independently of literary or pictorial associations" (quoted in Bernard, 1987, p. 6). This is quite the most radical stance found in all modern music.

The ideas of the cubists in dealing with objects had considerable significance for Varèse. Gombrich (1978) explains how Picasso confronted the problem of painting an impression of an object by "reduc-

ing the forms of nature to a flat pattern" and yet managing to "retain a
sense of solidity and depth" (p. 456). It led Picasso "back to Cézanne," who wrote in a letter to the young painter advising him to
"look at nature in terms of spheres, cones and cylinders" (p. 456).
Picasso and his associates took this advice literally and built their
paintings as "constructions" of geometric objects rather than as mere
copies of something. The problem then became one of juxtaposition
of shapes and ultimately of design. It was in such a context that the
influence of primitive art and design assumed such significance for
Picasso and the cubists. The designs they saw in Native American
totem poles, for example, provided some inspiration for dealing with
their own design problems. During the 1890s and 1900s several
groups of Native Americans traveled to Paris to demonstrate their
music, and carvings, and paintings. In particular the Kwakiutl people
of the Pacific Northwest, a tribe particularly famous for its carvings of
totem poles, made a big impact. The essential "paradox of painting,"
as Gombrich calls it, concerns the representation of depth on a two-
dimensional surface. "Cubism was an attempt to . . . exploit" this
paradox for "new effects" (Gombrich, 1978, p. 458). In fact, newness
for its own sake became a kind of watchword or rallying cry, and what
became important to artists were "problems of form . . . [and] . . .
form always comes first and the subject second" (p. 461).

Paul Klee (1879–1940) came to Paris in 1912 and found the city
"agog with cubism" (Gombrich, 1978, p. 463). He later explained
something of his technique, which is derived from cubist methods of
representing reality. He began by

> relating lines, shades and colors to each other, adding a stress here, re-
> moving a weight there, to achieve the feeling of balance or rightness after
> which every artist strives . . . forms emerging under his hands gradually
> suggested some real or fantastic subject to his imagination . . . he fol-
> lowed these hints . . . [so as not to] hinder his harmonies by completing
> the image that he had found. (Gombrich, 1978, p. 461)

More significantly, he likened this process to the same "mysterious power that formed the weird shapes of prehistoric animals, and
the fantastic fairyland of the deep sea fauna, which is still active in the
artist's mind and makes his creatures grow" (p. 462). This gives a clue
to the main force behind cubism: the process of creation whereby the
artist manipulates the shapes derived from an object being represented, thus creating a work of the imagination derived from the artist's
perception of the lines, shades, and colors. Process, then, is the most

important feature. There is no method save that dictated by the individual artist engaged in creational activity. Picasso put it this way: "art is not the application of beauty but what the instinct and the brain can conceive beyond any canon" (quoted in Gombrich, 1978, p. 463). He advocated ordered comparison and judgment rather than the instinctual mode of operating of the impressionists.

Varèse assimilated these ideas and applied them to music. He explained that

> Genius . . . is above morality: for its only duty is to create and consequently to live . . . beauty in art is a relative result obtained from a mixture of different elements, often most unexpected . . . novelty [is the only permanent element] . . . the demand is for freedom of conception, the renunciation of taught formulas, a tendency toward all that is new. (quoted in Bernard, 1987, p. 4)

He was also fond of quoting Debussy's famous aphorism that "works of art make rules but rules do not make works of art" (quoted in Bernard, 1987, p. 5), and Picasso's mocking comment about those who want to understand art—"everyone wants to understand art. Why not try to understand the song of a bird?" (quoted in Gombrich, 1978, p. 461)—seems to be never far away from his thoughts. Varèse disliked any attempt at analyzing his music and appears to have actively thwarted the efforts of those who tried. However, an insight into his thoughts can be obtained by considering his commitment to process, like the cubists, and to their predilection for presenting the geometric aspects of an object in various juxtapositions, including rotations, simultaneous presentation in layers, and variants on these processes.

Varèse applied this to music by utilizing elements such as rhythm, pitches, chords, blocks of sound, and timbres in the same way as cubists used geometric shapes in their painting. One important feature he developed was a sense of the vertical aspect of structuring sound, vertical in the sense of pitch in blocks of sound. According to Bernard (1987), this is possibly the most important clue both to his compositional processes and to understanding the structures he produced.

Initially, Varèse—not surprisingly—had some difficulty in applying cubist principles to musical composition. But this was mainly because of the limitations of the available instruments. He had only the traditional orchestral instruments, designed to play symphonic music, and the array of percussion instruments he could muster from many different sources. As a result, the kinds of transformations he attempted were extremely difficult to bring off. It was only when he was able to use electronically generated and controlled sound sources, during the early 1960s, that he was fully able to develop and explore his unique and highly revolutionary ideas for music. Nevertheless, he composed some extraordinarily challenging music for conventional instruments during his first stay in America, from 1915 to 1928 (when he returned for a short time to Paris, returning to America in 1933). He was aware, however, of the need for new instruments, that would enable him to realize his ambitions. His interest in science, which predated his move to America, led him to study the works of Helmholtz and other scientists who wrote about acoustics and to become acquainted with the ideas of Busoni.

For Varèse, the idea of a scientific explanation of musical sound and auditory perception was especially appealing, particularly in view of his concern to create musical structures that utilize sound in such novel ways. Such explanations not only gave him insights into the problems and limitations of existing instruments but also suggested ways of constructing new instruments and new scale systems as well as how these might be processed by the human ear. Clearly, he ignored the implications of Helmholtz's theory concerning pitch perception, concentrating instead on the broader applications, which opened up a new field of musical composition utilizing knowledge about all the parameters of sound, not just pitch.

He traveled to Germany, met Busoni, and was particularly impressed with Busoni's "Sketch of a New Aesthetic of Music" (1911/1962), in which he found ideas similar to his own. This statement, which appeared in 1911—at the time when Varèse was beginning to formulate his own new aesthetic—described a new music that rejects the existing system of tonality and instrumentation in favor of a greater freedom for the composer: "Music was born free; and to win freedom is its destiny" (p. 77). Busoni placed music above poetry in its "untrammeled immateriality," for "even the poetic word ranks lower in point of incorporealness" (p. 77). Thus Busoni used an old Platonic argument to new ends—a new musical aesthetic based on the world of musical sound set free from existing theory. However, Busoni was still a Platonist at heart in one sense: "but all arts, resources and forms ever aim at one end, namely, the imitation of nature and the interpretation of human feelings" (p. 77).

Varèse did not go along with this sentiment entirely, for he always maintained that his works represented nothing outside of music. The aspects of Busoni's theoretical stance that most attracted him were those that rejected Pythagorean harmonics as the basis for musical composition and advocated new scale systems based on microtonal intervals and new instruments to play such sounds. In this he found Helmholtz's great tome of immense value, for Helmholtz went into considerable detail about different scale systems across the world and the possibilities inherent in building scales on intervals other than the diatonic.

After criticizing the continued adherence to Pythagorean proportions as the basis for melody, Busoni (1911/1962) stated that "all signs presage a revolution, and a next step toward that eternal harmony" (p. 95). He went on to explain his use of quarter tones and other divisions of the whole tone. Then he commented on the value of electronic generation of sounds: "I refer to an invention by Dr. Thadeus Cahill [the Dynamophone of 1906]. He has constructed a comprehensive apparatus which makes it possible to transform an electric current into a fixed pitch and mathematically exact number of vibrations" (p. 95). But Varèse's interest moved from acoustics to science in general, and it was from the broader world of science that he drew his inspiration in composition.

The clue to Varèse's compositional structures and his musical expressionism lies in his lectures given across the United States during the 1920s and 1930s. In 1917 he wrote: "I dream of instruments obedient to my thought and which with their contribution of a whole new world of unsuspected sounds, will lend themselves to the exigencies of my inner rhythm" (quoted in Schwartz & Childs, 1978, p. 196). It is in such statements as these that one senses the full impact of cubist thought on Varèse's emerging compositional style and processes. His strivings with conventional instruments and the aesthetic problems this caused is reflected in a speech he gave in Santa Fe in 1936:

> When new instruments will allow me to write music as I conceive it, the movement of sound-masses, of shifting planes, will be clearly perceived in my work, taking the place of linear counterpoint. When sound-masses collide, the phenomena of penetration or repulsion will seem to occur. (quoted in Schwartz & Childs, 1978, p. 197)

The advances in his thinking beyond cubism and into the purely musical realm are shown in his identification of three dimensions in music: "horizontal, vertical, and dynamic swelling and decreasing" (quoted in Schwartz & Childs, 1978, p. 197). He speculated on the addition of a fourth, sound projection, likening sound to a beam of light making a journey through space.

Further, in the same speech, he indicated that these four dimensions are to be regarded as equal partners in the process of composition and, by implication, in the aesthetic perception of his music: "the role of colour or timbre would be completely changed from being incidental, anecdotal, sensual or picturesque—it would become an agent of delineation . . . an integral part of the form" (quoted in Schwartz & Childs, 1978, p. 197).

In a lecture given at Princeton in 1959, entitled "Rhythm, Form, and Content," he described electronic generation and control over sound as "our new liberating medium." He redefined rhythm as "the element in music that gives life to the work and holds it together. It is the element of stability, the generator of form . . . that intervenes at calculated, but not regular, time lapses . . . it is too often confused with metrics" (quoted in Schwartz & Childs, 1978, p. 202). He went on to liken his compositional processes to the formations of structure found in crystals: "Crystal form itself is a resultant rather than a primary attribute. It is the consequence of the interaction of attractive and repulsive forces and the ordered packing of the atom" (p. 203). This, he said, "suggests, better than any explanation I could give, the way my works are formed . . . the possible musical forms are as limitless as the exterior forms of crystals" (p. 203). He likened the processes of atoms, which are limited in scope and number but are manipulated to form the various exterior shapes we know as crystals, to those he employed in various manipulations of musical "atoms"— pitches, rhythms, timbres, durations—within the four dimensions of musical space—horizontal, vertical, dynamic, and projection into space.

Bernard (1987) explains in detail how these ideas can be extracted from the musical scores of Varèse. He examines several possibilities, including the notion of pitch symmetry formulated through fixed relationships based on the equally tempered scale and their possible rotations. In this each pitch interval is not interchangeable in the normal manner: fourths are not seen as inversions of fifths, for example, but as distinctly different pitch classes. Various other processes involve ways of using pitch intervals in rotation, inversion in the strict sense, and expansion.

The analogies with cubist conceptions of visual space are obvious. In the program notes to the first performance of *Déserts*, in 1954, Varèse mentioned his self-generated method of composition and the way order grows from within, just as in crystallization. At the first performance of *Integrales*, in 1925, he asked his listeners to "visualize the changing projection of a geometrical figure on a plane, with both plane and figure moving in space, but each with its own arbitrary and varying speeds of translation and rotation" (Ouellette, 1968, p.

83). The spatial qualities of *Integrales* are clearly the most significant. The work, which lasts just under twelve minutes, is scored for small wind orchestra and percussion—two piccolos, two clarinets, oboe, horn, trumpet, piccolo trumpet, three trombones, and seventeen percussion instruments. Projections in space in different planes was how Varèse (Ouellette, 1968) described its structure, and the term *sonic beams* seemed to express most aptly how he viewed the work. As Ouellette (1968) points out, the term *spatial music* was first formulated in relation to this work, making the year of its first performance an important event in the history of music. However, an interesting insight is given by a pupil of Varèse, Marc Wilkinson, who intimates that Varèse "lacked the facilities he needed" (Ouellette, 1968, p. 82) and was hampered by the limitations of conventional performance—the instruments available and their capabilities.

In 1931 Varèse completed a work considered by many to be one of the "masterpieces of twentieth century music" (Ouellette, 1968, p. 120)—*Ionisation*. The title refers to the process by which atoms and molecules, by becoming ions, enable a solution or matter to conduct electricity. Varèse found the process attractive by virtue of its generative implication for producing a great variety of structures, just as he had come to see another chemical process, crystallization, as a metaphor for his compositional process. The piece is for percussion instruments only. The absence of traditional musically pitched sounds proved to be quite startling. However, Varèse was able to demonstrate that his structural methods were not at all dependent upon pitch and that his notion of vertical blocks moving through temporal space could be applied to blocks of percussive sounds. Thirty-seven percussion instruments are required, including two sirens, brake-drums, and gongs, to be played by thirteen percussionists. It was first performed in New York in 1933. Another performance in Havana, later that year, moved a Los Angeles critic to comment that "emotional depths are touched by *Ionisation* as by a sculptural masterpiece of geometric abstraction" (quoted in Ouellette, 1968, p. 121). It seems clear, however, that Varèse's conceptions of process and form could not be fully realized until he had more complete controls over the sounds he was sculpting in space.

The nearest he came to having at his disposal the ideal instruments was in 1956 for the performance of his *Poème électronique* at the Philips pavilion at the World's Fair in Brussels. Here he had the most up-to-date electronic technology available, yet still it seemed inadequate to him for realizing fully the conceptions he had. He collaborated with Le Corbusier in the construction of the pavilion and the music. It was Corbusier who insisted on having Varèse, rather than Walton, Copeland, or Landowski; Xenakis fully supported this choice, which was not popular with the Fair officials.

But by this time Varèse's ideas were becoming known by the younger generation of composers in Europe—Boulez, Stockhausen, and Xenakis in particular. And it was through such contacts that his ideas have lived on after his death (in 1965) to become a major force in what can be described as *thinking in sound*—the new approach to composition following the growth of electronic- and computer-assisted compositional techniques.

THE USE OF NUMBER IN METHODS OF ORGANIZING
THE SONIC OBJECTS OF MUSIC

The so-called twelve-note method of composition developed by Schoenberg and his school in the early decades of this century provided the departure point for later composers in the middle of the century to develop new ways of organizing sound. Since the elements of music had been expanded from the fixed pitches of the diatonic system to include all elements of sound, it was necessary to find ways to structure compositions. The use of number series was an obvious step forward from random or intuitive juxtapositions of sounds. Although Varèse never resorted to any method of serial composition, as far as is known, it was inevitable that a new generation would include those who required something more structured than mere intuition or incipient chaos.

Olivier Messiaen, in the early years after the Second World War, carried the message of integral serialism, a method of organizing all elements of musical sound, to the younger generation. But this method was not entirely new; Webern had intimated its possibilities earlier. Basically, the idea is to submit the four very basic elements of musical sound—pitch, rhythm, dynamics, and timbre—to organization by means of number series. Each element in the four would have a number series of its own, and its extent would depend upon the number of items in the element. For example, in the case of traditional musical instruments, each octave comprises twelve semitones, therefore the numbers 1–12 are used; there may be seven levels of dynamics, in which case the numbers 1–7 are used, and so on. Each item in each element would be assigned a number, not necessarily coinciding with the order in which each item might appear on the instrument. The various number series, that is, one for each of the four elements, would then be organized into various orders of numbers and the arrangement of numbers could then be translated into sounds. In a most prosaic manner, this is essentially how serialism works in theory. In practice it is usually less prosaic and simplistic, a fact that can only be appreciated by analyzing the construction of an actual piece of music.

In the concluding three sections of this chapter, this is precisely what we will do. The work to be examined—Stockhausen's Piano Piece No. 1—is an illustration of how the notion of the autonomy of sound can be described as a logical step forward, musically, from the notion of the autonomy of music mentioned in Chapter 4, and how this newer notion has been achieved in the practices of musical composition.

Karlheinz Stockhausen's early piano works contain illuminating examples of the process at work. In particular, the Piano Piece No. 1 shows how the young Stockhausen applied the process to an acoustic instrument, the piano. This is a much more difficult task, considering the nature of the piano, than applying such processes to electronically generated and controlled sound. The technology of the 1950s was not sufficiently sophisticated or accessible to enable such application to occur, and one gets the feeling that Stockhausen demanded more in theory than it is possible for acoustic instruments to realize in practice. The composer himself suggested this during discussion of his work at a Cambridge University seminar (Stockhausen, 1971).

The piano has certain limitations because of its structure and mechanism (via a complex mechanism, strings tightened on a metal frame are struck by hammers activated by fingers hitting keys), making the realization of some resulting sounds very difficult in execution. The details of the analysis below illustrate the comparative inadequacy of existing instruments in responding to the possibilities for organizing sounds of which these new compositional procedures are capable.

The complexity that results from these procedures, for both performer and listener, have led many to conclude that serialism itself too readily succumbs to extreme esotericism or obscurantism, resulting in music that is artistically moribund. Its products, however, have never been fully understood or appreciated. This has partly to do with their complexity and partly to do with the emergence, during the 1960s and 1970s, of freer, more improvisational styles. With the rise to prominence of the microcomputer, digital synthesizers, and the Musical Instrument Digital Interface (MIDI) since the early 1980s, various serial techniques, or at least their derivatives, have come back into fashion. Greater controls than ever are now possible with this new microchip technology. And there seems to be no known physiological or psychological information indicating that humans cannot cope with the complexity produced by such compositions.

Stockhausen's Piano Piece No. 1 applies integral serialism less rigidly than the theory might suggest. Its complexity is unquestionably a hurdle to be overcome, but familiarity with the piece and its constructional contents reveals a rich palette of musical ideas.

An Overall Structural Principal

The work is one of a set of four composed in 1952–1953. It was first performed at Darmstadt Summer School in 1954 by Marcelle Mercenier. Stockhausen (1964) describes the significance of the piece and the impact it had on the musicians who heard it at that first performance. He reports that the audience responded by whistling their own improvised "groups," a group being defined by the pause that precedes and follows a series of sounds. The group stands alone, much like the collection of sounds that Debussy employed in his incipient use of group form in works such as *Jeux*. There is no functional relationship in the diatonic sense between the groups or within groups. The pause between groups draws its character from the groups that surround it. Stockhausen (1964) states that

> one of the ways into the music is to pay particular attention to when and how the pauses occur, and how relatively long or quiet they are felt to be. This depends upon the group both before and after; whether the sounds are dense, or thinly textured and so on. The aim is to experience in these sudden silences, or gradual pauses, as much as we experience in the notes themselves. (p. 19)

He adds that whoever senses this experiences the music much more deeply as a result. He further explains that a group is a "definite number of notes which through related proportions are connected to a quality of experience or a higher order . . . it is necessary to listen to every detail rather than try to relate to some vast pre-ordained scheme. A group has an atomized structure" (p. 63). In defining a group as a definite number of notes, he is merely saying that the notes that occur, whether they are single notes, dyads, triads, or whatever, comprise the group. At first this appears to be a stark, somewhat tautological, and rather banal statement, like saying that what you see as you look in a certain direction comprises the elements of the scene you are looking at. But it does have certain implications for the perceiver; it is necessary to listen very carefully to every detail contained in the sounds and to impose meaning purely in terms of the acoustic events themselves through the impact of these juxtaposed details. He goes on to give some hints on how to do this and the message is clear: he is propounding the nature of the listener's auditory perception of theoretical relationships based upon the atomization of sounds. What follows is a fairly detailed analysis of the structure of Piano Piece No. 1.

A New Musical Language

Stockhausen maintains that this is a new musical language; and this piece, the first conscious example of it, became a stimulus for others to compose in similar style. An experience of a higher order is achieved, we are told, as one perceives the relationships formed by individual sounds into groups, the groups into series of groups, and the series of groups into the whole piece.

There are no ethical considerations involved in the experience; it relies on what can only be termed a value-free sensory experience of sound, wherein the auditory perceptual apparatus is dealing with stimulation for which there is no precedent musically, no value system aesthetically, and no ethical tradition to explain it, save the science of acoustics and psychoacoustics. It is, in fact, structure per se that one is asked to consider, but a structure filled with sounds that are themselves semantically autonomous.

In order that one may perceive the natures of both the micro- and macrostructures, Stockhausen (1964) gives certain hints and points of departure. He explains that "there are six series of groups in this piano piece, each with six groups in a series, making 36 groups in all" (p. 68). However, he only gives details of the first two series of groups, as follows:

Series 1	*Series 2*
Group 1 = bar 1	Group 7 = bar 8
Group 2 = bar 2	Group 8 = bars 9 and 10
Group 3 = bar 3	Group 9 = bar 11
Group 4 = bar 4	Group 10 = bar 12
Group 5 = bars 5 and 6	Group 11 = bar 13
Group 6 = bar 7	Group 12 = bar 14

This shows the beginning of the macrostructure of the piece. The microstructure is contained in the number of notes in each group. The first group, or bar 1 (see Figure 5.2), has ten attacks (i.e., ten different sounds), which go from lowest to highest pitch register in a climbing movement. More of the auditory scenery in this first bar, which is

FIGURE 5.2 Group 1 from Stockhausen's *Piano Piece No. 1*

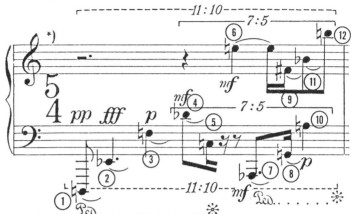

Nos. 1-6 = first hexachord
Nos. 7-12 = second hexachord

Group 1, is described: two intervals are falling, thus dividing the group into two subgroups. In the first subgroup the notes are distinguished by wide dynamic variation, whereas in the second they are more similar in dynamics. The use of pedal builds up a large cluster or chord as each attack is added. Stockhausen describes Group 2 similarly, and from this kind of detail he derives what he terms correspondences between groups.

By correspondences he means a complex set of relationships between different parameters of sound that may affect several groups in different ways. A correspondence does not mean repetition of previously used groups in the sense of thematic correspondence, nor variation, but rather correspondence in a kind of structural connection between elements of the sounds. It occurs in many different ways, and the listener should refer back to groups already heard to perceive, for example, elements like the average dynamics of Group 1, or the average tempo in Group 2, or the length of time that Group 3 lasts. These comprise the type of information from which correspondences can be perceived. Stockhausen provides some examples: Group 3 corresponds to Group 8 by means of individual lengths of sounds and silence. Other correspondences can be deduced from studying the score: Group 5 reminds one of Group 11 in that the rhythmic structure of each is similar (see Figure 5.3).

One is not an exact copy of the other, but the nature of correspondence might be described thus: in Group 11 the first half is identical in note values to that of Group 5, whereas the second half relates 32nd notes to an identical length of time expressed in 16th notes. The pitch

FIGURE 5.3 Examples of correspondence in Stockhausen's *Piano Piece No. 1*

Group 5 2/4

Group 11 2/4

range of both groups is almost identical: Group 5 spans six octaves and Group 11, six octaves. In dynamics, one reflects the other but at a lower level of intensity: in Group 5 dynamics levels are *f*, *ff*, *sffz*, and *fff*, while in Group 11 they are *mf*, *f*, and *ff*. Correspondence could be suggested in that the range from *f* to *fff* is similar to that from *mf* to *ff*.

The whole piece can be analyzed into six series of groups comprising thirty-six groups, as suggested by Stockhausen, although he does not supply details of such an analysis. Figure 5.4 shows an analysis worked out from the hints and clues provided by the composer. He talks of proportional relationships between the six groups of the first series and gives them as follows:

Group 1 = $5/4$
Group 2 = $2/4$
Group 3 = $3/4$
Group 4 = $3/8$
Group 5 = $4/4$
Group 6 = $6/4$

This gives the proportions $5 : 2 : 3 : 1 : 4 : 6$, a set that corresponds to the number of quarter notes contained in each group ($3/8 = 1/4$). Accordingly, the analysis is carried out based on the relationship between quarter-note equivalents within each series of six groups. The definition of groups by silences is also helpful in determining the identity of each group. The result is a fairly clear progression of groups into six series. The scheme of related proportions of quarter notes in the six series spanning the whole piece becomes as follows:

Series 1 = 524146
Series 2 = 365421
Series 3 = 264315
Series 4 = 146253
Series 5 = 651432
Series 6 = 135264

FIGURE 5.4 The six series of groups in Stockhausen's *Piano Piece No. 1,* showing related proportions of quarter-note equivalents

Series 1

Group numbers	1	2	3	4	5	6
Bar numbers	1	2	3	4	5-6	7
Time signatures	5/4	2/4	3/4	3/8	2/4	6/4
Related proportions of quarter notes	5	2	3	1	4	6

Series 2

Group numbers	7	8	9	10	11	12
Bar numbers	8	9-10	11	12	13	14
Time signatures	3/4	4/4&2/4	5/4	4/4	2/4	1/4
Related proportions of quarter notes	3	6	5	4	2	1

Series 3

Group numbers	13	14	15	16	17	18
Bar numbers	15-17	18-19	20	21-22	23	24-27
Time signatures	1/8&2/8	6/8	4/4	2/4&4/16	4/16	5/16
Related proportions of quarter notes	2	6	4	3	1	5

Series 4

Group numbers	19	20	21	22	23	24
Bar numbers	28	29-32	33	34-36	37-38	39-41
Time signatures	4/16	4/16	6/4	4/32&5/16	5/8	8/32
Related proportions of quarter notes	1	4	6	2	5	3

Series 5

Group numbers	25	26	27	28	29	30
Bar numbers	42	43-45	46	47	48-50	51-52
Time signatures	6/4	2/4&2/8	2/8	4/4	4/16,5/16,6/32	4/16
Related proportions of quarter notes	6	5	1	4	3	2

Series 6

Group numbers	31	32	33	34	35	36
Bar numbers	53	54	55-56	57	58-60	61
Time signatures	1/4	3/4	5/8	2/4	2/4	4/4
Related proportions of quarter notes	1	3	5	2	6	4

Note: The scheme of related proportions of quarter notes in the six series is as follows:
(1) 523146, (2) 365421, (3) 264315, (4) 146253, (5) 651432, (6) 135264.

It should be noted that these series utilize the numbers 1 to 6 only in defining the rhythmic structure.

Several other, and similar, correspondences between groups can thus be identified from this analysis. By reference to the bar numbers in the score, as indicated in Figure 5.4, using the information relating to Figure 5.3 as a model, and their place in the series as indicated in the full analysis as a reference, other correspondences can be observed from the notations. Further examples are as follows:

1. *Groups that remind the listener of other groups*
   - Groups that build up chords of varying characteristics through the use of pedal: Groups 1, 18, 27, 28, 29.
   - Groups that start with a chord and gradually release notes: Groups 9, 15, 32. They relate in other ways, too, however. Group 9 mirrors Group 32 in pitch placement and dynamics: pitch is high in the former and low in the latter. Dynamics range from *mf* to *fff* in Group 9 and from *pp* to *fff* in Group 32.
   - A high-pitched chord sounding against other activity in Group 21 is mirrored by a lower-pitched chord sounding against other activity in Group 14.
   - There is similarity between Groups 8 and 9 and between Groups 31 and 32 in the way they display movement from a simple chord to a highly complex one.

2. *Correspondence where different parameters relate across groups*
   - Groups 24 and 29 have similar average dynamics: *pp* to *f*.
   - Groups 1 and 30 have similar average dynamics: *pp* to *fff*.
   - Groups 16 and 25 have the highest average dynamics: *fff* to *sfffz* in range.
   - Group 8 comprises a four-note chord followed by two widely spaced single notes. Group 34 is even more widely spaced, comprising a high dyad followed by a low single note, then a widely spaced dyad followed by a high single note.

Although many other types of correspondence can be identified, these examples are meant to illustrate how complex the cross-referencing system is, both as observed from the notations and certainly as heard in performance. However, there are people who both perform and hear such correspondences, accepting them as information from the piece equivalent in function to the tonal relationships found in historical Western music using diatonic intervals and harmony.

The Organization of Pitch

The pitch organization of the piece illustrates the use of serial structure based on different orderings of the two hexachords of the chromatic scale. Each hexachord contains, of course, six notes, so the numbers 1–6 can be applied to each note in the hexachord and used in determining the serial structure. This division into hexachords is maintained throughout the piece, even though at times they overlap in performance. There are 720 possible ways of varying the order of the numbers 1–6 (numbers corresponding to the note-row). Stockhausen's choice of just 36 ways of ordering the numbers 1–6 for each hexachord is shown in Figure 5.5.

This figure shows every pitch utilized in the piece but substitutes a number for the actual pitch. The number is assigned to the pitch as determined by the first appearance of the note in bar 1. The first hexachord is easy to identify in proper order, since the six notes are played in succession. The second hexachord is more problematic in that some notes are played simultaneously; these are presented as underlined. Certain discrepancies are exposed in the form of notes missing from the series at certain points or notes being repeated, as indicated in Figure 5.5. The 36 appearances of the hexachord do not correspond with the 36 groups shown in Figure 5.4; groups and pauses between groups occur at any point in the appearance of the note-row.

A second method of setting out the pitches indicating the appearances of the note-row, or hexachord, is shown in Figure 5.6. This reduces the pitch distance to within an octave above middle C and indicates the actual note names of the hexachords in each appearance. Figures 5.5 and 5.6 can thus be seen as two parallel ways of looking at the pitch organization. The intriguing question is how Stockhausen arrived at the particular order for this piece from the 720 possible orderings of numbers 1–6. It is possible that he used some computer-generated random selection procedure of numbers, or merely selected them from the actual note orderings in an intuitive fashion. Either way, the choice does not appear to have any particular significance: it seems to be entirely without pattern from within the 720 possible orderings. One clue is that the notes at their true pitch level cover the whole range of the piano, just over seven octaves from A two octaves below the bottom space in the bass clef to B two octaves above the top of the treble clef, and this in itself becomes an important piece of information within the scheme of things.

FIGURE 5.5 The 36 successive re-orderings of the note-row used in Stockhausen's *Piano Piece No. 1*, with pitches designated 1–6

Note-Row Order Number	First Hexachord (C-F)	Second Hexachord (F#-B)
1	1 2 3 4 5 6	1 2 3 4 5 6
2	4 5 1 3 6 2	5 3 6 2 4 1
3	6 2 5 1 3 4	4 6 5 2 1 3
4	1 4 5 6 2 3	1 6 2 4 5 3
5	3 5 6 4 1 2	5 5 3 4 1 2 6 *(extra note 5)*
6	4 2 3 1 5 6	4 5 6 3 2 1
7	4 5 1 3 2 *(#6	1 6 3 5 4 2
8	3 6 4 2 5 1 missing)*	5 3 2 1 4 6
9	2 1 6 5 3 4	4 6 3 1 2 5
10	6 5 3 2 4 1	1 5 4 6 3 2
11	4 6 5 1 2 3	2 6 3 1 5 4
12	2 1 6 4 3 5	6 3 2 4 5 1
13	2 6 5 1 4 3	2 6 1 4 5 3 *(sounding with*
14	*(sounding with* 5 2 6 4 2 3	4 5 3 6 2 *1 next hexachord)*
15	*prev. hexachord)* 3 5 1 4 2 6	5 6 2 3 1 4
16	2 3 6 4 1 5	1 6 4 3 2 5
17	4 1 6 2 5 3	3 5 2 4 6 1
18	3 1 6 4 5 2	3 4 6 5 1 2
19	1 4 5 6 2 3	4 1 3 6 5 2
20	3 5 4 6 2 1	2 5 4 6 1 3
21	5 3 1 6 4 2	4 5 1 2 6 3
22	1 5 3 6 4 2 *2 (extra*	1 6 2 5 3 4
23	5 4 1 2 3 6 *note)*	4 5 1 6 3 2
24	5 4 3 6 2 1	3 1 4 6 2 5
25	5 4 1 6 3 2	5 2 6 4 1 3
26	4 1 2 6 5 3	2 6 4 5 3 2 *(#1 missing; #2*
27	6 1 2 4 5 3	4 2 3 1 5 6 *appears twice)*
28	6 2 1 3 4 5	6 3 5 1 2 4
29	2 3 1 6 5 4	4 6 3 1 5 2
30	2 4 5 3 1 6	1 2 6 5 4 3
31	6 5 3 4 1 2	6 1 2 4 3 5
32	6 5 4 3 1 *(#2*	3 4 6 1 5 2
33	1 6 3 5 4 2 *missing)*	6 2 3 1 4 5
34	6 3 5 1 4 2	6 2 4 1 5 3
35	1 5 2 3 4 6	1 5 6 2 3 4
36	4 2 5 3 1 6	3 4 6 4 1 2 *(#5 missing; #4 appears twice)*

FIGURE 5.6 The 36 successive re-orderings of the note-row used in Stockhausen's *Piano Piece No. 1*, with pitches shown on the staff and all intervals reduced to within the scope of one octave

FIGURE 5.6 *Continued*

FIGURE 5.6 *Continued*

Use of Dynamics

The range of dynamics used comprises six different levels: *pp, p, mf, f, ff, fff*. Apart from the occasional addition of *sffz* (once) and *sfffz* (five times) to make a seventh and eighth level, the six basic levels predominate throughout. Little evidence can be deduced from the score of any kind of number series using 1–6 for ordering the appearances of the dynamic levels. The use of dynamics, therefore, becomes one susceptible to the composer's random will, or artistic intuition. Indeed, some of the juxtapositions of dynamic levels are exceedingly difficult to reproduce as indicated on the piano. Group 9 at bar 11 (see full score) is an example of closely positioned pitches high up on the piano requiring that differentiation in dynamic levels be executed by different fingers—a technical feat of extreme difficulty. However, these pitches lie between approximately 500 Hz and 2,000 Hz, an area of great sensitivity for the human ear. Physiologically, therefore, there is no reason why humans should be unable to perceive such differences, even though the notes are clustered together. Difficulty of execution cannot be cited as reason for dismissing new music, as can be demonstrated in the life of Liszt. Given time and an audience's acculturation to new sounds, they can become acceptable.

Physically there is no reason that the information Stockhausen presents in this piece in the different parameters of sound cannot be perceived, and ultimately appreciated, by a wide range of the populace. The austerity and uncompromising nature of the structural schema, its application and execution constitute a feat of musical thinking commensurate with the application of fugal procedures in the keyboard works of J. S. Bach. It is worth noting that we have not earned a good track record, so to speak, in recognizing such musical ingenuity, considering the time it took for general understanding of the music of St. Thomas's cantor to be achieved. This claim for the music of Stockhausen may be greeted with less than wild enthusiasm or approbation by some, but time will tell, to finish with a cliché. It is my bet that time will prove Stockhausen to be the nearest the twentieth century has come to producing its version of J. S. Bach.

Cross-Cultural Comparisons

Since the nineteenth century, there has been an ever-increasing scientific interest in the music of different cultures across the world, reflected in the large number of studies and reports that exist on many different aspects of musical sound and behavior, ranging from the nature of the elements of musical sound to the cultural beliefs surrounding their use. A belief common to practically all cultures appears to be that concerning the power of musical sound to exert some influence over our physical and mental states. A ubiquitous version of this is the belief in the power of songs to heal physical and mental sickness; equally pervasive is the belief that certain sounds are inextricably linked in some way with the character, or *ethos*, of an object, person, tribe, nation, or other group of people. So although Plato articulated the theory of *ethos*, he did not invent the notion (see Chapter 4). In Western traditions, the belief that particular musical elements contain characteristics that betray more general behavioral traits goes back to the very cradle of Western culture; it arose even earlier in the ancient Chinese civilization (see Chapter 3).

MUSIC IN THE AFRICAN-AMERICAN TRADITION

The rise of rock 'n' roll in the United States in the 1950s sparked a storm of protest based on strongly held views that this music had power to corrupt. Hamm (1979) cites a psychiatrist who described rock 'n' roll as "a communicable disease" and a "cannibalistic and tribalistic" (p. 398) form of music. A judge in Florida (Hamm, 1979, p. 399) prepared warrants for the arrest of Elvis Presley on charges of impairing the morals of minors. Further, the *New York Times* carried a column in 1956 complaining that the "selfish exploitation and com-

180

mercialized over-stimulation of youth's physical impulses is certainly a gross national disservice" (Hamm, 1979, p. 400). And in 1961 the great Spanish cellist Pablo Casals described rock 'n' roll as "poison put to sound—a raucous distillation of the ugliness of our times. . . . It is against art, against life. It leads away from the exultation and elevation of spirit that should naturally spring from all good music" (quoted in Hamm, 1979, p. 400). Hamm (1979) further quotes Howard Hanson, who described the music as "acoustic pollution," asking "is this progress? We have lost our sense of values" (p. 400).

All this was little different from the continual criticism leveled at jazz in the United States during the 1920s and earlier. It was described variously as "doing a vast amount of harm to young minds and bodies not yet developed," as "the explanation of America's enormous crime rate," and as having the "power to turn modern men, women and children back to stages of barbarism . . . an activity which may be analyzed as a combination of nervousness, lawlessness, primitive and savage animalism and lasciviousness" (Merriam, 1964, p. 242).

This is all very Platonic, proving that ancient Greek views of music as possessing powers to influence behavior are still alive and well in the twentieth century. Today, toward the end of the twentieth century, one would have to be somewhat bigoted and blind still to hold such views about rock 'n' roll. It is now the staple musical diet of young people all over the world, whatever their class or creed. Various establishments shower awards on rock stars. Various Christian churches have espoused its sounds by using them in religious music, even the celebration of the mass. We can safely say that there is little evidence that rock 'n' roll has corrupted anyone. Elvis is something of a national hero, a show-business demigod, and the Queen of England bestowed one of her honors on the Beatles.

Springing from the sensuous sound of rhythm and blues, rock 'n' roll caught the imagination of white youth during the 1950s and has held it ever since. Here was sensuous music almost at the polar extreme to the intellectual music of the Western traditions, and it provoked a head-on clash between those who supported the intellectualist traditions of Western culture and those attracted by a more sensuous musical practice. The popularity of rock 'n' roll upset the comfortable and traditional belief in Western models of taste and balance in music and confronted the deeply entrenched Platonic belief in the primarily intellectual appeal of music.

Rhythm and blues arose from a musical culture alien to European traditions. It reflected certain African traditions that were kept alive by the descendants of the slaves brought to America from the seventeenth to nineteenth centuries. These traditions, excluding the more serious religious musical practices banned by the slave owners, are from a nonliterate oral musical culture in which music performed functions central to life in agrarian or hunting societies. Charters (1981) found some of the same "traditions of street dancing found in New Orleans Mardi Gras mornings of the late 1950s" (p. 68) in the Mokolo Dance that he witnessed in Banjul in present-day Gambia, on the West African coast. He recognized a technique of performing on the halamkatt that was "very much the same as the banjo players in Virginia and Kentucky" (p. 60). Although these were predominantly white banjo players, they all admitted that they had learned how to play from a black neighbor or from black musicians traveling through. Miller (1980) describes a style called rocking and reeling found in Mississippi Sanctified or Holiness churches during the 1920s and 1930s. This was based on archaic ring shouts and contained "rhythmic singing, a hard-driving beat, a bluesy melody, and the improvised, stream of consciousness words . . . all anticipating key aspects of rock and roll some twenty years later" (p. 3). He cites some 1929 and 1936 recordings by the Mississippi Jook Band that featured "fully formed rock and roll guitar riffs and a stomping rock and roll beat" (p. 3).

The rural origins of rhythm and blues go back to the days of slavery and the psychological influences exerted on the black consciousness from those days. Black music of those times consisted of spirituals, plantation songs, work songs, banjo music, and fiddle tunes and dances—the only music they were allowed to perform, because slave owners felt that to allow music and rituals to be performed would result in slaves' being unwilling to do as they were told. In effect, the owners were determined to destroy all semblance of cultural identity and impose Western ideals on the slaves. Many contemporary accounts describe how the African slaves brought with them their cultural habits of music and dance. Oakley (1976) cites an early-nineteenth-century description of behavior in a newly arrived shipload of slaves:

> They have great amusement in collecting together in groups and singing their favorite African songs; the energy of their action is more remarkable than the harmony of their music . . . we saw them dance and heard them sing. In dancing they scarcely move their feet, but throw about their arms and twisted and writhed their bodies into a multitude of disgusting and indecent attitudes. Their song was a wild yell devoid of all softness and harmony, and loudly chanted in harsh harmony. (p. 12)

A description such as this tells us more about the musical beliefs of the observer than the music itself. It is also redolent of the descriptions of Elvis Presley in his early days:

> When the music started, he'd begin wriggling and he wriggled so hard that quite a few cities banned him for obscenity. "Elvis Presley is morally insane" shrieked a Baptist pastor from Des Moines. (Cohn, 1969, p. 25)

Without doubt Presley "derived his whole approach and style from the negro rhythm and blues performers" (Keil, 1966, p. 44). The words of a Clara Smith song from the 1920s illustrate the origins of Presley's style of movement: "You move most everything 'cept your feet/Called whip it to a jelly, stir it in a bowl" (Oakley, 1976, p. 121).

Clearly black music had nothing to do with Western notions of morality or immorality. It was merely the way blacks did things, an innate and spontaneous outpouring of musical activity from their cultural origins. It may well be futile now to try to identify elements in contemporary African musical practices that might relate to those characterizing black rhythm and blues and derivative music, but the links are real enough. Charters (1981) describes his searchings for the African roots of the blues and admits that "I understood, finally, that in the blues I hadn't found a music that was part of the old African style and culture" (p. 127). However, there were clear signs of connections in other ways. "Things in the blues had come from the tribal musicians of the Old Kingdoms, but as a style the blues represented something else. It was essentially a new kind of song that had begun with the new life in the American South" (p. 127).

The American slaves found themselves in a society motivated by Platonic views on life; everything they did was interpreted through this intellectual filter. An account from the London *Times* correspondent at the time of the Civil War explains how "it struck me more and more . . . as I examined the expression on the faces of slaves, that deep dejection is the prevailing, if not universal, characteristic of the race" (quoted in Oakley, 1976, p. 14). This reflects a Platonic belief in the universality of specific physiognomic properties in all things, including human faces—a revealing of the internal by the external. The same interpretation was put on music. A description from the same period of slaves singing while rowing a party of whites across a river explains how "the tone of voice in which this boat-song was sung was inexpressibly plaintive, and, bearing such a melancholy tune and such affective words, produced a very pathetic affect. I saw tears in the eyes of the young ladies, and could scarcely restrain my own" (quoted in

Oakley, 1976, p. 17). But it should not be surprising that the black new Americans fell back on the African habit of basing songs on rhythms derived from their activities. The strokes in rowing would be slow, in turn producing a slow tempo for their singing. The chants would make use of whatever melodies the rowers knew, including the hymns taught them by their slave masters and owners; many of these hymns were, melodically, sad by design. To Western ears this would add up to a song about the sadness of their plight.

It is clear, however, that black American music did not and does not revolve around such things. Blues songs and slave songs were spontaneous expressions much in the traditions of newspapers; all kinds of activities, feelings, and happenings were sung about in the same way that the popular press reports on varied events. Black songs that are descriptive and light-hearted in their use of words are little different in musical content from those that use sad words or expressions of despair. Tempo and melody are not such clear pointers to the mood of a song or the singer in black American music as they are in European-based music. In fact, it can be said that one reason why the rock 'n' roll movement in music has gained such enormous worldwide popularity and support is that it provides a function for music that is entirely free from intellectualized aesthetic content, one that uses music as an expression of the energy and movement of life, be it as a slave or as an affluent teenager in today's consumer society. It is a reflection of human energy and lifestyle. It is not prescriptive in the sense that Western music derived from Platonic views is.

Bowra (1962) points out that "primitive song is an enhanced art of words," and as far as music is concerned "words, music and movement present a single unity and each element can be judged at its full worth only when it is at work with the others" (p. 28). He maintains that a primitive song arises from movement and to physical movement is owed its important characteristics. Music in such cultures serves to record immediate events, and the response is quick and spontaneous. Keil (1966), writing about the contemporary blues scene in urban black culture in the United States, describes it as a living, growing, developing artform that communicates values and lifestyles. He points out that "overt responses by the audience with the performer are important and vital features of blues musical expression" (p. 213). Most interestingly, he explains that there is a "general deficiency of specified relationship between blues syntax and blues semantics" that would "take a lifetime to close completely" (p. 213). He goes on to state that "it is entirely possible that the most significant aspects of some musical styles are physiological and biocultural . . . music must be seen in many instances as validating movement in much the same way that myth validates ritual'' (p. 214).

The African-American musical traditions are a mixture of Western musical elements and African musical traditions. The black American used the instruments available, which were designed to play Western scales—instruments such as the trumpet, clarinet, piano, trombone, guitar, banjo, and violin. These sounds, although they can be notated in Western notations, do not, however, reflect the beliefs implicit in such notations, and it is a mistake to take the connection any further. The African-American musical traditions represent a blossoming of a musical function entirely in contrast with that of the Platonic role given music in Western culture. It would be a mistake, therefore, to regard it as a musical fusion of traditions. It is more like a new form entirely, with roots in both but more strongly, semantically, in the African traditions of music as a social bond.

ACCEPTANCE VERSUS VERIFICATION
OF MUSIC'S POWERS

In some cultural traditions associations between musical elements and people's behavior is accepted because of belief in the importance of song ownership. A person is given a song and by virtue of this giving also receives the powers of the song, be they behavioral or medicinal. Ownership of the song means ownership of the powers of the song, such that there is a link between the capabilities of the person and the nature and power of the song. In Western traditions, ownership has been less important than either the power of the song or the links between song and behavior. Plato's explication of the *ethos* theory distinguished between the different powers of different songs by linking the character of musical elements with that of the people who performed or listened to such songs. Some songs were considered worthy in that they imitated good or noble attributes; others were not. In other cultural traditions, such distinctions emanate from the intended function of the song rather than its musical propensities and are accepted as the inevitable outcome of the giving; these traditions are less concerned with the concept of comparative worthiness of musical elements than with the actual power of songs and their ownership.

To this extent, music has always held a most important place in life in all cultures. It serves various needs in the relatively mundane as well as the most salubrious aspects of life and in the culturally crucial activities found in all societies. These latter activities, together with the music that inevitably accompanies them, are important markers or expressions of cultural belonging, and what gives them this importance and in fact ties them together is a sense of unanimity of purpose, intent, and symbolic importance in expressing the culture. Even the most technologically advanced societies will not conduct weddings, funerals, sporting events, state occasions, graduation ceremonies, and similar events without some suitable musical accompaniment. The idea of holding such ceremonies in silence is unthinkable and certainly rarely seems to occur in practice. And before the advent of modern medicine it was to music that humanity turned for cures to many types of illness, as the testimony of many writers from ancient Greek and Roman times through to the medieval period indicates.

The inquisitive and investigative proclivities in the Western psyche have long fueled attempts to discover precise correlations between musical sounds and their supposed powers. Some other cultures, accepting traditional beliefs on face value, are less concerned about investigating and explaining the source and nature of such powers than in preserving such traditions and beliefs. The Renaissance introduced into Western thought a skepticism toward most traditional beliefs that both undermined their validity and led to searches for empirical verification of such claims. If any sharp division exists between different cultural attitudes, it is that between a mind which accepts traditional beliefs without question and one which predicates their acceptance on some objective proof and explanation. Societies untouched by Renaissance thought have less difficulty accepting a traditional belief in the power of music to cure ills or contact the world of spirit beings. They are not driven by a desire to verify such powers and identify physical correlates between such phenomena and actual musical elements. In fact, to do so would, in some societies, be considered a serious insult to the spirit from which such powers emanate. These societies know the power of music—know in the sense of believing and accepting the veracity of experiencing music's powers.

In contrast, the path of Western thought since Plato and Aristotle has been one of attempting to classify and systematize all phenomena in order to explain and gain control over any such powers as those, for example, thought to reside in musical sound. Because of the central role of music in early scientific thought, musical phenomena were among the first to be systematically defined and catalogued. Ever since the beginnings of systematization in Western melody and rhythm, from the modal system of ancient Greece through to medieval systems of pitch and rhythm, there has coexisted the much older belief in music's powers. This created a sort of fusion of influences and effects whereby the newer inquisitiveness, the older belief, and the introduction of systems in melody and harmony have come together to create an edifice of theory about music that combines the objective and analytical with the traditional and superstitious, as explained in Chapters 3 and 4.

One result has been the attempt to understand the latter through the tenets of the former, often as though it were a simple matter of investigating cause and effect. Ancient beliefs, however, rely on ancient rites, on ancestors with special powers, or on spirit beings communicating, often through musical sound, in suitable conditions and with appropriate accoutrements. They imply the exclusion of nonbelievers and skeptics and suggest a complex web of interactions and influences that preclude the establishment of simple cause-and-effect mechanisms. One can, of course, no more prove that Roman music was capable of curing a Roman's sciatica, as many ancient writers claimed, than one can demonstrate the transcendental properties of Liszt's music for his nineteenth-century followers. It might be agreed, even by the most skeptical observer, that music has some effect on us; but from our current cultural standpoint in a highly technological and economically sophisticated society, such effects as curing illness and mental transportation can seem like products of wishful thinking. Nevertheless, for those societies, and many across the world today, such effects of music were, and are, precise and powerful.

COMMON BELIEFS IN THE SUPERNATURAL
SOURCE OF MUSIC

Common to many aboriginal societies is the importance of dreams and the communications that occur in this state. One of the most important functions of dreams in many such societies is to facilitate the transmission of complete songs. If anything compensates for lack of an objective or methodological basis upon which to found a theory of musical knowledge and practice, it is the role of dreams in transmitting the musical artifact in a complete and perfect state, requiring only replication. It is commonly reported in many ethnological studies of the Australian aboriginal culture, for example, that Australian aboriginals considered the role of the Dreamtime absolutely crucial to their survival. The Dreamtime is regarded as the truly creative time of their existence. It is the time when they make contact with the supernatural forces that shaped their universe. It is also regarded as the source and repository of songs and, indeed, all artistic activities. Through their ability to dream, the Australian aboriginals can tap what is to them this source of immense power and knowledge. They regard the songs given to them in dreams as having special powers and their own role as re-creating them as faithfully as possible. Wild (1975) reports that the Walbiri people of the Northern Territories do not attribute artistic creativity to any individual, past or present, outside of the Dreamtime. All artistic productions are believed to be re-creations of Dreamtime events, and exact reproduction rather than interpretation is the ideal.

In such a belief system, creativity, as Western thought has defined it, cannot exist. There is no place for the individual as "creator" of his or her own music. This represents a significant and qualitative difference between an aboriginal musician and a Western composer such as Liszt. The latter seeks to create original music that represents a mystical experience so that listeners can indulge their own imagination accordingly. The former sings the songs of the spirits given in a dream, thus replicating, not representing the power of the spirit world. The latter seeks to invent the voice of divine truth as interpreted by the composer, the re-creator, not as given by the source, the creator. One replicates the sound of divine power; the other creates an original and personal impression of it. One is subservient, receiving music from the divine powers through mystical dreams and trances; the other is assertive, creating music to represent divine providence.

However, in other respects certain similarities appear to exist between the Pythagorean notion of the music of the spheres and the aboriginal notion of the music of the spirit world. In both, the role of humans is to create in their own environment the music in which resides the power of forces in another dimension. The Pythagorean belief in the role of numbers as a means of expressing this power and realizing it in musical sound is the Western equivalent of the aboriginal belief in dreams as communication from the spirit world. The former has led to the development of a complex edifice of theory and practice designed to explicate and facilitate the physical realization of the special powers thought to reside in musical sounds. As expressed in the concept of harmony (explained in Chapter 3), these special powers, thought to be of cosmic origin, are supposed to influence the mental and physical state of humanity. The practices of the aboriginals have remained intuitive, a response to personal experience with the songs of the spirit world encountered in states of awareness different from everyday consciousness. Powers from the spirit world, given in song form, are believed to have many different effects on humanity, encompassing everything that happens on a day-to-day basis. There is no evidence in aboriginal cultures of a concern for establishing a systematic relationship between specific musical elements and the powers they hold. This is in marked contrast to the beliefs surrounding Western musical traditions, which, under the inexorable influence of Western rationalism, hold that such relationships, if they exist, should be capable of investigation and identification.

The central importance of dreams is also a feature of life among the Pacific Northwest Indians (Boas, 1888/1964; Densmore, 1939; Halpern, 1967, 1981). Many researchers report that Indians describe how particular songs were given to them in dreams or visions, often by long-dead ancestors or famous chiefs. Among the Indians there exists the practice of ownership of songs. No one who does not own a particular song is supposed to perform it without permission. Ownership can be bestowed, as in marriage gifts, or it can be bought and sold. A person who buys a song is also believed to buy the special gifts associated with it. On the other hand, Indian mythology tells of heroes who were given songs in dreams and visions as a special reward, indicating that the recipient was important and highly esteemed by the spirit people. Halpern (1981) reports Indian song makers' descriptions of how songs are composed. The "skeleton of the song" is the drum rhythm, and syllables become the framework for the melody (p. 12). Sounds from nature, such as wind or rain, form the model for imitation in the conscious act of song creation. But there are powerful subconscious forces at work as well, intrusions from experiences in dreams and trances. Song makers often report that they wake up from sleep, and dreams, with the whole song complete in their head.

To the Indians, songs are the most important means of communicating with powers they consider significant to their existence. There are songs for performance at almost every event in their lives. Just as they believe that supernatural power could exist in humans if they managed to fuse their being with that of the natural world around them, so they also believe that this power is manifest in songs. As Halpern (1967) puts it, "the Pacific North West Indian believed that supernatural power resided in man as well as in nature, and that to be one with nature meant a fusion of power into one being, resulting in the creation of a song" (p. 5). An intervening variable is the role of the animal world in mediating between the spirit world and the realm of human existence. Animals are thought to be capable of a higher level of contact with the spirit world than humans, as well as being closely connected to humans themselves. They are considered either to have been human, as in the case of the bear, and evolved to a higher plane of existence nearer to the spirit world, or to be spirits in concrete form, as certain sea creatures are believed to be (Densmore, 1939).

The notion among the Pacific Northwest Indians that music facilitates contact with the spirit world might be equated with the Western belief that the perfectness manifested in the interactions of the planets can be experienced in related and derivative, perfect musical sounds. The latter notion of power (i.e., perfectness) is rooted in a pseudoscientific explanation of how natural things should ideally relate and interact with one another in perfect harmony, as exemplified in the motions of the planets in the Pythagorean belief system.

MUSICAL TRANSMISSION FROM THE SUPERNATURAL TO THE HUMAN REALM

For societies such as those of the Pacific Northwest Indian or the Australian aboriginal, music contains the essence of powers that exist in the spirit world, and men and women are the purveyors of this power through their ability to sing the power into existence. With such a source for cultural transmission of music, one would imagine that there would be a great deal of flexibility in the interpretation of precise details. One cannot be sure, for example, that the practices perceived in dreams can be accurately reproduced, or even that they are capable of being reproduced. There can be no systematic criticism of performance, since one either knows or does not know, especially in the performance of privately owned songs received in this fashion. There seems no option but to accept that the owner of the song is giving the definitive performance; such performers are, therefore, always right in that they, and only they, know how a song should be performed. But this does not mean arbitrariness. Song makers and song owners among the Pacific Northwest Indians know instantly when a mistake has been made, as many researchers have consistently reported—from Boas in the late nineteenth century to Halpern more recently. They are all clear on one thing: the musical activities of such song makers and owners are not arbitrary in the sense that they do not make up their songs each time they are performed, as some early European travellers believed. Their music making is the product of an orderly musical system, and mistakes in performance are not taken lightly. In fact, punishments for mistakes were formerly quite severe, since musical mistakes are believed to result in misappropriation of the special powers that accompany song performance.

In creating power through singing it into existence, the song owner is considered to have access to the source of life. Thus musical knowledge is power, and such knowledge is omnipotent. This much is clear from the many accounts of those who have collected and studied the music of the Pacific Northwest Indian. This is not to say that their music comes exclusively from dreams. Songs are composed by song makers for various occasions, but central to their religious life and beliefs are the songs that come to certain people in mystical circumstances.

Western equivalents to the notions that music provides access to the source of life and that one can create power by singing it into existence are found in ancient Pythagoreanism. Here music re-creates the harmony of the spheres, the secret of life's power, and musical performance creates this power of harmony. Pythagorean beliefs encapsulate the notion that the harmony of life's power is actually present in musical harmony, with the latter representing or imitating the former in live performance.

Frances Densmore (1939, 1972) reports on numerous songs of the Pacific Northwest Indians that were given in dreams and believed to contain special powers emanating from the spirit of an ancestor or some other entity in the spirit world. These powers range over the whole gamut of existence—from hunting, to marriage, to the cure of illnesses. Such dream songs are also believed to enable their owners to perform socially useful acts, such as locating missing persons or lost articles. Others are used in contests between possessors of magic powers, with song performance forming the nature of the battle.

Such powers cannot be conjured up without performance of the song. It is only in the re-creation of the song in performance that the power residing in the sound can be summoned. Significantly, the musical elements in these songs do not appear to symbolize or represent power; they actually *are* the power. This is substantially different from the notion of representation found in modern Western musical traditions. From Plato onwards, the Western intellect has grappled with various complications of the Pythagorean belief that musical and cosmic harmony are closely linked. It was argued both that music represented or imitated such powers and that musical elements contained intrinsic properties associated with such powers (see Chapters 3 and 4). And by the nineteenth century the notion that music provides access to other realms of existence and knowledge provided further complications: music was neither power per se nor an imitation of it; it became, rather, a means of mental transport to other states of awareness in transcendental works by composers such as Liszt.

SOME FUNCTIONS OF MUSIC ACROSS
DIFFERENT CULTURES

Ida Halpern (1967) reports how Mungo Martin, a famous Kwakiutl Indian carver and song maker of British Columbia, was reproached by other chiefs for giving his songs to her for ethnological study. They felt he had compromised the trust given him by the spirit world in singing his songs to a non-Indian researcher. He replied that he was a sick man when he started singing for her and that "now after a year's singing I sang myself to health and am well again" (p. 4). The songs had such power that the physical production of the sounds in performance was able to restore his health.

This is an important concept and marks a difference from the beliefs of ancient Pythagoreans, who held that the true music of the spheres is inaccessible to human ears; the ideal music and its power is grasped only through contemplation of its nature and perceived only through a study of proportional theory. For the Kwakiutl medicine men, however, the power is evoked or summoned only in the physical act of performance—in fact, in the actual reproduction of the sounds. This is not the same as saying that the power lies in the musical elements irrespective of who performs the song. Although the power of healing, for example, does lie in the sounds, it lies only in the sounds made by the person who owns them. Thus, although there seems to be a need for the ritual act of singing in order to summon the power, the effectiveness of the act is contingent upon the person doing the singing. The apparent lack of any systematic linking of specific musical elements with specific powers might suggest that the elements of music themselves are less important for summoning the power than the involvement of the correct human vehicle. A possible parallel in modern Western music is the perception that only those who sing with the right kind of sound can be said to render a musically "proper" performance of a song: just anybody cannot do so.

Despite a certain need for "proper" performance, there has evolved in the West a belief in the paramount importance of musical elements as the conveyors of extramusical power or meaning. Thus there are certain musical elements deemed appropriate for funerals, others for weddings, yet others for healing sickness, and so on. It is this kind of systematic linkage between specific musical elements and their function that has not yet been discerned in aboriginal music.

Densmore (1939) lists many functions for music in the lives of Native Americans. These include songs connected with legends; songs for potlatch ceremonies, contests of physical strength, various types of dancing and celebrations, and social gatherings of various kinds;

war songs; children's songs; and songs used in the treatment of the sick. Some of these songs were composed by men and women, while many others were received in dreams.

The act of composition is described as intuitive in the sense that the composer merely tried some phrases one after the other until they sounded right. In practically all the activities in which the performance of a song is used to summon certain powers, the performer also carries out associated activities, such as dancing, and dresses according to custom. With such a variety of functions for music, all relating to the complex organization of lifestyles and belief systems, it is difficult to accept that the use of musical elements is entirely random and that intuitive musical behavior signals no systematic use of musical elements.

The Australian aboriginals use a musical system that acts as a kind of mnemonic device for recalling the meanings and associations inherent in the song. The word they apply to this device is *mayu* (Ellis, 1984), which refers to the rhythmic and melodic features of the song, particularly the former. It appears that certain *mayu*s crossed many different language barriers as well as vast tracts of land to become a sort of aboriginal *lingua franca*, enabling different aboriginal tribes to carry what they call song lines, common to a variety of tribes, across the vast Australian continent. It also appears to be a sort of cartographic device, enabling the song maker literally to sing his way across great distances. In this function for song, certain musical elements appear to be associated with specific geographic locations. The *mayu* represents a kind of basic component of a song, which appears to be in the form of certain rhythmic characteristics. Some tribes of Native Americans (e.g., the Ojibwa song scrolls) utilized a system of notating some aspects of songs as a form of musical mnemonic useful in remembering performance details.

However, such practices are far removed from comprising an abstract, systematic theory that determines the organization and use of such elements as melody and rhythm in musical practice. They reflect instead the practical functions and essential use of music in an intricate belief system involving the land, its physical characteristics, the plant and animal life, and the role of humans within these.

IDENTIFYING SPECIFIC MUSICAL ELEMENTS
AND THEIR FUNCTIONS

Western musical theory enables us to classify and identify musical elements with some precision, and from this stylistic features can be identified. In this way it is possible to point with some precision to particular musical elements that are supposed to convey certain meanings, or powers. For example, the transcendental intentions of Liszt's music can be traced, as it were, to specific melodies and harmonies and described technically in musical terms. Provided the belief is there in the mind of the listener, such musical elements will convey the intended meaning. The composer invents the music and applies the meanings, and the listener needs to believe in these meanings. Objective testing for evidence of such meanings is, therefore, rather futile.

Aboriginal cultures attribute much more potent powers to music than does modern Western society. But since these cultures have neither written theory nor systems of musical notation, it is difficult to identify what musical elements are believed to have what powers. The music of such cultures is produced and performed intuitively, but, as has been pointed out, this does mean randomly. On the face of it, it seems unlikely that any culture uses musical elements randomly in the exercising of music's powers, despite the lack of a written systematic theory and notational system. The problem lies in the selection of appropriate analytical tools for identifying any such connections between musical elements and their supposed powers. The use of Western notation as such an analytical tool has obvious limitations, as will be discussed in detail below. For the moment, this is the crucial distinction: one musical practice is supported by theoretical premises and notations for expressing them; others are supported by intuitive acts of communication and expression.

Western music theory reflects a culture that values the predictive and descriptive functions of scientific method—and the resultant ability of humans to shape their destiny and environment. Such a music theory is capable of defining and predicting which musical elements have certain effects. Thus Western man or woman is able to generate at will, without the intervention of superhuman powers, the special effects of music. Western rationalism can approach the question of the functioning of these powers because of the existence of its musical theory. Through it one can attempt to answer questions about the powers of musical elements by empirically establishing psychophysical correlates between acoustical and psychological phenomena. In effect, the Western ideal is the harnessing and controlling of the power of music through a scientific understanding of the precise correlations between musical sound and resultant human behavior.

The other cultures discussed here perceive the role of humans quite differently in relation to what they believe to be the special powers of the spirit world contained in musical sound. Man or woman becomes a willing repository, as it were, for the power of the spirit world. The very existence in memory of songs is evidence of the spirit world's desire to pass its powers on to humanity. Humans thus work in sympathy and partnership with these powers rather than seeking to take charge of them. In such a world, there is no need for a systematic method of analyzing musical elements for the purpose of matching them with specific powers. But is there any substance to the notion of a subconsciously or intuitively derived system of linking specific powers with specific musical elements? In other words, must such a system be consciously organized, as well as written down and codified in the Western manner, in order to exist?

What can be confidently asserted is that all cultures tend to believe that their respective musical practices reflect their respective value systems as both symbols and as more than symbols. They regard musical sound as intrinsically possessing certain powers that pertain to the most important things in life—whether to a notion of scientifically defined perfectness or to the source of ultimate power and creation itself emanating from a spirit world. The ambivalence in Western intellectual traditions about whether musical sound actually contains or merely reflects certain powers is testimony to both a specific Western rationalism and a universal belief in the supernatural origin and power of music. The place of music in the belief systems of all cultures suggests that music itself must be, to some degree, systematically organized, just as the society to which the music contributes such a powerful force is systematically organized.

It might be expected that the subtle yet crucial distinction between a musical practice based on predictive and prescriptive theory and one based on transmission from and response to an intuitive source of musical inspiration would produce musical elements of substantially different character in each. Different, that is, in that the former is created in the human realm while the latter is created in the supernatural realm. But, again, the Western ambivalence intrudes, for as we have seen in Chapters 3 and 4, Western beliefs in respect to music include the notion of divine inspiration for musical behaviors. The question, then, concerns the degree and nature of musical differences between cultures.

But can it be that all music-making is essentially driven by the same or similar forces of belief, that the rise of systematic theory in music has not substantially altered this, and that systems exist in the music of all cultures? Certain aspects of Western theory would seem to support the first two such notions, particularly in the tenets of Pythagoreanism. If so, Western theory might provide some useful ways of identifying the nature of relationships between powers and musical elements that are applicable across all cultures. A brief summary of some attempts to establish the presence of systems in different musical cultures illuminates the difficulties.

From the early nineteenth century onwards, researchers have attempted to discover laws that might indicate the nature of musical systems. Inspired by the utilitarian qualities of Western musical notation, which not only facilitates performance and provides a means for recording music for use after the death of the composer but also enables the identification of correlations between Western musical sound and its effects on people, researchers have attempted to apply this notation to aboriginal music for the same purposes. Western notation, however, is not an objective record even of Western musical sounds. It is a product of Western musical theory and relates to the actions musicians must take to produce sounds from instruments or voice. Nevertheless, despite these drawbacks, some useful information has been gathered, without which all trace of some music from various non-Western cultures would have been lost.

During the 1880s a number of studies presenting songs from various Pacific Northwest Indians as well as the Canadian Inuit were published. Densmore (1926) reports that Carl Stumpf of Vienna published a pamphlet of songs of the Bellacoola Indians of British Columbia in 1886 and mentions that in 1888 Franz Boas published twenty-three Inuit songs with analytical notes. She also reports that, in the same year, 1888, Boas published some songs by the Kwakiutl Indians of the Pacific Northwest. The kind of analysis made from these records of songs can be seen in Franz Boas's monumental studies. From the Western notations of Inuit and Kwakiutl songs, he was able to identify the use of various scales, including the pentatonic, derived from the Western equally tempered system (Densmore, 1926). One is described as identical to Helmholtz's major pentatonic (the black notes on the piano starting on C#); another, to a minor form of this scale (starting on D#).

In analysis of songs of the Inuit, the use of both the pentatonic and the diatonic minor scale is identified (Boas, 1964). Further, Boas cites a Professor Succo, who "calls attention to the fact that the relation of the melodies to their key note resembles that of the Gregorian chants" (p. 244). This was purely an intuitive observation, however, and has little basis in empirical fact or analytical deduction.

The search for organizational systems in the music of non-Western cultures paralleled the search for systems underlying organization of all facets of life. Boas suggested that the formation of a system of social organization and classification of the human universe is a necessary condition of totemism—a most potent force in the life of North American Indians (Lévi-Strauss, 1969). It is unthinkable that music should be the only aspect of human life without any systematic organization and structural use of elements in any culture. The problem lies in identifying its principles in intuitive acts of music-making.

In 1889, Jesse Fewkes and Benjamin Gilman published articles on the songs of the Zuni and Hopi people (Densmore, 1926). These songs became the subject of two varying interpretations. Judging from these songs Fewkes and Gilman denied the existence of any evidence for a sense of scale, as Westerners know it, among these Native Americans. In contrast, John Filmore believed that the Indians have a "subconscious sense of harmony similar to that which is developed in the music of the white race" (quoted in Densmore, 1926, p. 83). Gilman was of the opinion that "in this archaic stage of the art [of music], scales are not formed but forming" (quoted in Densmore, 1926, p. 81). Filmore actually harmonized the Indian melodies in their notated form in the style of Christian hymns in an attempt to demonstrate his thesis that

> sense of key-relationships and of harmonic relations . . . is at least subconsciously present in the Indian mind. For when the melodies are given in the correct pitch [that is in the form of Western notations of major and minor modes] and with natural harmonies the Indians soon come to recognize and enjoy them. (quoted in Densmore, 1926, p. 81)

Without doubt, the work of Boas is of monumental significance in anthropology. His careful recording and description of every facet of life of the Indian and Inuit communities across North America has become a most important source of information about these cultures. Moreover, his resistance to the application of existing theories of universals has influenced such figures as Lèvi-Strauss (Gardner, 1985). He was certainly able to appreciate the subtleties of aboriginal music, but he was unable to record it as objectively and accurately as other facets of their life. For instance, he measured lengths of weapons and tools and weighed various domestic objects. And even his transcriptions of spoken language by means of Western letters and additional symbols probably provide a much more sensitive record of their language than Western music notation does of their music.

More recent work using modifications of Western notations as the basic tool for analysis have produced some interesting insights into stylistic features and structural uses of musical elements. Halpern

(1981), who carried out extensive studies of the music of the Pacific Northwest Indian over a period of nearly forty years, was able to deduce from her modified transcriptional use of Western notations some clear stylistic differences between different song genres. Noting that the Indians themselves "classified songs by genre rather than title" (p. 6), she found, for example, that songs for the potlatch ceremonies all have structural features in common, as do *hamatsa* songs (see below) and social songs.

Potlatch songs are strophic and generally constructed with two basic sections for each verse. The first section tends to have three parts, comprising an introduction, "sustained notes with some embellishments," followed by what she termed "cadence units" (Halpern, 1981, p. 39). The second section has an introduction, followed by what she terms "chain patterns" (p. 39)—that is, repeated patterns of short duration—followed by a cadence section.

She notes that the melodic style of potlatch songs is less complex than that of other genres, particularly the hamatsa songs and that, generally, they use scales with only five or six notes. Considering the nature of potlatch ceremonies, this seems quite significant as an indication of a sense of systematic use of musical elements.

The potlatch was, and is, the central social event of the Indians' life. It is when the host demonstrates his generosity by giving to all his guests: the more he gives, the more prestige he acquires. Potlatch ceremonies can last for several days, weeks, or months, and invited guests come from many miles away. It seems sensible that songs for these ceremonies ought, therefore, to be relatively simple in construction, free from the sort of sophistication that implies secret and individual tribal practices and beliefs, in order that a broad cross-section of people might enjoy them without too much effort. In this sense they might be compared to the communal songs found in many Western traditions, which also tend to be simple in construction in order to facilitate mass involvement. Included in such communal music is modern popular music, with its essentially simple musical structure and content.

In contrast, the hamatsa ceremonies are partly secret and very special to a particular tribe. According to Halpern (1981), the complexity of the music reflects this intimacy and secrecy, which in turn is an intimation of the importance and profundity of the hamatsa traditions. Again, this has parallels in Western musical practices: the music of the Catholic mass, for example, which includes the transubstantiation of bread and wine into the body and blood of Christ, is profound, and often of the highest artistic complexity.

The hamatsa is an initiation rite that apparently began with the

Kwakiutl Indians and spread to other groups, such as the Nootka and Haida (Halpern, 1981). A young man or woman is sent into the forest for a period of time ranging from four or five months to four years. During this time the initiate is to live in a wild state, learn many secrets of spiritual life, and acquire some contact with the natural world of plants and animals. In some ways it is a parallel to, as well as an antecedent of, the Western practice of sending young people on journeys, "grand tours," or to the university.

On the young Indians' return to their families there is a ceremony in which the whole band, or village, welcomes the "wild" man or woman back home. The first part of the ceremony is a secret initiation, but during the second part, which is public, the title "hamatsa" is bestowed on the recipient as a mark of distinction (Halpern, 1981). This ceremony is a culturally important one for the Kwakiutl people, and the artistic complexity of the music reflects both the importance of the ceremony and the secret cultural symbols and beliefs held by the people.

In studying many hamatsa songs, Halpern (1981) found them generally to contain three types of melody: descending melodies; melodies with angular leaps; and pendulum-like, undulating melodies. Variation within these basic styles is considerable and appears in two forms. These Halpern describes as "microtonal pitch migration (as a continuous process in the song) and internalized variation of sections" (p. 24). This basis for construction is capable of yielding enormously complex structures. The continual pitch migration to which Halpern refers, along with the continuous variation of short sections or musical cells within each verse and between verses, creates a structure sensitive enough to symbolize this most secret and sensitive practice and ceremonial.

Songs in the social genre, but not part of the potlatch group, tend to have a comparatively large melodic range, up to a tenth or a twelfth (Halpern, 1981). This is a much wider range than either the hamatsa or potlatch songs possess. In love songs the melodic contour is a descending one, but their typical opening involves an ascending interval. The constructional patterns of these songs are "significantly less intricate than in the Hamatsa genre and less extended than in the pattern-based Potlatch genre" (p. 38). Halpern provides an example of the structure of a love song. It is a strophic song, and each verse comprises two basic sections. In the first section a single motif, or idea, is varied a number of times. In the second section, three different motifs are sung in succession. Between the two sections there is what Halpern terms a "migratory note, without a fixed pitch" (p. 38).

These structural analyses by Halpern constitute a major breakthrough in the search for systematic use of musical elements in the music of the Pacific Northwest Indian. The clear differences by genre that Halpern describes indicate that these people, although lacking a written theory, nevertheless have developed a sophisticated system of music construction that clearly matches musical elements with meaning and function in a manner not entirely dissimilar to that employed in the Western traditions.

Some problems remain, however. As Halpern herself acknowledged, the use of Western notation, even with modifications to account for many differences in intonation between the two musical scale systems, and even with the best of intentions, does obscure some of the nuances of tuning. It is not possible to tell, for example, whether a microtonal change in pitch ought to be regarded as a new pitch or as an intended or accidental modification of the previous one. It can be regarded as either and notated accordingly. Halpern (1981), realizing this, introduced measurements of frequency using a pitch extraction routine whereby precise measurements in cents could be obtained of all pitches.

She was, sadly, unable to follow up this line of inquiry any further due to illness and her subsequent death. Another researcher (Ellis, 1965) had also introduced electronic analysis of frequencies as an aid to identifying pitches and scale systems in aboriginal music, but with the music of the Australian aboriginal.

Following the identification of differential structuring for songs for each genre or type of event in the lives of people such as American Indians or Australian aboriginals, a necessary next step is to identify more precisely the differing characters of the musical elements, particularly pitch. This is difficult enough with the use of microtonal intervals; but considering the proclivities of humans to perceive both language and musical elements in categories (see Chapter 2), it is necessary to take account of these as well.

CATEGORICAL PERCEPTION AND MUSICAL BEHAVIOR

Ellis (1965) provided information on pitch from both intervals and individual pitches. Transforming intervals into cents, she attempted to show how these might be broken down into categories in order to yield scale patterns. However, the problems caused by the human tendency to categorize meant that it was not possible to determine any systematic use of particular intervals from the cent values. There was too much overlap and spread of cent values to provide any coherent pattern. Turning to the individual frequencies instead, she found that a pattern was discernible from the number of times particular frequencies appeared.

In this manner she noted that the distances between the most frequently recurring pitches, or frequencies, could be described arithmetically, rather than logarithmically as in Western scales. She noted that the most predominant intervals tended to be "30 plus 30 plus 15 Hz apart" and that there was evidence of "an arithmetic progression with a basic interval of 5 Hz" (p. 132). There was, therefore, some evidence of a scale system quite different from that used in Western music.

However, the problem of natural human variations in performance makes the task of identifying unknown scale systems extremely difficult. Looking at evidence from Western musical practices as far back as Seashore (1938), there is ample indication that even the most highly trained singers and instrumentalists vary their pitches, admittedly within narrow confines, when performing. In other words, instead of accurately reproducing the intervals of, say, the perfect fifth as 702 cents each time it is performed, it is quite normal for variations to occur around the expected standard, that is, both less and more than 702 cents. In perception of musical intervals, as in the perception of speech phonemes (see Chapter 2), there is evidence of a similar tolerance around an expected norm. Thus in both musical performance and perception it appears that humans will accept nearly correct musical intervals or speech phonemes as being the correct one.

In studies of pitch accuracy in the performance of Western opera singers, I have observed some clear indications of both the existence of this phenomenon and its extent. Assuming that all human behavior is similar in this respect—that is, assuming that no human being will reproduce accurately and precisely the same musical interval with no differences each time it is sung—it would follow that if some pattern of deviations from the expected norm could be derived from studies of Western musical practices, where all the parameters are known, then, by extrapolation, it might be possible to deduce scale patterns from similar data obtained from musicians of other cultures.

Pitch data from three Western singers were obtained and analyzed in the manner explained below. From recordings of actual performances, pitch extraction was carried out on suitable passages and expressed in Hz values. Data were compiled whereby every pitch interval was listed and compared with the known standard tunings. From these it was possible to suggest a normally expected deviation from the expected tuning of any musical interval in singing.

The opening bars of the "Dirge" from Benjamin Britten's *Serenade for Tenor, Horn, and Strings* were chosen both because this work was available in three different commercial recordings, all of which were used in the analysis, and because the tenor soloist is required in this passage to sing unaccompanied. The instrumentalists join him when he reaches the tonic, thus ensuring that he maintains accuracy of intonation throughout and compatibility with the instrumentalists in this respect. The notes sung are shown on the staff in Figure 6.1. The assumption is that all these notes are related tonally and that intervals can, therefore, be calculated between all of them in combination. Accordingly, a matrix of interval relationships was prepared whereby each note formed an interval with each other note irrespective of their position in the melody. The frequency of each sung note was extracted using a pitch extraction routine that has a high degree of accuracy (*Mslpitch*, 1987). These frequencies formed the data in the matrix. From this matrix, interval ratios were calculated between the frequencies of all possible pairs of notes. These ratios were translated into cents using the formula log (base 10) of the ratio of the pair of frequencies divided by the log of 1 cent (see Chapter 2). Since all intended intervals were known, it was possible to match each sung interval with its intended one.

From these data mean scores and standard deviations from the intended cent value, using equal temperament as the standard, were calculated. It became clear that the mean values for each interval class (i.e., semitone, tone, etc.) varied around the intended value considerably. Standard deviations, in cent values, ranged around 20 to 30 cents. This means that one can expect highly trained professional Western singers to deviate by as much as this from an expected interval, as defined by equal temperament, and still sound in tune. This can be characterized as categorical behavior. Such a finding is not new. Seashore (1938) noted considerable deviations in the professional singers he studied, and many investigators since have made similar observations. However, it does supply us with some sort of standard by means

FIGURE 6.1 The pitches sung in the opening bars of the "Dirge" from Britten's *Serenade for Tenor, Horn, and Strings*

of which we might study the intervals sung by singers using unknown scale systems. The details of the deviations and the means scores are shown in Figure 6.2.

Since the cent values are constant throughout the pitch range, irrespective of their actual value in cycles per second, or Hz, it is possible to reduce all values to within 100 cents. Thus an interval of 720 cents intended to be a perfect fifth (700 cents in equal temperament) can be shown as 120 cents, just as an interval of 220 intended to be a whole tone (that is, 200 cents) can be shown similarly as 120 cents. This was done for ease of comparison. Accordingly, all cent values have been reduced in Figure 6.2 to deviations around 100 cents. Mean values for each interval sung were calculated by taking the mean of all intervals sung in each class. Thus all the fifths sung contributed to the mean score for fifths, and so on. Each mean shown in Figure 6.2, therefore, represents several sung intervals.

It can be seen that most of the mean values observed range approximately 10 cents on either side of the expected mean value. Thus one might expect mean values of singers of unknown scales to deviate the same amount around their expected interval. The standard deviations show the kind of ranges one might expect from several performances of the same interval.

Using these data as a guide, similar data were extracted from an Indian singer for comparison and possible identification of the Indian scale the melodies were based upon. The singer was a Coast Salish Indian from British Columbia, a woman in her 70s, who sang three children's songs her mother had taught her before the First World War. One of these songs had five verses. Thus it was possible to compare data derived not only from the three different songs but also from the five verses of the same song wherein the melody was repeated, albeit with some modifications caused by different words being sung.

A similar process was employed to that used in the analysis of the three Western performances of Britten's "Dirge"; that is, a matrix was prepared of all notes sung within each song, and, based on the assumption that all notes interrelated with each other to form a sort of scale, as in Western music, all possible intervals from pairings of notes were calculated in cents. The idea that only the intervals directly adjacent to each other should be used for data analysis was rejected because it was clear that in the performance of the songs each phrase employed many different ways of ordering the same pitches, suggesting the use of a scale.

Table 6.1 shows the suggested intervals, in cent values, that might make up the scale being employed by this singer. The data are derived

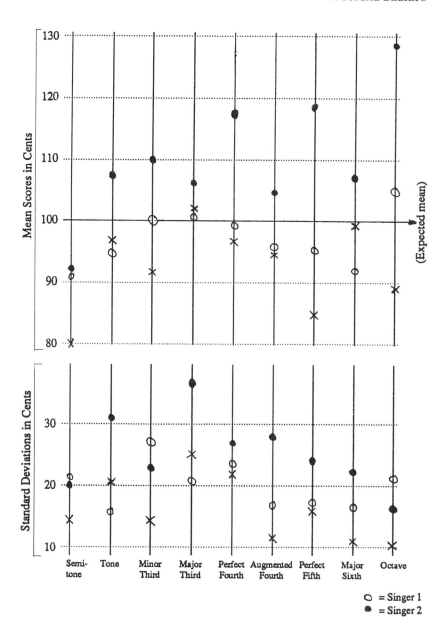

FIGURE 6.2 Deviations from the expected mean for the musical intervals in the opening bars of the "Dirge" from Britten's *Serenade for Tenor, Horn, and Strings* as sung by three tenors, with standard deviations shown for comparison

TABLE 6.1 Suggested intervals used by the Salish Indian singer, shown in cent values

Number	Cents	Number	Cents
1	33	11	701
2	56	12	740
3	80	13	790
4	244	14	215
5	284	15	497
6	320	16	547
7	361	17	588
8	404	18	1023
9	450	19	1071
10	664	20	1385

from mean scores of all interval classes identified. The problem of identifying the interval class is, however, considerable. Several assumptions underlay the choices made. These were as follows:

1. Expected standard deviations from the intended interval of about 20 to 30 cents
2. An expected range of mean scores above and below any intended interval of about 10 cents
3. An expected use of microtonal intervals as reported by all observers of Indian singers from Boas onwards
4. An expected close proximity of several different interval classes, making choice difficult

To facilitate the identification of intervals, all cent values were marked on graph paper, as shown in Figure 6.3. When depicted in this way, certain obvious groupings of intervals suggest themselves, as indicated in Figure 6.3. By marking off each group in this manner across all the intervals sung, and by calculating mean interval values in cents for each interval group, as indicated, a set of means was obtained. It was noted that the ranges were generally narrower than those obtained from the Western singers; but since microtonal intervals were expected, this was not considered a problem, particularly in view of the fact that Western diatonic intervals are very wide in comparison.

Using these obtained mean scores, clusters of interval classes began to suggest themselves merely by virtue of their proximity and distance from each other. Admittedly, some of the identifications were less problematic than others, and some required a certain leap of faith

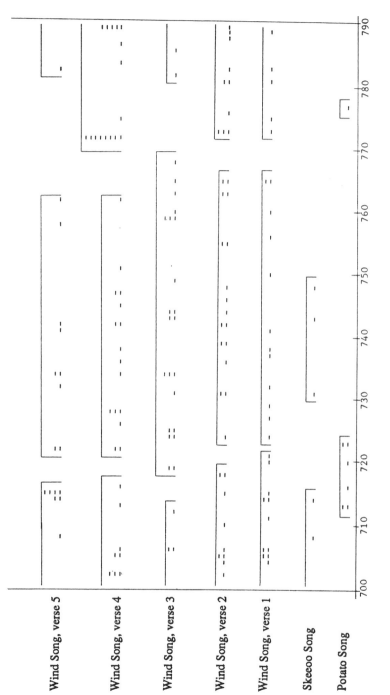

FIGURE 6.3 Distribution of intervals sung by a Salish Indian singer, shown as cent values

rather than purely objective deduction. However, using these obtained means, the classes of intervals shown in Table 6.1 are suggested for this singer. The variation observed in the performance of each single intended interval is an example of categorical behavior. Note the use of three intervals within the space of a semitone between unison and 100 cents and between 200 and 300 cents. This tends to confirm the subjective reports of the collectors from Boas onwards that these Native Americans used small intervals, of much less than a semitone, freely in their melodies. Most of the intervals tend to lie lower than the perfect fifth; and as the interval gets larger, the spaces between them increases. Only a very few intervals lie above the octave.

The problem remains concerning the model used for obtaining these intervals. Were they just reproduced intuitively, out of nothing common to humans, or are they a product of some underlying physiologically and psychologically based process common to all humans? It is to our current knowledge of the relationship between pitch perception and spectral content that we now turn to try to suggest some answers to this particular problem.

RELATIONSHIPS BETWEEN SPECTRAL COMPONENTS OF SUNG AND INSTRUMENTAL SOUNDS ACCORDING TO THEORIES OF PITCH PERCEPTION

Applying current knowledge of pitch perception, particularly what might be termed the "hardware" (that is, the ear mechanism) involved, it seems likely that nonintegrally related scales could easily be devised. If perceived pitch is determined by pattern recognition processes reacting to the spectral content of a waveform, then it would follow that scale systems should relate to such patterns.

In Chapter 2, the ability of the ear to resolve individual harmonics in a complex sound was referred to. Helmholtz claimed to be able to resolve up to the 16th harmonic in a complex sound with integrally related partials, and although this has been shown to be improbable, it does highlight the proclivity of the ear to resolve partials. If the complex wave comprises inharmonic partials, then the problem of resolution should be different from that posed by harmonic partials. The evidence seems to point that way (Benade, 1976).

In complex sounds that contain inharmonic partials, such as those from a drum, the partials do not fuse at about the 8th, as with harmonic spectra. This being the case, it seems probable that the ear can learn to pick out individual partials much higher than the 8th. In view of the demonstrated role in pitch perception of the harmonic spectra of sounds, this is of considerable importance in understanding the scales invented by cultures that use drum sounds as accompanying instruments.

Pacific Northwest Indian cultures are just such musical cultures. A comparison between the partials of the drum accompanying the Coast Salish singer referred to above and the intervals she sang clearly reveals some evidence of similarities. I am not claiming that the drum she used is the definitive source of the scales she employed. It is not certain that the drum she accompanied herself with was the original drum used by her mother, from whom she learned the songs. But there is sufficient evidence to arouse interest in a drum as a contributing, even if not the sole, source of her scale system.

In Table 6.2 the twenty intervals identified in the songs are shown in bands, numerically, in cent values. They can be seen as falling into categories by virtue of the frequency of their occurrence in the songs. There are twelve main intervals suggested, designated as such because each occurs at least 50 times. It is difficult to decide what might constitute a "main" interval; 50 occurrences, therefore, seems as good a criterion as any. Located close to some of the intervals are what might be termed satellite intervals—small clusters of intervals lying just outside the main band width of cent values. Eight subsidiary intervals follow the main ones. These are designated as such because they occur 48 times or less; admittedly, a somewhat arbitrary division designed merely to facilitate analysis.

TABLE 6.2 **The 20 intervals contained in the sample of Salish Indian songs and their frequency of occurrence**

Main intervals (occurrences > 50)			Subsidiary intervals (occurrences < 50)		
Number	Cents value	Occurrences	Number	Cents value	Occurrences
1	30-36	117	13	209-222	38
2	54-58	57	14	492-502	35
3	76-84	63	15	532-562	34
4	230-257	78	16	583-594	20
5	275-294	89	17	780-800	48
6	314-327	73	18	1020-1025	35
7	359-363	83	19	1062-1081	20
8	401-408	76	20	1340-1431	3
9	445-455	81			
10	650-677	59			
11	697-705	80			
12	736-745	79			

In Figure 6.4 the distribution of intervals is shown graphically, and the semitones of the equal temperament Western scale system are shown as 100-cent markers serving as reference points. It can clearly be seen how unlike the two systems are: only a few intervals used by this singer seem to be common in Western traditions. The most frequently occurring intervals in the Salish musical system are clearly unlike those of the Western system. This can be seen by observing the information in Table 6.2 and Figure 6.4. The most frequently occurring Salish interval is that lying the narrow band of 30–36 cents. This occurred 117 times. Other frequent intervals lie at 359–363 cents (83 occurrences), 445–455 cents (81 occurrences), 736–745 cents (79 occurrences), and so on. The use of the fifth was, however, quite predominant. A band ranging from 697–705 cents, coinciding with the natural and equal fifths of Western tuning, occurred 80 times.

A table of drum partials was prepared for comparison (Table 6.3). This was derived from Fourier analysis of the sounds of the drum, about twelve inches in diameter, used in accompanying the Salish songs. These Fourier components varied over time considerably, and this was accounted for in the calculations by using the components that had the strongest amplitudes. The drum sound faded very quickly, and on listening carefully it became apparent that only the beginning of the sound provided sufficient information to make interpretations regarding pitch. This impression was confirmed by three very experienced musicians. Amplitude levels of the spectral components further confirmed this.

Consequently, the Fourier components for the first 30 ms of the sound were used to calculate a set of numbers that might represent human perception of the drum partials. After the first 30 ms of sound, the components varied wildly. The resultant components cannot be presented as the definitive match between subjective human perception and the actual acoustic event, if only for the reason that even during the first 30 ms of the sound there was variation in the components' frequencies. Accordingly, an average frequency value was taken for each component. For example, the fundamental rate was observed to vary between 77 and 93 Hz, and the average was calculated to be 80 Hz. In Table 6.3 these averages are shown in ascending order of partial number from the fundamental upwards. Included is the ratio formed with the fundamental, in each case expressed as a proportion. From these proportions it can clearly be seen that the partials of the drum are not integral multiples of the fundamental, as Western musical theory demands of accompanying instruments. The distance in cents above the fundamental frequency is also shown, but this has been

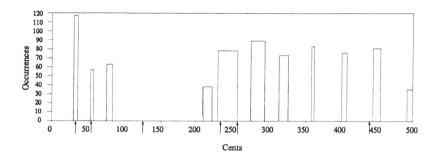

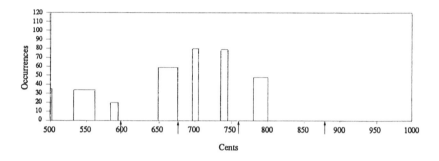

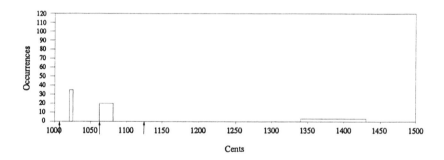

↑ = Drum partial

FIGURE 6.4 Distribution of intervals, in cents, in the sample of Salish Indian songs, with drum partials marked for comparison

TABLE 6.3 Fourier components of pressure waves caused by one beat of the drum used by the Salish Indian singer

Number	Ratio of Fundamental	Hz value	Cents value
1	1	80	0
2	1.48	119	686
3	3.53	283	987
4	4.9	397	371
5	6.23	499	767
6	7.42	594	1069
7	8.26	661	54
8	9.3	744	259
9	10.38	828	444
10	11.3	904	597
11	13.27	1061	875
12	14.32	1146	1007
13	15.36	1229	1128
14	16.31	1305	33
15	17.28	1383	133
16	18.37	1470	238
(and so on up to No. 19)			

Note: Values relate to the loudest part of sound near its inception.

reduced to within one octave for easy comparison with Western intervals.

Thus it would seem that if a singer is acculturated to sounds such as those of this drum, then, according to the theories referred to in Chapter 2 (e.g., Divenyi, 1979; Terhardt, 1974), the scales developed will reflect these inharmonic partials, as in the music of Bali and Java. In Figure 6.4 the relationship between some drum partials and intervals in the songs are shown. The most frequently occurring interval in the song is that lying at 30–36 cents, and this corresponds with the 14th drum partial (33 cents). Another frequently occurring song interval is that lying at 445–455 cents. This corresponds to the 9th drum partial (444 cents).

Absolute accuracy is, of course, not possible in ascertaining the drum partials, and this applies also to some extent to the song intervals, for the reasons given above. These facts, together with the human proclivity for categorical perception and categorical behavior referred to earlier, make these figures even less precise. However, there seems to be sufficient evidence of correspondence between the sung intervals of the Salish singer and the drum partials used in accompanying her singing to suggest that their similarity is more than incidental.

It can be postulated, therefore, that the use of different drums throughout the immensely long history of the Pacific Northwest Indian would provide other kinds of intervals of a similar nature, that is, having nonintegral relationships with the fundamental frequency and between each partial.

As further evidence that the songs of this Indian singer contain some indication of deliberate structural use of musical scales, it can be observed how the main intervals of these songs, intended for children, lie below 700 cents, or the fifth in Western terms. Such a narrow range is found in Western children's songs, as well as those of other cultures. This in itself is not that surprising, since it is obvious that the undeveloped vocal apparatus of children cannot easily cope with wider pitch ranges. What is of significance is that this suggests evidence of the Pacific Northwest Indians' capability for selecting and organizing pitches on a systematic basis. So although there is no written evidence of the use of scales in such music, it seems clear that there is a systematic use of musical scales and song material that suit the purposes for performing songs. It might, therefore, be possible that such musical practices include beliefs in intrinsic semantic properties of musical sounds: a systematic set of relationships between musical elements and their significance. There is no written record, of course, and the further possibility is that knowledge of such systematic relationships is passed on orally.

CHAPTER 7

Towards a Pancultural Approach for Music in Education

The human tendency to invent cultural metaphors was mentioned in Chapter 1, where the invention of musical beliefs that motivate men and women to produce music was presented as a way of viewing the theoretical constructs that guide musical activities. Seen in this way, the enormous edifice of Western musical theory and practice can be placed alongside all other musical cultures as one out of many marvelous examples of human artistic ingenuity. A basic argument throughout this book has been that in order to understand the place of music in human life, it is necessary to understand the belief system within which music is produced. Human belief systems are developed over long periods, and those affecting music form an integral part of the cultural history of any group of people. This history is an important part of the history of human intellectual activity in general; it reflects our pragmatic knowledge base, our beliefs about the world and ourselves, and our interactions with both our own kind and the powers that historically were believed to lie above human existence and knowledge. This was discussed in earlier chapters concerning Pythagoreanism and the belief systems of the Kwakiutl Indian.

In practically all cultures, music, more than other artforms, has held a unique place in the human quest to rise above the immediate environment. The practices of the art of music reflect ideas and beliefs relating both to human aspiration and superhuman powers. Music has traditionally been regarded as both the key to knowledge lying beyond the human domain and the source of that knowledge itself. Equally traditionally, music has held an important role in education in all cultures for precisely these reasons.

In fact, of all subjects in the curriculum, music is one of the oldest and most important. In the West it has been a part of educational practice from the time of the Pythagoreans onwards. In other cultures music plays a significant role in initiation rites, for which young children are prepared from an early age. In early Western culture, it was an essential part of the main fabric of the curriculum; indeed, as explained in Chapter 3, the theory of harmonics dictated the subjects chosen for the school curriculum which were relayed through time to become the *quadrivium* of medieval Europe.

Music became an essential part of knowledge not only in and of itself but as a central element in the scientific knowledge of all things. A study of music, specifically Pythagorean harmonics, was, therefore, considered crucial for the educated mind, an idea that has lingered in Western educational practices for 2,000 years. Even when scientific knowledge advanced to the point where Pythagorean harmonic theory was rendered mathematically no more than superstition and esotericism, music still retained its central and unique role in educational practices, as explained in Chapters 3 and 4.

Throughout the growth of Christianity, and well into the twentieth century, music has remained a main subject in education, certainly more so than any of the other arts. Visual art was distrusted by Plato as comprising deceptive images of reality, and poetry was turned into the science of rhetoric by Aristotle. Music alone remained central because of both its expressive powers and the belief in its centrality to scientific understanding of the human and superhuman.

INSTITUTIONALIZED MUSIC EDUCATION
IN WESTERN TRADITIONS

In the early stages of Western civilization, music was studied as a subject with a demanding intellectual theory as well as a practical performance component. It was Aristotle who raised the issue about the relative importance of practical performance versus a study of theory combined with listening (Chapter 4). In *The Politics* he asked whether it was necessary actually to play musical instruments, in view of the amount of work involved, in order to derive the desired educational benefit. Later commentators were more scathing about the role of performance in music education (Chapter 4).

Thus at the beginnings of Western educational practice there were seeds of doubt concerning the need for including performance instruction in musical education. It was, however, generally agreed that the theories of harmonics and *ethos* as applied to music were essential components in the education of the young. Not until the Christian era was musical performance affirmed as equal to, if not more important than, theory. Music was used as a means of inducing proper spiritual contemplation, and this was achieved, as explained in Chapter 4 and as intimated by Augustine, through the effects of musical sounds on the sensibilities, thereby softening the intellect for more serious spiritual activity.

In modern education, with churches playing a leading role in establishing schools for universal compulsory education, music retained this latter role in the curriculum. During the nineteenth century, music education, by which was meant singing religious songs, hymns, and psalms, was the main educational means of spreading the Christian gospel. The need to civilize people, who were showing alarming tendencies in the new cities of the Industrial Revolution all over Europe and North America, was seen by church authorities as an important mission, and indeed it was. It was through singing that children best learned Christianity, and music theory was taught to the children of the working classes purely as a means of facilitating the learning of religious music. By this time the theories of harmonics and musical mimesis had become sufficiently complex, as explained in Chapters 3 and 4, that study of them was thought fit only for the wealthy and privileged.

Following the First World War, as general education became more secular in intent and as municipal authorities began to take over the running of schools, the functions of music in education remained essentially the same; although they lost much of their specifically religious thrust, they remained virtually untouched in musical terms. In other words, musical performance, as instituted by the religious authorities, remained as the core activity in music education.

This, then, is the legacy of music in Western education, a legacy of elevating music to a most distinguished role in educational practice. But this legacy also includes the underpinning theory, which has no place in modern science. Thus the legacy is something of an anachronism, educationally, and therefore problematic for music educators. A further problem in music education is that concerning the relative importance of musical performance versus theories seeking to explain music. Performance has retained the supremacy it achieved from Augustine onwards as a useful tool in the processes of disseminating the Christian gospel, but it does so today without the underpinnings of either Christianity or Pythagorean harmonics. The study of the ideas that drive musical practices, although regarded by the ancient

Greeks as the real essence of music, has become regarded more as an adjunct to performance—a reversal of roles, in fact.

In schools today, music still retains a prominent role, particularly in the education of young children, but only by virtue of being regarded as part of a block of subjects generically described as the visual and performing arts. The rationale for their inclusion in the curriculum is usually given as something to do with educating all aspects of the personality, or with providing a full range of educational experiences for the child to develop from. Although this is a significant departure from the traditional role for music in education, educational practices remain tied to performance as the main focus. Thus a traditional historical activity is tied to new theoretical underpinnings, producing an uneasy partnership.

It is not my intent, however, to examine in detail the history and evolution of the school curriculum. Instead I want to provide a general context within which to discuss the implications for music education of the notion that music is an invented cultural artifact. We can best understand its significance for us by understanding the belief systems that have nurtured musical practices throughout history and across different cultures. It was necessary to provide a brief historical perspective on music education for two reasons: first, because of the obvious and close historical links between educational practices and the belief systems themselves; second, in order to understand the present situation in music education more profoundly.

DEFINING EDUCATIONAL EXPERIENCE IN MUSIC

The central importance of what have been termed *musical beliefs* to our understanding of music holds some implications for educational practices. It raises a number of issues that are fundamental. If the aim of music education is to promote understanding of musical practice, then the question arises as to the best way to achieve this. Musical performance alone cannot promote such understanding; some purely intellectual activity that attempts to provide a framework for explaining and predicting musical actions is needed. But the term *understanding* is ambiguous, as well as somewhat vague, in this context. Traditionally in music education, it meant understanding the theory of Pythagorean harmonics, understanding how the theory explicated the natural order of the elements in the cosmic scheme of things, and understanding how humans, through their experience of music, could be made privy to the secrets of the universe. Having access to such knowledge would, in turn, provide individuals with the secrets of the good life and enable them to function more effectively and perfectly as human beings. In Plato's scheme this was tied to the notion of the ideal political state, where all the citizens live in a state of goodness and perfect harmony induced by the perfect harmony of their surroundings and their artifacts, which include music. This socializing role for music was taken up by Christianity and retained in educational practices until fairly recently.

This is, however, not the understanding of musical practice we hold today, unless we accept such beliefs and their cultural ramifications. Today, we talk of aesthetic experience as some force that is somehow good for us in the sense of providing our brains and bodies with a sufficient variety of experiences to enable us to develop fully— the aesthetic dimension, irrespective of what it is, being a part of that variety. In reality this is merely an echo of Platonism without its essential ingredients. Asking us to accept this kind of role for music without asking us to believe in the tenets of Pythagoreanism or the Platonic theory of *ethos* is asking us to perform half the task. If we do not know the tenets referred to, then to be educated in the music produced by people who did must mean either that we rely on some form of cultural osmosis for providing knowledge of the tenets or that we regard the music as some kind of behavioral activity that can be presented devoid of its intended semantic function.

If we abjure critical study of the tenets, encountering them only osmotically through general acculturation, we are likely to accept Western musical theories and beliefs as universal truths, not cultural artifacts; and if we avoid formal study of its elements, we are equally likely to view Western music itself as an exemplification of universal truths. Thus, unless we approach the whole edifice of Western music from the perspective of Pythagorean and Platonic theory, we fall into the trap of ethnocentric thinking by assuming that the cultural perspective we have grown up with is in fact the objective truth. The problem is that the popular cultural perspective of the West has lost its focus as far as music is concerned; remnants of Pythagorean and Platonic theory, kept alive by the popular media, coexist uneasily with intrusions from other cultural traditions.

Popular music, for example, is an uneasy mixture of Western aesthetic ideals and almost totally alien musical practices from other cultures. The result most often is confusion, rather than fusion, of cultures. Rock 'n' roll in its original pure form as blues music is a genuine cultural artifact that stands on its own, apart from Western traditions, worthy of attention. Popular music that mixes Western music and rock into a homogenized product presents a semantically confusing message to listeners; where there are elements of Platonic *ethos* operating, these are juxtaposed or even nullified by the effects of a musical tradition in which the notion of *ethos* has no place. The African traditions from which American blues music sprang rely on an entirely different role for music: it is more a social, collective expression, with an immediacy of semantic purpose that the more theoretically motivated and introspective traditions of Western art music do not recognize. The two are not easily fused into an artistically convincing whole. On the other hand, a fusion of Western and Native American or Australian aboriginal musical traditions, based on an artistic use of acoustic elements of both traditions, is a more legitimate cross-cultural activity. From the twentieth-century standpoint of autonomy of musical sound, a number of composers have succeeded in doing this. Stockhausen, with his electronic composition *Telemusik*, written for the World Fair in Osaka, Japan, is a famous case in point.

If we do approach Western music through its historical and contemporary theoretical underpinnings and belief structures, then we see it as reflective of the growth and development of Western rational thought; consequently we see it not as *the* definitive musical artifact but as a product of particular ways of thinking. Other ways of thinking about the world, or different conclusions about nature, its structure, and the interdependence of the elements that make up our world—such as those held by certain aboriginal groups across the world—can be viewed, consequently, as capable of producing music equally valid as artforms and understandable in their own terms.

In this way music can be seen as truly representative of the culture that produced it—not in the fashion desired by Plato and Aristotle in their explication of the *ethos* theory, but in the context of more recent knowledge and understanding of human auditory functioning and mental proclivities to invent belief systems for explaining our behavior. As I argued earlier (in Chapters 3 and 4), the introspective and analytical traditions of the West have produced a musical theory system wherein superstition and objectivity had been intermingled to such a point that, as far as music is concerned, they became almost indistinguishable. That they are now not quite totally so conflated is due both to our ability to trace the origins and development of musical theory and behavior throughout the course of Western history and to modern knowledge of auditory functioning.

When knowledge of the complex behavior of the pressure waves we call musical sound was as incomplete as knowledge of human auditory functioning, it remained possible for successive generations of theorists to re-confirm the tenets of Pythagorean harmonic theory. Thus Zarlino, Rameau, and Helmholtz could exert enormous influence over musicians and educators, since it was possible to state, without fear of scientifically provable refutation (as opposed to logical arguments based on common sense, such as those of D'Alembert and Rousseau discussed in Chapter 3), that Pythagoras had indeed discovered the true secrets of musical harmony and its relationship to the natural workings of the human ear. It could be asserted, as Helmholtz did, that the ear responds more sympathetically, and therefore more naturally, to sounds comprised of integrally related spectral components. From such an idea, it requires only a short step to posit that Western music has evolved toward the state of perfection implicit in Pythagorean theory. Such a view not only provides a single standard for assessing and categorizing the work of any composer; it also allows the music of non-Western cultures to be classified as at some inferior stage in their evolution toward Pythagorean standards.

That composers contemporary with Helmholtz, as well as those of succeeding generations, paid little or no attention to these particular implications of his empirical and speculative work is testimony to two major influences on the course of Western music during the last hundred years or so: (1) recent knowledge of the pattern recognition proclivities of human auditory functioning, whereby any waveform pattern, harmonic or inharmonic, can be assimilated by the auditory system, and (2) the newly established autonomy for music as an expression in its own right. Both suggest a more all-embracing use of sound for its intrinsic acoustic properties than was possible under Pythagorean influence.

THE NEED FOR NEW PRACTICES IN MUSIC EDUCATION

The practices of music education have not, however, responded to the two major influences described above. The views of Helmholtz concerning pitch perception still hold sway as the single most significant scientific influence on music education practices. Primarily, the Helmholtzian role assigned to the fundamental frequency of a complex waveform in the acquisition of pitch concepts is still the major theoretical underpinning for children's music-making in schools. Instruments such as the recorder, chime bars, and glockenspiel retain their preeminence as school instruments. These conform well to Helmholtzian views in that most spectral energy in waveforms produced by these instruments lies at the fundamental or the 2nd harmonic, with little or no perceivable energy in the spectrum above these. The proclivities of the ear mechanism for pattern recognition of the events occurring in the transmission of the total spectral envelope is thus underutilized in the perception of such sounds.

There is, however, a more curious aspect to the prevalence of such instruments in the schools, in view of the fact that school music tends to favor historical uses of melody, rhythm, and harmony. Since Pythagorean harmonic theory in its more modern form stipulates that the harmonic (that is, integral multiples of the fundamental rate of repetition) components of a musical pressure wave contain the essential ingredients for the construction of Western musical harmony and scales (see Chapter 3), it is surprising that educational practices have arisen which provide children with experiences of sounds that contain no such harmonic components. In other words, only a musical diet of sounds rich in harmonic content will ensure that children develop the appropriate auditory gestalts (see Chapter 2) for Western music. Strangely enough, the sounds of typical school instruments do not provide this type of auditory experience.

Modern knowledge of auditory functioning tells us that acquisition of Western musical concepts of pitch, melody, and harmony is dependent upon experience at an early age of sounds rich in harmonic content. Ideally, these should come from authentic musical instruments and trained singers. The ancient and medieval musical practices that survive in contemporary choir schools are in fact most appropriate for developing these musical concepts. *Ab initio* singers learn from highly experienced choristers, who are able to produce sounds rich in harmonic content, as well as from the richly harmonic sounds of the organ that accompanies performance.

It is clear that children will learn from whatever experiences they encounter. If they have experiences only in inharmonic sounds, as in Bali, Java, or the Kwakiutl Indian culture, then they will reproduce these types of sounds. If they have experience only in sounds devoid of rich harmonic spectra, as in the "school music" sounds described above, then they will produce similar sounds in their music-making. The problems they encounter later have to do with the fact that "school music" sounds do not exist outside school; consequently, the school experience is likely to be quickly discarded as unrelated to the real world of musical sound.

Modern psychoacoustic research tells us quite clearly that there is no natural progression from learning pitch concepts from simple waveforms to learning pitch concepts from complex waveforms (see Chapter 2). What we learn about pitch from any type of waveform is what we come to accept pitch to be. Pitch, as explained in Chapter 2, is a concept produced by pattern recognition of the activities of the pressure wave, not simply a process of extracting periodicity from the fundamental component. Chapter 2 reports on studies showing that different waveforms with the same fundamental repetition rates will induce different subjective pitch sensations, making it clear that the waveform, not the fundamental, is the true conveyor of pitch. The implications are clear for music educators: we should educate children in the particular cultural pitch gestalt we deem appropriate. We cannot readily expect children to assimilate ones different from those we train them in. The same would apply to all aspects of musical sound.

THE PANCULTURAL APPROACH TO MUSIC EDUCATION

The question as to which cultural sounds are most appropriate for educating children musically is a critical one nowadays in view of the cultural mixing occurring across the world. We have only two realistic choices: one is to confine children to the genuine sounds of one culture, a difficult enough task considering today's pervasive entertainment media and society's cultural mix; the other is to approach music education from a pancultural perspective, treating the study of a single musical culture as a special unit within a broader definition of music education. There is little need to dwell on the former approach. European and Native American cultures have been successfully doing this outside its school systems for thousands of years. In the West, the models of the apprenticeship system, whereby a student learned from a practicing master, and the special music schools set up by the medieval monastic authorities cannot be improved upon as purveyors of musical culture. They have kept the Western musical traditions alive. Similarly, initiation practices in other societies have kept their traditions alive. Schools of today, however, are an entirely different type of institution serving entirely different needs; their pupils live in societies having no single cultural focus, where their lives are full of auditory images from a wide variety of sources, including the entertainment media in all its guises. Thus a pancultural approach seems more appropriate. To succeed, such an approach demands certain fundamental changes in the practices of music education. But, as is argued above, existing practices are, in any event, inappropriate for the purposes they serve.

To approach music education panculturally rather than uniculturally requires, initially, the development of auditory gestalts that relate more to the autonomous qualities of sound per se than to the sounds of any single musical culture. The modern cultural environment is so culturally mixed and confusing that it is necessary to educate the ear in the subtleties of the autonomous qualities of sound prior to an education in the sounds of a particular musical culture. In this way, the distinct and unique acoustic properties of different musical cultures can best be approached. Such an approach is possible nowadays only because technology has advanced sufficiently to enable us to have at our disposal both the knowledge of these autonomous qualities of sound and the equipment to produce any of them relatively easily.

The danger of the pancultural approach is that children might grow up knowing *no* particular musical culture. The advantage is that they can grow up knowing more about both their own and other musical cultures than present practices permit. The *foundations* of the approach should, therefore, be rooted in no specific cultural tradition; rather, they should contain hints and elements of many different cultures in order that these can be expanded upon throughout the child's development. The ear's ability for pattern perception of pressure waves should be exploited to its fullest capacity in order that the child can appreciate auditory experiences beyond those of a single culture. Children should have experience in the sensations of both harmonic and inharmonic sounds, and they should have at their disposal equipment enabling them to manipulate as full a range of different waveforms as possible. Such equipment can be in the form of a variety of acoustic instruments, ranging from typical school instruments, to "junk" instruments (such as old metal piping and automobile brake-drums), to conventional authentic musical instruments. The equipment can also be in the form of electronic synthesizers and samplers.

The purpose of such a variety of sound sources is to develop in the child as wide a range of auditory gestalts as possible. It should be borne in mind that no single musical culture uses more than a very narrow range of the sounds to which the human ear can respond, and the entertainment media today present a wider range of auditory expressions than those of any single traditional musical culture. The child is, therefore, already being assaulted with an enormous variety of sounds. There are, I suggest, two foundations upon which the approach can be based:

1. Experience of as wide a variety of culture-free sounds as possible

2. Experience of the cultural sounds of music in the context of their belief systems

Each of these foundations will be discussed below.

Experiencing a Wide Range of Sounds

The pancultural approach subsumes the sounds of all possible cultures. The fundamental premise upon which the approach is built is that it is initially necessary to provide educational experiences in the full range of sounds to which the human ear is responsive in order to enable the child to cope with the sounds heard in the entertainment media and from different cultures.

Educational experience in a wide range of sounds implies that some kind of musical activity is taking place in these sounds. Children will go through three basic stages, or aspects, as far as music education is concerned (Paynter, 1971; Schafer, 1967; Walker, 1976, 1984):

1. The children will explore the capability of the instruments to no particular purpose other than to find out what the instruments are capable of, or just to make a noise. Having presented both children and adults with collections of instruments, I can state empirically that this first stage will inevitably be tried by all age groups.
2. This stage is marked by a desire to impose some personal controls on the instrument and the sounds it can produce. Students will become dissatisfied with merely making sound for its own sake and look for organizational structures in the sounds and behaviors they produce.
3. In this stage they attempt to make the instruments expressive of their personal, inner desires and needs. It is at this point that frustration can set in as they seek to make the instrument produce sounds it is not capable of or realize that they have inadequate technique to produce the sounds they want.

Guiding students through these stages is a highly professional task, requiring a wide knowledge and understanding of music on the part of the teacher as well as a commitment to the broader educational goals of panculturalism in music education. The stages are not to be regarded as inexorably sequenced, or discrete. They are guidelines to expected learning and behavior, no more. A detailed description of each stage follows.

Exploration. This first stage is one in which all aspects of sound can be explored, identified, described, and manipulated. These aspects concern acoustic phenomena such as timbre (or waveform), pitch, duration, loudness; general aesthetic impression arising from interactions of these aspects; and identification of predominant features from among these aspects. For example, when an automobile brake-drum is struck by a piece of metal used as a beater, the sound may have an ambiguous pitch (rather like a bell), a short duration, and a high onset characteristic, yielding a sharp, sudden, loud sensation. Quite independent of cultural meaning, these aspects of sound can be discussed, listened to, identified, described using appropriate language of either a technical or subjective nature, and expressed using visual metaphors—in other words, drawing or painting what the sounds "look like" (Walker, 1978, 1981, 1985, 1987a, 1987b).

In this way, from the initial exploration and discovery of what the instruments are capable of doing, there arises a more structured approach whereby students are required to identify aurally different acoustic characteristics of sound, to focus on these, and to be able to describe and understand such distinctions in a coherent manner.

This is an essential component in the basic musical abilities of anyone, whether performer, composer, or listener. This activity should continue throughout the educational process. It is not something that can be satisfactorily completed at a certain age and then abandoned. It is also important to remember that children have greater sensitivity to acoustic phenomena, particularly to the higher frequencies in the spectral envelope of complex pressure waves, than do adults (see Chapter 2). Children will, in fact, hear more than adults in activities such as this, which makes it imperative that adult teachers know from a technical viewpoint what the sounds being studied actually contain. They cannot rely on the ear alone. But perhaps most important, this stage is akin to the autonomous use of sound found in contemporary music. Teachers should at all times be on the lookout for opportunities to relate activities to contemporary music.

Seeking Personal Control. At the second stage attempts are made to gain personal control over both the instrument and one's own actions. At this stage teachers can introduce exercises to help students develop a sense of musical structure. Knowledge of contemporary music, particularly of its wide variety of structures and compositional procedures, is important to this stage. The simplest kind of structure of a pancultural nature is that involving two contrasting sounds. They may simply be different or they may be more specifically related—by being opposite, for example. Pairings such as high versus low in pitch, loud versus soft in dynamics, and so on are more specifically related than a soft tap on a drum paired with soft tap on a cymbal. Once each student has had the opportunity to produce two contrasting sounds and to explore this task to his or her own satisfaction, it is then almost obligatory to let the whole class hear each individual's pair of contrasting sounds. This can be done in conjunction with further discussion, as a whole class, about the acoustic properties of the two sounds.

Following this, further structure can be suggested by means of both full-class and small-group improvisation based upon the pair of contrasting sounds. Simple group or class improvisations can be achieved by a basic conducting procedure: the conductor, either student or teacher, can bring in a pair of sounds from an individual and eliminate them at will by means of a simple hand movement. In this fashion, students can construct their own improvisations by making their own selections of sounds to juxtapose. At this stage, there are no cultural components. Students are dealing with sound patterns as auditory sensations. Alternatively, they can be asked to improvise with schemes based on twentieth-century art music by various composers.

Inevitably, however, questions of taste will arise, even if in a most rudimentary form, such as "I like that" or "I don't like this." These situations provide teachers with opportunities to explain and demonstrate cultural values in music, and to present an introduction to the belief systems that sustain such values.

Personal Expression. In the third stage students are asked to produce expressive pieces using the variety of instruments available, including electronic instruments and recorded sounds. Class organization can cater to individuals, to groups, or to whole-class participation. The teacher can both impose specific tasks and allow for individual creativity in the activities of students.

It is at this point that there arises a need for some specific cultural focus. If, for example, students are asked to compose music that expresses some particularly tragic incident in a story or poem, it is imperative that they subsequently be introduced to the work of specific composers who have overtly expressed something similar—Beethoven, Tchaikovsky, Mahler, as well as various opera and film composers spring to mind. In this way students can be made aware of the sounds they have chosen to represent certain meanings in comparison to the choices made by Western composers. Such comparisons facilitate a study of the contents of works such as Mahler's "Resurrection" Symphony and Beethoven's *Egmont* overture. Children will be better able to confront the complexities of such works after having gone through the task of creating their own sounds to imitate such meanings. The same applies to any meaning the teacher asks the children to create music about, and comparisons can be taken from contemporary musical works or the standard repertoire.

Hearing the different musical sounds that different cultures use to express similar events (such as tragic ones) can highlight the uniqueness of each musical culture as well as indicate the significance of cultural uses of music and the role of theory in helping our understanding, as well as determining the nature, of musical expression. Non-Western cultures without a theory of *ethos*, for example, have different roles for music than mere imitation or representation, and this shows up in the sounds utilized. Only after having studied the acoustic properties of a wide variety of instruments can students understand this. Without this focus on a study of sounds, listening becomes a passive endeavor, without much educational merit.

It is possible to introduce overtly pancultural musical aspects such as those described above during the first two stages. However, pancultural aspects should not form a separate "unit"; they should be interspersed with the study of musical sounds from specific cultures. The musical sounds of all cultures produce patterns that can be perceived in a pancultural rather than a culture-specific manner. Examples of patterns or musical structures from a variety of cultural sources can introduce students to the concept of culturally derived variety. For example, teachers can relate an improvisational piece based on pairs of contrasting timbres or pitches to the gamelan traditions of Bali and Java. They can relate one based on contrasting durations to rhythmically based African traditions. They can relate one based on long silences or slow-moving events to the mystic traditions of Tibet, or, in another cultural context, one where the contrasting sounds are pitches using microtonal intervals between them to Kwakiutl music or the music of most other aboriginal cultures. It is up to the individual teacher to introduce such cultural experiences from essentially noncultural sounds found in the students' improvisations. At all times the opportunity to introduce students to the work of contemporary composers should be sought.

Understanding Cultural Uses of Musical Sounds

The second foundational premise of panculturalism concerns the progression from noncultural uses of sound to an *understanding* of cultural uses of sound in musical acts. The essence of panculturalism in music education is, therefore, to begin from a noncultural, objective, acoustic standpoint so that the extent of the different parameters of sound can be fully explored and understood; only then should specific cultural uses of various sound parameters be introduced. Once students have explored and discussed sounds themselves, they can bring an intellectual analysis and understanding to listening to the music of other cultures. A specific non-Western musical culture should be isolated for study at this stage, so that students will not grow up with Western music as their only reference point in musical studies, even though Western music might dominate in their out-of-school life. Thus they will be encouraged to develop respect and understanding for all human musical cultures in all their richness and diversity.

The broad goal of the pancultural approach is to promote a more profound understanding, of specific cultures, their belief systems, their special musical sounds, their special meanings, and the ways in which all these things can induce meanings. However, it is not the only goal. By developing a keen auditory awareness, these activities bring auditory functioning to a refined level, which, in turn, increases students' own enjoyment of music by making them more demanding and informed listeners. And this enjoyment should extend to music of the twentieth century.

The most important thing about cultural uses of sound in musical acts is that the sounds, as well as the actions needed to produce them, are inextricably involved with cultural beliefs. These beliefs concern every aspect of life and death, and music is the vehicle that presents them for personal verification, reinforcement, and nurture, as well as for communication with others who hold similar beliefs. Therefore, to approach the music of any culture in a manner insensitive to both the importance of beliefs and the links between music and belief is to be ill-educated and musically crude. Learning to understand the pleasures of auditory sensation by enjoying sound for its own sake, as in the activities described for first foundation, is a necessary stage of involvement. It has parallels to language development, where very young children imitate speech sounds of their parents for the pure joy of making sounds with their vocal tract. This exploration of sound should not be confused with the artistic use of sound found in twentieth-century art music. They are not the same, as explained in Chapter 5. But exploration of sound should precede learning about how sound is used as a means of communication, whether in speech or in music. Omission of such exploration creates impediments in later acts of communication, as has been shown in studies of speech development—children deprived of opportunities to babble and freely make sounds before speech develops show learning difficulties in their speech activities.

Exploration of sound itself, however, must lead to learning about how human societies imbue sounds with intended meanings so that humans can communicate with one another adequately and effectively. The so-called second foundation is, therefore, intended to begin this introduction to the specific culturally applied meanings that humans have attributed to musical sounds. The focus here is on learning about the music theory and beliefs of a particular culture, which, in turn, have motivated the invention, composition, and performance of music. Three main aspects should inform and enlighten students in their involvement with this second foundation:

1. Working with the theory and belief of a particular culture
2. Creative activities emanating from students' understanding of the theory and belief
3. Hearing and, if possible, becoming personally involved in, the genuine music of a particular culture

These three aspects should not be seen as sequential; they are no more than approaches to be used by the teacher as an organizational ploy. Nor should they be seen as discrete; the activities emanating from each overlap with the other two. The teacher needs to decide, depending on the students, which aspect, or aspects, should precede the others. An outline follows of what each aspect might involve in practice. Two distinct musical cultures are dealt with from within the framework of these aspects: Western musical culture and that of the Pacific Northwest Indian.

WESTERN MUSICAL CULTURE

Working with the Theory. Essentially, Western musical culture is based on arithmetic, on proportional theory and its associated beliefs, including a supposed relationship between ideal proportions and ideal sounds. Simple proportional lengths of a variety of materials should be explored and introduced. The easiest material to start with is a length of violin or guitar string, or some similar material suitably stretched so that it can be "stopped" by the fingers at any point, as on a soundboard or with frets on a guitar. School instruments often include a simple harp or zither that can be used for this purpose. The teacher, or the students, can construct a kind of monochord such as the Pythagoreans used in their empirical studies of proportional theory.

The string can be divided into simple proportions and made to produce sounds relating to the ideal musical ratios (i.e., 2 : 1, 3 : 2, etc., as explained in Chapter 3). Other materials, such as those used on chime bars or xylophones, can also be used to explore the concepts of melodic and harmonic relationships derived from the simple proportions of Western musical theory. These relationships, in other words, concern both successive sounds, as in melody, and concurrent sounds, as in harmony.

Pythagorean beliefs concerning the music of the spheres, explained in Chapter 3, should be introduced. The belief system surrounding proportional theory and its musical applications should form the content of this aspect of the work, and it should be extended, if students are capable, into a study of the spectral content of sound.

Some materials, when set into vibration, yield spectral contents that are integrally related, or nearly so. Other materials yield nonintegrally related spectral contents. Experiments with different materials should be performed in order to educate the ears and minds of students in the range of sounds between the two extremes and in various types of noise. The use of electronically generated and manipulated sound is especially useful in this activity, and microcomputers and samplers with sound analysis capability would enhance the educational experience.

Further stages should involve the introduction of the Platonic theory of *ethos* together with the various historical and contemporary examples of music composed to conform to the theory, as explained in Chapter 4.

Creative Activities. Students should be encouraged to work with different materials, devising proportions from lengths of string, size of chime bars, or even lengths of tubing made from scrap metal. They should be encouraged to compare melodies made with these different materials and to make judgments based on Pythagorean proportional theory about their relative beauty. Sounds with the most perfectly related harmonic partials will appear most beautiful according to the theory. In order to demonstrate examples of the application of the belief, the introduction of Western musical instruments should follow these exploratory activities.

Combinations of different sounds to form harmony in the Western sense should also be experimented with. Two, three, and four sounds played simultaneously should be listened to intently for their aesthetic appeal, their beauty in the Pythagorean sense. The students' responses should be guided by the Western theory of beauty in sound. That is, the most beautiful harmonies should be found from combinations of sounds where Pythagorean proportional theory has been applied to both melodic and spectral components in the sound.

Students' experiences with the difficulties of finding and shaping materials in order to make them conform to the Pythagorean ideals should enable them to appreciate something of the enormous effort that underpins the development of Western technology in musical practices.

An obvious further development from these activities is the introduction of basic theories of musical harmony, starting with cadence figures and progressing to more complex harmonic sentences. Similarly with melody, students can be introduced to melodic structures, such as simple binary and ternary forms.

In combination with earlier activities in the first foundation, activities in the expression of Platonic *ethos* can form part of the learning experience. Developing full compositions that express, imitate, or represent various emotions, feelings, incidents, behaviors, and so on, as explained in Chapter 4, should be practiced. The use of poetry and stories as sources should be encouraged.

Hearing the Genuine Music of the Culture. It is essential that students be introduced to the genuine cultural artifact—the actual sounds of Western art music. After the preceding activities, and as a part of them where appropriate, students should hear and take part in performances of Western art music. The teacher can select and structure this variously. There is no reason that the music of any particular historical period or genre should precede any other, but it might be helpful to introduce this music by linking some of the early listening to activities described above. For example, as the students struggle to develop sounds that are proportionally related in pitch, the teacher can introduce the earliest attempts at melody with examples of ancient Greek melody. This is not to imply that the latter is experimental in the same sense; but the profusion of ways of dividing up the tetrachord, as explained in Chapter 3, can best be understood after students have themselves attempted to construct scales in this manner. This may be followed by examples of medieval Gregorian chant to show a stage when scale selections had been made and narrow restrictions were applied. Recordings of both ancient Greek music and Gregorian chant are readily available.

Vis-à-vis the spectral content of sound, a comparison of the sounds of ancient and modern instruments will illustrate some differences that technological advances, as well as theoretical changes in perspective, have brought about. The people who lived contemporaneously with ancient instruments thought they sounded beautiful. We, today, feel our modern instruments sound beautiful. This is because we as well as they have been acculturated to the theories and sounds of our respective times.

MUSIC OF THE PACIFIC NORTHWEST INDIAN

Working with the Theory. A non-Western musical culture should be studied in some depth. Here I use the Indians of the Pacific Northwest of America so as to be able to cite specific examples. Obviously general principles can be extrapolated and applied to any non-Western musical culture about which sufficient information exists. Beliefs of various tribes from the Pacific Northwest should be studied from a general perspective. The role of myth in recording and passing on these beliefs should be a focus. There are many published versions of Indian legends that could introduce students to the traditional beliefs of these Indians regarding the supernatural, their relationships with all living things and their natural environment, their various practices in day-to-day living, and their ways of celebrating, as in potlatch and hamatsa ceremonies. Their belief in the role of the spirit world in communicating songs to them is of special importance.

The materials available should include photographs, films, copies of actual Indian artifacts, and recordings of speech and song, all of which are readily available through a variety of sources, including libraries and commercial outlets.

The essential elements in their beliefs concerning music are those that indicate the role of natural sounds, the special vocal sounds they make, the influence of the drum on their music-making, and the sociopolitical function of songs they perform. Reference to Chapter 6 will supply some of the details.

Creative Activities. There are three basic aspects of the musical practices the Pacific Northwest Indian that can be used in creative activities. These are:

1. Melodies based on nonintegral relations
2. Inharmonic partials in the sound spectra of drums
3. Rhythms based on nonmetric patterns of duration and combinations of sound

Creative activities with materials similar to those mentioned in connection with Western music in the previous section can be used

here. Melodies based on nonintegral relations can be approached crea-
tively by having students explore the sounds of strings or lengths of
materials that are proportionally related in nonintegral terms; that is,
in fractional numbers, such as 0.5, 1.73, 2.83. For example, a length
of string 12 inches long could be stopped so as to make two different
lengths of 7.5 inches and 4.5 inches. This would produce an interval
whose proportion is 1.66 (i.e., 7.5 : 4.5). This interval sounds larger
than the perfect fifth, whose proportion is 1.5 (i.e., 3 : 2). Stopping
the string is done in the same way as is done on the violin to produce
the octave or fifth according to proportional theory.

Students can devise melodies using such proportions and thus
gain experience of nonintegral relationship in melodic expressions. As
many different proportions should be tried and melodies constructed
as student intuition can create.

Similar such relationships can be explored further in the sound
spectra produced by bells, automobile brake-drums—in fact, drums of
any sort—and any pieces of metal or wood that produce inharmonic
spectra. If possible, the students should be shown examples of harmonic and inharmonic spectra in graphic form, such as can be obtained from some samplers and spectral analysis programs on microcomputers.

The class should explore rhythms that combine a regularly beating
sound, on a drum for example, with a variety of nonmetric improvisations that do not reflect a desire to fit in with the regular drum beats.
Complete independence from the drum beat should be practiced.

Hearing the Genuine Music of the Culture. There are many recordings available of authentic sounds of Pacific Northwest Indian
music. Some are cited as references in Chapter 6. These should be
introduced at various stages in the activities described above. It may
be better to first allow students to improvise their own nonintegral
melodies and spectral sounds, together with rhythms independent of
a regular drum beat. The natural inflections of spoken words could be
used as a basis for musical improvisation. This is not quite the same as
composing a melody to words since the spoken inflections become
the basis for melody. Following these activities, listening to the genuine sound of an Indian song can be very rewarding, much more so
than merely having such details pointed out theoretically and then
listening for them. Practical involvement in making music is the best
preparation for listening to the music.

The general approach indicated above in educating students in the
two foundations of panculturalism allows teachers to develop and

devise their own methods and select their own materials. The most successful teacher is, I believe, the most inventive and creative one, rather than the one who slavishly follows taxonomies or sequences of learning. Knowledge in music cannot be broken into neat, discrete parcels of experience and information. Neither can it be placed in a learning sequence that is applicable to all situations and all students' needs. These kinds of things are rightly the domain of the professional teacher, who is best situated to make decisions about sequencing activities and taxonomical progressions of experience. The teacher knows the needs of students best.

The above suggestions are guidelines, no more. It is hoped that they are sufficient to get the professional teacher going in a direction in general music education that, I believe, is the one most appropriate to the world we now live in.

References

Arnheim, R. (1969). *Art and visual perception*. London: Faber and Faber.

Baker, N. K., & Scruton, R. (1980). Expressionism. In *The new Grove dictionary of music and musicians* (Vol. 6, pp. 324–332). London: Macmillan.

Barbera, C. A. (1980). *The persistence of Pythagorean mathematics in ancient musical thought*. Unpublished doctoral dissertation, University of North Carolina, Chapel Hill.

Barbera, C. A. (1984). The consonant eleventh and the expansion of the musical tetractys: A study of ancient Pythagoreanism. *Journal of Music Theory, 28*, 191–223.

Barbour, J. M. (1953). *Tuning and temperament—A historical survey*. East Lansing: Michigan State College Press.

Beattie, J. (1974). *The philosophical and critical works of James Beattie*. New York: Georg Olms Verlag. (Original work published in 1790)

Beckman, M. E. (1988). Phonetic theory. In F. Newmayer (Ed.), *Linguistics: The Cambridge survey*. Cambridge, England: Cambridge University Press.

Bekesy, G. von. (1960). *Experiments in hearing*. New York: McGraw-Hill.

Benade, A. H. (1976). *Fundamentals of musical acoustics*. New York: Oxford University Press.

Bernard, J. W. (1980). The principles and the elements: Rameau's controversy with D'Alembert. *Journal of Music Theory, 24*(1), 37–62.

Bernard, J. W. (1987). *The music of Edgard Varèse*. New Haven, CT: Yale University Press.

Blom, E. (1954). Gluck. In *Grove's dictionary of music and musicians* (Vol. 3, p. 679). London: Macmillan.

Bloom, A. (Trans.). (1968). *The Republic of Plato*. New York: Basic Books.

Boas, F. (1964). *The central Eskimo*. Lincoln: University of Nebraska Press. (Original work published 1888)

Boer, E. de. (1976). On the "residue" and auditory pitch perception. In W. D. Keidel & W. Neff (Eds.), *Handbook of sensory physiology* (Vol. 5, Part 3). Berlin: Springer Verlag.

Bowra, C. M. (1962). *Primitive song*. Cleveland: World Publishing Company.

Boyer, C. J. (1968). *A history of mathematics*. New York: Wiley.

Bruner, J. (1973). *Beyond the information given: Studies in the psychology of knowing*. New York: Norton.

Bryant, P. (1974). *Perception and understanding in young children*. London: Methuen.

Buelow, G. J. (1980). Rhetoric and music. In *The new Grove dictionary of music and musicians* (Vol. 15, pp. 793–803). London: Macmillan.

Bundy, R. S., Columbo, J., & Singer, J. (1982). Pitch perception in young infants. *Developmental Psychology, 18* (1), 10–14.

Bunt, L. N. H., Jones, S., & Bedient, R. (1976). *Historical roots of elementary mathematics*. Englewood Cliffs, NJ.: Prentice-Hall.

Busoni, F. (1962). Sketch of a new aesthetic in music (T. Baker, Trans.). In *Three classics in the aesthetics of music*. New York: Dover. (Original work published 1911)

Butler, C. (1970). *The principles of music*. New York: Da Capo. (Original work published 1636)

Butler, G. (1977). Fugue and rhetoric. *Journal of Music Theory, 21* (1), 49–111.

Carse, A. (1948). *The orchestra from Beethoven to Berlioz*. Cambridge: Heffer.

Charters, S. (1981). *The roots of the blues*. New York: Putnam.

Chung, D. Y., & Colavita, F. B. (1976). Periodicity pitch perception and its upper frequency limit in cats. *Perception and Psychophysics, 20* (6), 431–437.

Clarkson, M. G., & Clifton, R. K. (1985). Infant pitch perception: Evidence for responding to pitch categories and the missing fundamental. *Journal of the Acoustical Society of America, 77* (4), 1521–1527.

Clifton, R. K., Morrongiello, B. A., Kulig, J. W., & Dowd, J. M. (1981). Newborns' orientation to sound: Possible implications for cortical development. *Child Development, 52,* 833–838.

Cohn, N. (1969). *Pop from the beginning*. Birkenhead, England: Willmer Brothers.

Cooke, D. (1959). *The language of music*. London: Oxford University Press.

Cynx, J., & Shapiro, M. (1986). Perception of the missing fundamental by a species of song bird. *Journal of Comparative Psychology, 100* (4), 356–360.

Davies, J. B. (1978). *Psychology of music*. Stanford, CA: Stanford University Press.

Davison, A. T., & Apel, W. (1964). *Historical anthology of music*. Cambridge, MA: Harvard University Press.

Debussy, C. (1962). Monsieur Croche the dilettante hater (B. N. Langdon Davies, Trans.). In *Three classics in the aesthetics of music*. New York: Dover. (Original work published 1927)

Densmore, F. (1926). The study of Indian music in the 19th century. *American Anthropologist, 28,* 77–86.

Densmore, F. (1939). *Nootkan and Quileute music*. (Bureau of American Ethnology, Bulletin No. 124).

Densmore, F. (1972). *Music of the Indians of British Columbia*. New York: Da Capo.

Denvir, B. (Ed.). (1987). *The impressionists at first hand*. New York: Thames and Hudson.

Divenyi, P. L. (1979). Is pitch a learned attribute of sound: Two points in support of Terhardt's theory. *Journal of the Acoustical Society of America, 66* (4), 1210–1213.

Eimas, P. D., Siqueland, E. R., Jusczyk, R., & Vigorito, J. (1971). Speech perception in infants. *Science, 171*, 303–306.

Ellis, C. (1965). Pre-instrumental scales. *Ethnomusicology, 9*, 126–137.

Ellis, C. (1984). The nature of Australian aboriginal music. *International Journal of Music Education, 4* (Nov.), 47–51.

Eves, H. W. (1964). *Introduction to the history of mathematics*. New York: Holt, Rinehart & Winston.

Farmer, H. G. (1969). The music of ancient Egypt. In *The new Oxford history of music* (Vol. 1, pp. 255–279). London: Oxford University Press.

Fergusson, F. (Ed.). (1961). *Aristotle's Poetics* (S. H. Butcher, Trans.). New York: Hill and Wang.

Fiske, H. (1989). Musical imagery. *Canadian Music Educator: Research Edition, 30* (1), 5–21.

Fry, D. B. (1979). *The physics of speech*. Cambridge, England: Cambridge University Press.

Gardner, H. (1985). *The mind's new science*. New York: Basic Books.

Gillings, R. J. (1962). *Mathematics in the time of the pharaohs*. Cambridge, MA: MIT Press.

Goldstein, J. L. (1973). An optimum processor theory for the central formation of the pitch of complex tones. *Journal of the Acoustical Society of America, 54*, 1496–1516.

Goldstein, J. L. (1978). Mechanisms of signal analysis and pattern perception in periodicity pitch. *Audiology, 17*, 421–445.

Gombrich, E. H. (1978). *The story of art*. New York: Dutton.

Gregory, R. (1966). *Eye and brain*. London: Weidenfeld.

Halpern, I. (1967). Indian music of the Pacific Northwest coast [Notes to Ethnic Folkways Album FE 4523]. New York: Folkways Records.

Halpern, I. (1981). Kwakiutl Indian music [Notes to Ethnic Folkways Album FE 4122]. New York: Folkways Records.

Hamm, C. (1979). *Yesterdays—Popular song in America*. New York: Norton.

Hanslick, E. (1957). *The beautiful in music* (G. Cohen, Trans.). New York: Bobbs Merrill. (Original work published in 1854)

Helmholtz, H. (1954). *On the sensations of tone*. New York: Dover. (Original work published 1885)

Henderson, I. (1969). Ancient Greek music. In *The new Oxford history of music*, Vol. 1, edited by E. Wellesz. London: Oxford University Press.

Heninger, S. K. (1974). *Touches of sweet harmony*. San Marino, CA: Huntington Library.

Houtsma, A. J. M. (1971). What determines musical pitch? *Journal of Music Theory, 15* (1), 138–157.

Houtsma, A. J. M., & Goldstein, J. L. (1972). Perception of music intervals: Evidence for a central origin of the pitch of complex tones. *Journal of the Acoustical Society of America, 51*, 520–529.

Hyland, D. A. (1973). *The origins of philosophy.* Atlantic Highlands, NJ: Humanities Press.

Javel, E. (1980). Coding of AM tones in the chinchilla auditory nerve: Implications for the pitch of complex tones. *Journal of the Acoustical Society of America, 68* (1), 133–146.

Jusczyk, P. W., Rosner, B. S., Cutting, J. E., Foard, C. F., & Smith, L. B. (1977). Categorical perception of non-speech sounds by two-month-old infants. *Perception and Psychophysics, 21* (1), 50–54.

Kearsley, R. B. (1973). The newborn's response to auditory stimulation: A demonstration of orienting and defensive behavior. *Child Development, 44*, 582–589.

Keil, C. (1966). *Urban blues.* Chicago: University of Chicago Press.

Kennedy, G. A. (1980). *Classical rhetoric and its Christian and secular tradition from ancient to modern times.* Chapel Hill: University of North Carolina Press.

Kuttner, F. A. (1965). A musicological interpretation of the twelve *lu*s in China's traditional tone system. *Ethnomusicology, 9* (1), 22–38.

Lang, P. H. (1978). *Music in Western civilization.* London: Dent.

Lennenberg, H. (1958). Johan Mattheson on affect and rhetoric in music. *Journal of Music Theory, 2* (2), 193–236.

Levin, F. R. (1972). Synesis in Aristoxenian theory. *Transactions and Proceedings of the American Philological Society, 103*, 211–234.

Lévi-Strauss, C. (1969). *Totemism.* London: Penguin.

Liberman, A. M., Harris, K. S., Hoffman, H. S., & Griffith, B. C. (1957). The discrimination of speech sounds within and across phoneme boundaries. *Journal of Experimental Psychology, 54*, 358–368.

Locke, S., & Kellar, L. (1973). Categorical perception in a non-linguistic mode. *Cortex, 9*, 355–369.

Magee, B. (1983). *The philosophy of Schopenhauer.* Oxford, England: Clarendon Press.

Marks, L. (1978). *The unity of the senses.* New York: Academic Press.

Mendelssohn, F. B. (1956). Letter [1842] to Marc-André Sochay. In S. Morgenstern (Ed.), *Composers on music.* New York: Pantheon.

Merriam, A. P. (1964). *The anthropology of music.* Evanston IL: Northwestern University Press.

Messiaen, O. (1944). *Technique de mon langage musical.* Paris: Alphonse Leduc.

Meyer, J. (1978). The dependence of pitch on harmonic spectra. *Psychology of Music, 6* (1), 3–13.

Miller, J. (Ed.). (1980). *The Rolling Stone illustrated history of the blues.* New York: Random House.

Miller, G. (1964). *Psychology—The science of mental life.* New York: Hutchinson.

Morley, T. (1952). *A plain and easy introduction to practical music (1597)* (A. Harman, Ed.). New York: Norton. (Original work published 1597)

Mslpitch (1987). [Pitch extraction program for IBM microcomputers]. Center for Speech Technology Research, University of Victoria, Canada.

Muir, D., & Field, J. (1979). Newborn infants orient to sound. *Child Development, 50* (1), 431–436.

Newman, E. (1949). *Wagner nights*. London: Putnam.

Oakley, G. (1976). *The devil's music—A history of the blues*. New York: Harcourt Brace Jovanovich.

Ohgushi, K. (1978). On the role of spatial and temporal cues in the perception of pitch of complex tones. *Journal of the Acoustical Society of America, 64* (3), 764–770.

Olsho, L. W., Schorn, C., Sakai, R., Turpin, R., & Speduto, V. (1982). Auditory frequency discrimination in infancy. *Developmental Psychology, 18* (5), 721–726.

Ouellette, F. (1968). *Edgard Varèse*. New York: Orion.

Outler, A. C. (Ed.). (1955). *Augustine: Confessions and Enchiridion*. Philadelphia: Westminster Press.

Patterson, R. (1986). Spiral detection of periodicity and the spiral form of musical scales. *Psychology of Music, 14* (1), 44–61.

Paul, C. B. (1975). Music and ideology: Rameau, Rousseau, and 1789. *Journal of the History of Ideas, 32*, 392–415.

Paynter, J. (1971). *Creative music in the classroom*. Unpublished doctoral dissertation, University of York, England.

Plomp, R., & Level, W. J. M. (1965). Tonal consonance and critical bandwidth. *Journal of the Acoustical Society of America, 38*, 548–560.

Radocy, R., & Boyle, D. (1979). *The psychological foundations of musical behavior*. Springfield, IL: Charles C. Thomas.

Rainbow, B. (1967). *The land without music*. London: Novello.

Read, H. (1967). *The true voice of feeling*. London: Faber and Faber.

Reese, G. (1977). *Music in the renaissance*. London: Dent.

Ritsma, R. J. (1962). Existence regions of tonal residue. *Journal of the Acoustical Society of America, 34*, 1224–1229.

Rivera, B. V. (1978). The Isogogue (1581) of Johannes Avianus: An early formulation of triadic theory. *Journal of Music Theory, 22* (1), 43–65.

Roederer, J. G. (1979). *Introduction to the physics and psychophysics of music*. New York: Springer Verlag.

Rousseau, J. J. (1966). Essay on the origin of languages. In *On the origin of languages* (J. H. Morgan & A. Gode, Trans.). Chicago: University of Chicago. (Original work published 1749—music sections only)

Schafer, J. M. (1965). *The composer in the classroom*. Toronto: BMI.

Schafer, J. M. (1967). *Ear cleaning*. Toronto: BMI.

Schoenberg, A. (1911). *Harmonielehre*. Vienna: Universal Verlag.

Schopenhauer, A. (1964). *The world as will and idea* (R. B. Haldane & J. Kemp, Trans.). London: Routledge and Kegan Paul. (Original work published 1818)

Schouten, J. F. (1940). The perception of pitch. *Phillips Technical Review, 5* (10), 286–294.

Schouten, J. F. (1970). The residue phenomenon and its impact on the theory of hearing. *Audiology, 1*, 7–10.

Schwartz, E., & Childs, B. (Eds.). (1978). *Contemporary composers on contemporary music.* New York: Da Capo.

Scott, J. F. (1960). *A history of mathematics from antiquity to the beginning of the 19th century.* London: Taylor and Francis.

Seashore, C. (1938). *Psychology of music.* New York: McGraw-Hill.

Siegel, J. A., & Siegel, W. (1977a). Absolute identification of notes and intervals by musicians. *Perception and Psychophysics, 21* (2), 143–152.

Siegel, J. A., & Siegel, W. (1977b). Categorical perception of tonal intervals: Musicians cannot tell sharp from flat. *Perception and Psychophysics, 21* (5), 399–407.

Sitwell, S. (1967). *Liszt.* New York: Dover.

Smith, A. (1967). Essays on philosophical subjects. In W. D. Wightman & J. C. Bryan (Eds.), *The early writings of Adam Smith* (Reprints of Economic Classics). Oxford: Clarendon Press. (Original work published 1795)

Smith, H., Stevens, K., & Tomlinson, R. S. (1967). On an unusual mode of chanting by certain Tibetan Lamas. *Journal of the Acoustical Society of America, 41*, 1262–1264.

Smith, P., & Jones, O. R. (1986). *The philosophy of mind.* Cambridge, England: Cambridge University Press.

Smith, P. E. (1951). *History of mathematics.* New York: Ginn.

Sparshot, F. E. (1980). The aesthetics of music. In *The new Grove dictionary of music and musicians* (Vol. 1, pp. 120–135). London: Macmillan.

Stockhausen, K. (1964). *Texte.* Vienna: Schauberg.

Stockhausen, K. (1971). [Seminar at Cambridge University, England].

Strunk, O. (1950). *Source readings in music history.* New York: Norton.

Sundberg, J. (1987). *The science of the singing voice.* Dekalb: Northern Illinois University Press.

Tartini, G. (1754). *Trattato de musica.* Padua.

Teas, D. C., Klein, A. J., & Kramer, S. J. (1982). An analysis of auditory brain stem responses in young infants. *Hearing Research, 7*, 19–54.

Terhardt, E. (1970). Frequency analysis and periodicity detection in the sensations of roughness and periodicity pitch. In R. Plomp & G. F. Smoorenberg (Eds.), *Frequency analysis and periodicity detection in hearing* (pp. 258–281). Leiden: Eijthoff.

Terhardt, E. (1972). Zur Tonhöhenwahrnehmung von Klängen II. Ein Funktionsschema. *Acustica, 26*, 187–199.

Terhardt, E. (1974). Pitch, consonance, and harmony. *Journal of the Acoustical Society of America, 55*, 1061–1069.

Terhardt, E. (1979). Calculating virtual pitch. *Hearing Research, 1*, 155–182.

Terhardt, E., Gerhard, S., & Seewann, M. (1982). Pitch of complex signals according to virtual pitch theory: Tests, examples, and predictions. *Journal of the Acoustical Society of America, 71* (3), 671–678.

Trehub, S. E., Bull, D., & Thorp, G. A. (1984). Infants' perception of melodies: The role of melodic contour. *Child Development, 55*, 821–825.

Trehub, S. E., & Rabinovitch, M. S. (1972). Auditory and linguistic sensitivity in early infancy. *Developmental Psychology, 6* (1), 74–77.

Truax, B. (Ed.). (1978). *Handbook for acoustic ecology.* Vancouver, B.C.: A.R.C. Publications.

Twining, T. (Trans.). (1934). *Aristotle's Poetics.* London: Dent. (Reissue of 1789 edition)

Wagner, R. (1981). *The invention of culture.* Chicago: University of Chicago Press.

Wagner, R. (1986). *Symbols that stand for themselves.* Chicago: University of Chicago Press.

Walker, R. (1976). *Sound projects.* London: Oxford University Press.

Walker, R. (1978). Perception and music notation. *Psychology of Music, 6* (1), 21–47.

Walker, R. (1981). The presence of internalised images of musical sounds. *Council for Research in Music Education, 66–67*, 107–112.

Walker, R. (1984). *Music education: tradition and innovation.* Springfield: Thomas.

Walker, R. (1985). Music imagery and musical concepts: Some evidence from the congenitally blind. *Council for Research in Music Education, 85*, 229–238.

Walker, R. (1986). Music and multiculturalism. *International Journal of Music Education, 8*, 43–52.

Walker, R. (1987a). The effects of culture, environment, age, and musical training on choices of visual metaphor for sound. *Perception and Psychophysics, 42* (5), 491–502.

Walker, R. (1987b). Some differences between pitch perception and auditory discrimination by children of different culture and musical background. *Council for Research in Music Education, 91*, 166–170.

Wallace, W. (1970). *Life of Arthur Schopenhauer.* London: Walter Scott.

Walliser, K. von. (1969). Correlation between sound stimulus and periodicity pitch. *Acustica, 21* (6), 319–329.

Ward, W. D. (1954). Subjective musical pitch. *Journal of the Acoustical Society of America, 26* (3), 369–380.

Welldon, J. E. C. (Trans.). (1883). *The Politics of Aristotle.* London: Macmillan.

Wightman, F. L. (1973). The pattern transformation model of pitch. *Journal of the Acoustical Society of America, 54* (2), 407–416.

Wild, S. A. (1975). *Walbiri music and dance in their social and cultural nexus.* Doctoral dissertation, Indiana University, Bloomington. (University Microfilms).

Winnington-Ingram, R. P. (1980). Greek music. In *The new Grove dictionary of music and musicians* (Vol. 7, pp. 659–672). London: Macmillan.

Wollheim, R. (1968). *Art and its objects.* London: Penguin.

Wormith, S. J., Pankerst, D., & Moffitt, A. R. (1975). Frequency discrimination by young infants. *Child Development, 46*, 272–275.

Index

243

About the Author

ROBERT WALKER has been a professor of Music Education on the Faculty of Education at Simon Fraser University in British Columbia, Canada, since 1981. He holds B.Mus. and Ph.D. degrees from the Music Department of the University of London, as well as diplomas from the Royal College of Music and the Royal College of Organists. Prior to joining the faculty at Simon Fraser University, he taught at grammar schools in England and colleges and universities in England, Australia, and Canada.

His previous publications include more than 40 papers on topics ranging from empirical research in the psycho-physics of music, music pedagogy, and auditory-visual perception. His research interests include acoustical studies of North American Indian and Inuit sung sounds, and the effects of culture and environment on visual imagery for sound. He is also the author of a critical analysis of modern pedagogy in music, *Music Education: Tradition and Innovation* (Charles C. Thomas, 1984), and the editor of the *Canadian Music Educators Journal* and the *Canadian Journal of Research in Music Education*.